D0380751

What Your
Birthday
Reveals
About Your
Sex Life

What Your Birthday Reveals About Your Sex Life

YOUR KEY TO THE HEAVENLY *Sex Life* YOU WERE BORN TO HAVE

PHYLLIS VEGA

Aadamsmedia

Avon, Massachusetts

Published by
Adams Media, a division of F+W Media, Inc.
57 Littlefield Street, Avon, MA 02322. U.S.A.
www.adamsmedia.com

ISBN-10: 1-4405-0596-9
ISBN-13: 978-1-4405-0596-6
eISBN-10: 1-4405-0991-3
eISBN-13: 978-1-4405-0991-9

Printed in the United States of America.

10   9   8   7   6   5   4   3   2   1

Library of Congress Cataloging-in-Publication Data
is available from the publisher.

This publication is designed to provide accurate and authoritative information with regard to the subject matter covered. It is sold with the understanding that the publisher is not engaged in rendering legal, accounting, or other
professional advice. If legal advice or other expert assistance is required, the
services of a competent professional person should be sought.
—From a *Declaration of Principles* jointly adopted by a Committee of the
American Bar Association and a Committee of Publishers and Associations

Many of the designations used by manufacturers and sellers to distinguish
their product are claimed as trademarks. Where those designations appear
in this book and Adams Media was aware of a trademark claim, the designations have been printed with initial capital letters.

Illustrations © iStockphoto/helgy716

This book is available at quantity discounts for bulk purchases.
For information, please call 1-800-289-0963.

Contents

Introduction — vii

Part 1: Signs and Numbers — *1*

Chapter 1: *The Twelve Signs of the Zodiac — 3*

Chapter 2: *The Nine Basic Numbers — 17*

Part 2: The 366 Birthdays of the Year — *21*

Introduction

Your birthday is more than just any old day during the year in which you were born. It is a defining factor of who you are and how you act and react in various situations. Astrologers and numerologists believe that each day in the yearly cycle emits distinct vibrations and contains unique characteristics. The influence of the day of your birth is one of the dynamics that distinguishes you from other people.

The book is divided into two sections. *Part One: Signs and Numbers* talks about the archetypes and traits related to each of the Sun signs and the characteristics of the nine basic numbers. *Part Two: The 366 Birthdays of the Year* gives a comprehensive sexual sketch for each birthdate, broken down into the following categories: *What Makes You Tick, Between the Sheets*, and *Tips for Your Ideal Lover.*

In *What Your Birthday Reveals about Your Sex Life*, the author draws upon the predictive powers of astrology and the ancient art of numerology to create a revealing summary of your sexuality that can help you enjoy a better love life. It is a lively up-to-date guide that provides you with fresh insights into yourself, how you react sexually, and what turns you on and off in bed. Moreover, the book is user friendly so you won't need to do any tedious astrological or numerological calculations. The month and day you were born is the only key you need to unlock the intimate sex secrets of your own birthday or that of anyone else.

Part 1

Signs
and
Numbers

CHAPTER 1

The Twelve Signs of the Zodiac

SUN SIGN CHART

Aries (Ruler: Mars; Element: Fire): March 21–April 19

Taurus (Ruler: Venus; Element: Earth): April 20–May 20

Gemini (Ruler: Mercury; Element: Air): May 21–June 20

Cancer (Ruler: Moon; Element: Water): June 21–July 22

Leo (Ruler: Sun; Element: Fire): July 23–August 22

Virgo (Ruler: Mercury; Element: Earth): August 23–September 22

Libra (Ruler: Venus; Element: Air): September 23–October 22

Scorpio (Ruler: Pluto; Element: Water): October 23–November 21

Sagittarius (Ruler: Jupiter; Element: Fire): November 22–December 21

Capricorn (Ruler: Saturn; Element: Earth): December 22–January 20

Aquarius (Ruler: Uranus; Element: Air): January 21–February 18

Pisces (Ruler: Neptune; Element: Water): February 19–March 20

Born on a Cusp?

The dates given in the Sun Sign Chart are only an approximation, because the Sun does not enter each of the signs on the same day or time every year. If you were born on a cusp (a day when the Sun changes signs), you will need to determine which sign the Sun was in at the time you were born. As long as you know your time of birth, you can have an accurate horoscope chart drawn up by an astrologer or chart-making service. However, if you were born on a cusp day and don't know the exact time you were born, you may never know for sure which sign is the correct one. In this case, you should read the interpretation for the adjacent sign as well as the one for your birthday to see which one is a better fit.

The Sun Signs

Fire (Aries, Leo, Sagittarius): Fire signs are romantic. You love extravagantly, passionately, and dramatically. Spontaneous, impulsive, and full of surprises, you're never boring. Since subtlety is not your style, you are very open about your feelings. Fire-sign natives are bold and usually willing to risk rejection. Your attitude is that there are lots more fish in the sea.

Earth (Taurus, Virgo, Capricorn): Earth signs are serious minded and practical. Your happiness lies in the material realm, and you derive great pleasure from a comfortable, settled home life. Cautious and controlled, Earth-sign natives take love seriously. Tactile and very aware of physical sensations, you have a well-developed sensual side and a strong need for physical contact.

Air (Gemini, Libra, Aquarius): Air signs flirt with love and romance. You want a relationship that provides intellectual stimulation, companionship, and witty, engaging conversation. Emotionally cool, you "feel" as much with your mind as with your body. Your real need is to connect on a mental level. For you, the exchange of thoughts and ideas is paramount in a loving union.

Water (Cancer, Scorpio, Pisces): Water signs are sensitive, emotional, responsive, intuitive, and empathetic. Psychically, there are few barriers between you and others, and you often pick up on what those around you are feeling. You tend to overuse your imagination, and the combination of intuition and imagination can make you feel exceedingly vulnerable in a romantic relationship.

Aries,
the Initiator

MARCH 21–APRIL 19

Symbol: the Ram

Planetary Ruler: Mars

More of a tiger than a ram where your sexuality is concerned, you get off on the hunt as well as the conquest. A decidedly physical and fearless lover, you've been blessed with the stamina to keep going all night long. In your quest for sexual pleasure, you enjoy variety, experimentation, and innovation. An open-minded bed partner is virtually a must because boredom is an anathema to you. Although eroticism matters, a mental connection with your bedmate is also truly important. Moreover, you are a closet romantic. In love, as in life, you definitely want it all.

Sexually, you're a fireball; when aroused, Aries can be more ardent and exciting than any sign in the zodiac, except possibly Scorpio. Your ego, however, is rather fragile and the best way to woo you is with a little flattery. Although you're usually open to straight talk outside the bedroom, the lover who is foolish enough to critique your performance between the sheets needs to choose his or her words very carefully. Where criticism is concerned, you are a lot more comfortable dishing it out than taking it. To you, even a slight hint that your lovemaking is less than perfect can be devastating.

Taurus, the Sensualist

APRIL 20–MAY 20

Symbol: the Bull
Planetary Ruler: Venus

Individuals born under the sign of the bull are deeply passionate, if somewhat shy and reserved. Fearful of rejection, you prefer to draw love to you rather than pursue it openly. Since those ruled by Venus are naturally charming, alluring, and sexy, you probably have little trouble attracting romantic partners. When intimately involved with someone, you make a caring, considerate lover. However, you require a lot of affection and consideration in return. Like Aries and Leo, Taurus natives thrive on flattery and compliments.

Essentially what you are looking for in a romantic relationship is stability, emotional security, and good sex. To you, good sex usually means a sensuous, passionate, but uncomplicated physical relationship. The sensible bull is romantic yet never fanciful. Your ideas about love tend to be traditional. You refuse to play games, and you don't make promises that you can't keep. You are naturally seductive, and when you overcome your inhibitions you're capable of depths of passion that will leave your lover gasping for breath (and begging for more). Once your libido has been let loose, you can be a very demanding lover. However, you're set in your ways and generally not given to kinky boudoir behavior or radical sexual experimentation.

Gemini, the Communicator

MAY 21–JUNE 20

Symbol: the Twins

Planetary Ruler: Mercury

Although apparently easygoing and relaxed about sexuality, Gemini can be as bold and daring in the bedroom as any Aries. Once you set your sights on a prospective lover, you know all the right things to do and say to gain his or her attention. With the mood upon you, you're capable of making love just about anywhere and you're glib enough to talk your way into virtually any bed. Flirting comes easy to you; when the sexual banter becomes hot and heavy, you may surprise a fairly recent acquaintance with an impromptu invitation to join you in a passionate night of lovemaking. However, once a new relationship progresses to the nitty-gritty of serious commitment, you're just as likely to hit the panic button.

The reward for the mate who ultimately catches you is a charming, free-spirited lover who shines at parties and is something of a devil in the bedroom. Still, you're almost always in control of your emotions, and no amount of physical passion causes you to lose your head completely. When it comes to romance and relationships you are analytical, and it is unlikely that you will ever experience the emotional ecstasy of being totally swept away by love.

Cancer, the Nurturer

JUNE 21–JULY 22

Symbol: the Crab
Planetary Ruler: the Moon

Cancer is a very physical sign, and sex with you is a sensuous experience. Typically, there is lots of tender foreplay, with aromatic massages, candles by the bedside, soft music in the background, and deliciously scented flowers everywhere. While you might be willing to try something new, you're not likely to be the one to suggest innovations. Even so, when your need for love and acceptance has been satisfied, you can be quite sexually creative. Since your sexuality is primarily directed toward the satisfaction of your partner, you generally go along with whatever your mate wants, so long as he or she is sympathetic and considerate of your feelings.

The emotional firepower aroused within you tends to manifest as sensual romantic fantasies rather than sexual acrobatics. Your typical mating ritual is like a slow ballet, yet a lover with the right moves can lead you in a torrid bedroom tango. Since you are quite intuitive, you sense what your partner wants and you're usually more than happy to provide it. With you, sex often equates with love, so that the bed partner who satisfies your need for security is the one most likely to unleash a volcanic eruption of sensual treats.

Leo,
the Performer

JULY 23–AUGUST 22

Symbol: the Lion

Planetary Ruler: the Sun

Passion burns in Leo's mind and body. You radiate sex appeal and self-confidence. Although you enjoy exploring the physical side of love, you need to be fond of your partner to truly enjoy the sex act. You prefer being in charge in bed. As befits a Fire sign, there is great energy and physicality in your lovemaking. White heat, ardor, and enthusiasm emanate from you. No other zodiac sign is as majestic, theatrical, or grand as Leo. As a result, there's no shortage of potential partners who are just longing to bask in your delightful solar warmth.

You respond passionately when your partner tells you that you are a wonderful lover. Moreover, you return the compliment by showing him or her just how much that praise means to you. Lions love seduction and erotic foreplay, and a well-placed mirror can add to your pleasure, since Leo's flowing mane and catlike quality are just begging to be watched. You crave action first and foremost, and you love being the center of attention in the bedroom and elsewhere. You are open to any manner of sexual interaction that clearly demonstrates your own desirability and rightful place at the heart of things.

Virgo, the Perfectionist

AUGUST 23–SEPTEMBER 22

Symbol: the Virgin

Planetary Ruler: Mercury

Since Virgo is not one of the highly sexed zodiac signs, you may not place all that much importance on the sex act itself. Kind words, kisses, and caresses make you feel warm and safe. Sex with you is typically slow and long lasting, as it can take you some time to get going. However, once the fire is lit, your bed partner can look forward to a passionate session of lovemaking that will not cool down very quickly. Actually, you can be quite intense in bed, especially with a mate you trust, for that's when you're able to relax and let yourself go.

You are not the type of person who is looking for a one-night stand. You prefer a committed union with Mr. or Ms. Right, and when you find it, sex with you is tender and romantic but also straightforward, with few fancy moves. As time progresses you become more sensual, and once a union is on solid ground, you're usually willing to experiment with different techniques of erotic foreplay. The stomach area is very sensitive in most Virgo natives. Stroking it, circling the bellybutton with a finger, or giving a light tummy massage is a sure-fire turn-on.

Libra, the Romantic

SEPTEMBER 23–OCTOBER 22

Symbol: the Scales
Planetary Ruler: Venus

Libra natives are extraordinarily romantic, and some actually seem to prefer the ethereal rituals of courtly love and romance to the unbridled passion of earthy sexual encounters. As befits your beautiful world, you adore being loved and lusted after, although you may initially prefer admiration from a safe distance. Once begun, sex with you is an enchanting, sensual experience with lots of gentle rubbing, stroking, and caressing. You are good at lovemaking and are typically willing to try something new as long as it is elegant and classy; coarseness and vulgarity turn you off.

Libras make very imaginative lovers. In bed, you are just as creative and artistic as you are in your daily life. You tend to view sex as an art form, and you're willing to explore different means of achieving intimacy. For you, sex involves not only the physical act, but the environment as well. You set the mood with lots of teasing foreplay and create ambiance with flowers, candles, scented massage oils, and soft music. If the mood is not right, even the sexiest Libra will not respond. The lower back is your most sensitive region and caressing it lightly can heighten and enhance your sensual experience.

Scorpio, the Extremist

OCTOBER 23–NOVEMBER 21

Symbol: the Scorpion
Planetary Ruler: Pluto

Scorpio is the zodiacal sign that is the most likely to act out sexual fantasies. Others may talk about it, but none fully throw themselves into their roles like scorpions. Fantasy or not, sex with you is a thrilling experience that is definitely not for the faint of heart. Sexually, Scorpio has one goal: to give and receive the greatest possible pleasure. You will use any means at your disposal to achieve this result. Moreover, you continue to seduce your partner even as the sex act continues.

The most sensually energetic of all the signs, Scorpios are passionate lovers. For you, union with your beloved is a sacrament, and your overriding urge is to use your innate power to go beyond everyday life and lose yourself completely in an almost mystical ecstasy. As a result, you are capable of the greatest heights of passion. Your feelings are so intense that the sex act becomes a total emotional and physical experience that can last all night long. Although the genitals are everybody's erogenous zone, they are supersensitive in Scorpios, so stroking and caressing them sets you on fire. Just touching these areas ignites a passionate flame that usually can't be extinguished without completion.

Sagittarius, the Adventurer

NOVEMBER 22–DECEMBER 21

Symbol: the Archer
Planetary Ruler: Jupiter

Archers are passionate and adventurous in other life areas, and this innate enthusiasm naturally carries over to their love lives. Although you don't appear to take romantic relationships very seriously, when you are at the height of passion, you behave as if each love affair is the real thing and destined to last forever. Sagittarius can be as impulsive as any Aries and as willing to jump wholeheartedly into a new romance (or out of an old one). While your physical desires are strong, sex alone rarely fulfills you. For you, no relationship is truly complete without mental compatibility and mutual understanding.

Sagittarians love novelty, and your desire to learn new things makes you a highly experimental and adaptable bed partner. You are turned on by exuberance and straightforward talk and actions, and turned off by superficiality and artificial behavior. Since you have no qualms about voicing your own wants, needs, and opinions, you appreciate equal frankness from your lovers. Archers are naturally equipped with a fear of intimacy; as a result, you value freedom and independence above all things. The mate who allows you plenty of breathing room is the one most likely to be repaid with lasting devotion and lots of hot sex.

Capricorn, the Pragmatist

DECEMBER 22–JANUARY 20

Symbol: the Goat

Planetary Ruler: Saturn

Those ruled by Saturn tend to hide their deepest feelings behind a mask of cool detachment. You may not be particularly romantic, but you're extremely passionate. Beneath your shell of protection, you sizzle with lusty sensuality. Although you crave love and affection, you tremble at the prospect of losing control or being placed in an emotionally vulnerable position. You never jump into a relationship without careful consideration, yet once committed you tend to stay that way. Goats want to be the boss and can be genuinely possessive, dictatorial, and demanding. However, as a friend or lover, no other zodiacal sign is as dependable.

Your lovemaking is very passionate and can be quite a surprise to a new lover who has only seen your refined exterior. Capricorn sexuality is robust, and the better you know your bed partner, the more willing you are to test the boundaries of passion. In bed, the goat is more than willing to experiment and try out new things. While you may be a bit too cautious and traditional to suggest any out-of-the-ordinary sexual practices on your own, you are eager to please your partner and will not hesitate to follow his or her lead.

Aquarius, the Innovator

JANUARY 21–FEBRUARY 18

Symbol: the Water Bearer
Planetary Ruler: Uranus

The only thing that's for sure in a close relationship with the typical Aquarian is the water bearer's tendency to view his or her romantic partner as a friend as well as a lover. Even in the most intimate situations, your first connection is invariably a mental one. One nice thing about your mindset is that you view your lover as an individual, not as a sex object. Although sex is truly important to you, it is rarely uppermost in your mind. Your deepest need is for a mate or partner who is able to satisfy you intellectually as well as physically.

Aquarius in bed is difficult to describe because the water bearer brings along a plethora of contradictions and paradoxes. Like the other Air signs (Gemini and Libra), the idea of sex is typically more exciting to you than the actual act. Your fantasies often involve getting caught having sex in unusual situations; you're attracted to people who are offbeat and a little odd. Imaginative and innovative in your approach to lovemaking, you appreciate a bedmate who is equally creative. Since you view sex as fun and not to be taken too seriously, you particularly enjoy spontaneous encounters and quickies.

Pisces, the Dreamer

FEBRUARY 19–MARCH 20

Symbol: the Fish

Planetary Ruler: Neptune

Like Cancer and Scorpio, the other Water signs, Pisceans are intense in their intimate relationships. Longing to explore the entire range of emotions, you immerse yourself completely in the experience. Idealism prompts you to merge your personality with that of your loved one, and when you fall, you fall hook, line, and sinker. Although fear of rejection can make you skittish and reluctant to make the first move, the telepathic signals you send out are unmistakable, and the object of your affection rarely has difficulty getting the message. Your soulful gaze speaks volumes and telegraphs the irresistible promise of earthly and heavenly delights.

Typically, fish make sensual, creative lovers who adore playful sex and wild romps through exotic fantasies. With a bed partner who indulges your flights of fancy, you're primed to keep going all night long. For you, love and sex together form a complete union that makes you feel safe and totally uninhibited. Once you overcome your innate shyness, you adore role-playing games where you can get completely involved and lose yourself in risqué encounters. Since the feet are Pisces' most sensitive body part, massaging your feet or sucking your toes gets you all steamed up and ready for action.

CHAPTER 2

The Nine Basic Numbers

The most widely used of the modern numerological systems is that of the Greek mathematician Pythagoras, who said, "All things can be expressed in numerical terms, because all things are ultimately reduced to numbers." Pythagoras saw numbers as the basis of all art, science, and music. He and his followers also believed that by contemplating numbers they would discover the spiritual key that leads to the divine.

The Root Numbers

There are nine basic or root numbers, and one of them is associated with your birthday. The sum of any compound number, when reduced to a single digit, is its basic or root number. The root number for your birthday is the day of the month on which you were born, reduced to a single digit. If your birthday is on the 28th day of any month, you simply add the two digits together: 2 + 8 = 10. Then reduce the result further, until you arrive at a single digit: 1 + 0 = 1. The root digit for the 28th day of any month is 1.

ROOT-NUMBER BIRTH-DATE CHART

Number 1: Born on the 1st, 10th, 19th, or 28th of any month
Number 2: Born on the 2nd, 11th, 20th, or 29th of any month
Number 3: Born on the 3rd, 12th, 21st, or 30th of any month
Number 4: Born on the 4th, 13th, 22nd, or 31st of any month

Number 5: Born on the 5th, 14th, or 23rd of any month
Number 6: Born on the 6th, 15th, or 24th of any month
Number 7: Born on the 7th, 16th, or 25th of any month
Number 8: Born on the 8th, 17th, or 26th of any month
Number 9: Born on the 9th, 18th, or 27th of any month

Number 1, the Leader

One is a leader and pioneer, and your dynamic personality prompts you to assume a primary role in all your endeavors. Ones also like to take the lead in love. You thoroughly enjoy the chase, and can be single-minded in your pursuit of a partner. Extended foreplay is not a prerequisite to your sexual enjoyment, nor do you especially like cuddling after sex. Even so, your bedmates find you an exciting, imaginative, innovative lover.

Number 2, the Diplomat

Twos are romantic, faithful, and affectionate, and they expect fidelity and devotion in return. In bed and out, you enjoy creating a pleasant atmosphere for your beloved. Between the sheets, you'll do whatever you deem necessary in order to keep the relationship running smoothly. Foreplay with lots of kissing and cuddling is important to you; it makes you feel loved and protected. A sense of emotional security is your key to a contented sex life.

Number 3, the Social Butterfly

You are an exciting, playful lover with tons of self-confidence, and your lighthearted attitude helps your partner relax and feel comfortable in the bedroom. You enjoy trying different sexual positions, and prefer spontaneous foreplay that is creative and imaginative. Always willing to experiment, you can be so uninhibited that you make your lover blush. Variety is a must; if the sexual relationship becomes dull or boring, you could decide to leave.

Number 4, the Realist

Although passionate and sensual, you're a practical romantic. In bed, you generally prefer sticking to the tried and true, especially during foreplay, where you tend to follow a set routine. As a lover, your movements are slow and sensual, and you enjoy drawing out the lovemaking in anticipation of a big finish. Even so, too much of the same old thing can be boring, and every once in a while, you will turn wild and crazy.

Number 5, the Adventurer

Fives are adventurous and enjoy variety and excitement in bed. In love, you need mental as well as physical stimulation. Spontaneity is a turn-on, and you like the thrill of trying new positions and finding new places for lovemaking. Role-playing during foreplay gives you a chance to experiment with innovative ideas and nontraditional bedroom activities. Although you are quick to adapt to ups and downs in a relationship, you may decide to leave if you get bored.

Number 6, the Idealist

Sixes have a deep dislike of discord. You work hard at maintaining peace and harmony in your intimate relationships. Pleasure is your aphrodisiac, and when you find someone you care about, indulging your carnal desires is a joy. Long sessions of foreplay that include being kissed and stroked all over are very much to your liking. The romantic atmosphere created by beautiful surroundings also creates an air of romance that turns you on.

Number 7, the Scholar

You crave a deep spiritual connection with your soul mate and can potentially reach levels of intimacy that are beyond most people's comprehension. On the other hand, you tend to be a little spacy and detached in bed, and your overanalytical nature can produce an almost clinical approach to love and sex. If your relationship goals are too lofty and unrealistic, you could be disappointed when the union inevitably falls short of your ideal.

Number 8, the Executive

Eights are typically practical and secure, and offer their mates safety and stability. However, if you treat an intimate relationship like a business deal, you can easily alienate your partner. You are competitive in bed and out, and you can get a little too wrapped up in the politics of sexual power and control. Any type of foreplay, including using sex toys, that gets your juices flowing and fires up your libido is okay with you.

Number 9, the Philanthropist

Nines are caring, involved, and sympathetic. You show your love by helping your partners and even assuming their problems. You tend to relegate your own needs to the back burner, while attending to those of your mate. In bed, however, your passion can be volcanic and your quiet, submissive nature can become quite demanding and sexually exciting. During foreplay, sexy eye contact, provocative conversation, and erotic attire all serve as tantalizing aphrodisiacs for your lovemaking.

Part 2

The 366 Birthdays of the Year

January 1, *Capricorn 1*

What Makes You Tick

Outwardly, you may appear to be a shrewd, cool operator, but you're anything but cool and collected on the inside. It goes without saying that you're an ambitious overachiever with an overwhelming desire to succeed in the workplace. However, family and friends also mean a great deal to you, and your loved ones know that they can depend upon your loyalty and support to help get them through whatever problems arise.

Between the Sheets

When you work you work hard, but when you play you expect a good time. Sexually, you tend to swing back and forth between the fiery passion characterized by the number 1, and the reserved detachment indicated by your Capricorn Sun sign. Behind closed doors, and with the right partner, you can turn into the quintessential sexy beast; in public, however, your refined dignity is all most people will see. Although inherently traditional in some ways, you have some very inventive ideas regarding lovemaking, and you want a partner who is as creative as you and as interested in keeping love fresh and alive. A mate who is clever, sexy, caring, and reliable can sustain your interest for a lifetime.

Tips for Your Ideal Lover

You may be emotionally reserved, but physically you're a powerhouse of sexual energy. Once you get started, you can continue all night long, and nothing keeps you going better than a bed partner whose erotic imagination, innovative moves, and sexual stamina are equal to your own.

January 2, *Capricorn 2*

What Makes You Tick

Although determined and competitive by nature, your material ambition has been tempered by a deep-seated desire to join your life to that of another person. In an intimate union, devotion, commitment, compatibility, and shared goals are essential to you. You like to take the time to assess all your options before choosing a mate, but once you find Mr. or Ms. Right, you'll happily settle in for the long term.

Between the Sheets

Simmering beneath your cool public exterior is a hot-blooded passion that emerges behind closed doors. You want a physical relationship that stirs your imagination and teases all your senses. Right from the beginning you need to feel the strong spark of chemistry, or it just won't happen. To sustain your interest, your bed partner must be both intelligent and sexy because you enjoy a lively conversation as much as a sensual romp. An ardent lover, you like to be the one in charge of the action, both in bed and out. In moments of shared intimacy, your animal-like physicality may be felt as a formidable presence as you move slowly and steadily toward the peaks of pleasure.

Tips for Your Ideal Lover

Once assured of your mate's affection, you make an eager lover, highly responsive to sensual delights. You flourish with an energetic bed partner who stirs your deeper sexual impulses. You particularly like it when your mate introduces new techniques that add to your mutual enjoyment.

January 3, *Capricorn 3*

What Makes You Tick

This combination of Capricorn's down-to-earth practicality and number 3's dramatic imagination is hard to beat. You work hard and you're dependable, yet you refuse to let family responsibilities or career obligations keep you from enjoying yourself. A fountain of ideas and energy, you will do whatever you choose to do in life in your own inimitable way. In a romantic relationship, you need a mate who lets you be yourself.

Between the Sheets

Sexually, you are passionate and sensual, yet you're rather inhibited emotionally. Although you may appear modest and reserved in public situations, you have a huge appetite for physical pleasures behind closed doors. Still, you're more comfortable engaging in the physical act of lovemaking than in examining the emotions it engenders. In general, you are more interested in sex than in romance, but you're too embarrassed to say so. Even so, you take great pride in your sexual prowess; with the right playmate, you throw off your hesitation and allow the lusty side of your red-blooded nature to surface. More than anything, you want a significant other who can keep up with you in the bedroom.

Tips for Your Ideal Lover

You are delightfully open to suggestion and sexual experimentation, and the idea of forbidden fruit enthralls you. Since you have an active fantasy life and a taste for naughty adventures, your physical responses are sharpened considerably by a combination of verbal foreplay and the lush imaginings of your fertile mind.

January 4, *Capricorn 4*

What Makes You Tick

Emotionally, you tend to build walls between yourself and others. Although your deepest need is to be loved, you don't always come off as especially lovable. Nevertheless, beneath your serious façade there's a protective, caring person who will do whatever is necessary to assist loved ones in trouble. When you make a firm commitment, it's usually for a lifetime, and your significant other can rest assured that you won't run off at the first sign of trouble.

Between the Sheets

When you let down your guard, your passion and lusty appetite for pleasure become apparent. Highly sexed and swiftly aroused, your approach to lovemaking is simple and straightforward. Endurance is your forte. Whatever you lack in the romance department, you make up for in skill and sexual prowess. The rough and tumble of ardent love invigorates you and provides an escape from the responsibilities of daily life. Moreover, you are able to communicate through your lovemaking the deep feelings that you cannot express verbally. You can be demanding and always like being in control, yet your kinder, gentler side is concerned with your partner's pleasure as well as your own.

Tips for Your Ideal Lover

A prospective partner who is inventive and skilled in lovemaking has a good chance with you. As someone with a strong sex drive, you appreciate a bedmate whose physical needs equal your own. You may think you prefer being the aggressor, but sometimes you really enjoy being seduced.

January 5, *Capricorn 5*

What Makes You Tick

The Sun sign Capricorn and the number 5 together produce a freedom-loving, unpredictable goat who seeks a relationship that includes both personal independence and traditional commitment. You are a patient suitor; you build trust slowly. An intimate union must challenge you intellectually, while providing much-needed emotional security. In social situations, you tend to hold back with people you don't know well, hiding any shyness you feel behind a quirky sense of humor.

Between the Sheets

Sexually, you're more open-minded than most others of your Sun sign, but you sometimes get so caught up in work or in pet projects that you completely forget about lovemaking. Although it usually takes only a gentle reminder to turn your attention back to the bedroom, your partner may be confused by your sporadic periods of sexual detachment. Still, once your attention is engaged, no one makes a more ardent or inventive lover. Communication and intellectual compatibility are as important to you as physical contact, and once you've achieved a mental connection, your passion swiftly intensifies. More than anything, you need a confident mate who understands your mood swings and is able to match your adventurous spirit both inside the bedroom and outside.

Tips for Your Ideal Lover

You're turned on by a mate who is imaginative and entertaining in bed; someone who takes an uninhibited approach to sex and likes experimenting. Once your sexual juices start flowing, your sensual nature comes to the fore and your lusty libido is revealed.

January 6, *Capricorn 6*

What Makes You Tick

Relating comes more naturally to you than to other Capricorns, and you probably don't feel complete without the companionship of a loving partner. Stability is very important to you, and you need to be with someone who not only attracts you physically, but also shares your interests and goals. Knowing that you can count on your mate through good times and bad is really what makes a relationship work for you.

Between the Sheets

Since frivolous flings hold little appeal, you have the patience to wait for the lover who fits into your life plans. Once you find your true love, your determined approach leaves little doubt about your intentions. The romantic side of you responds to beautiful surroundings and a pleasant, graceful atmosphere in which to make love. While you keep your passionate sexual impulses under wraps in public situations, you display your true nature as a lusty sexual partner in the privacy of the bedroom. Although you can be cuddly and affectionate at times, you may also appear cool and somewhat controlling at other times. That's part of your appeal; you're a bit mysterious and defy easy definition.

Tips for Your Ideal Lover

Your earthy sensuality grows richer over time, and your appetite for sexual pleasure tends to increase as you grow older. You're turned on by a lover who wines and dines you in classy places, and then stirs your imagination in private with a romantic ambiance and a full-body erotic massage.

January 7, *Capricorn 7*

What Makes You Tick

While you're not actually a loner, you do need to feel comfortable and secure with a romantic partner before you'll even think about building a permanent relationship. What you really want is an intimate union that takes you to a higher place physically, intellectually, and spiritually. Rejection cuts you to the core, and when things go wrong, you are easily discouraged. Consequently, you would rather be alone than involved with the wrong person.

Between the Sheets

Despite your strong sex drive, you are an extremely private person. Getting past your protective armor may take some time; but once it is breached, your latent desire quickly grows into a torrent of passion. You take great pride in your sexual prowess. So once your juices get flowing, your lucky partner is in for a night of ardent lovemaking. You're a born sensualist, and lovemaking restores your vital energies and opens you to deep intimacy. When you unleash your innate eroticism, it is difficult to go back to acting controlled and reserved. Even so, you have a way of directing every situation without appearing to be in control, and you never quite let go completely.

Tips for Your Ideal Lover

Although you won't be dominated in any way, you can be seduced quite easily. You don't like to be rushed into sex. The slow-moving, patient lover knows how to ease you into a state of relaxed sensuality with sweet talk and highly erotic foreplay.

January 8, *Capricorn 8*

What Makes You Tick

You have big dreams, and you make sure that nothing stands in the way of achieving your ambitions. You take relationships as seriously as other aspects of your life. Although you proceed with caution, you are a loving and devoted partner once you are committed. In public, you're reserved, but in private, you are an openly demonstrative powerhouse of sexual energy.

Between the Sheets

For you, the ideal intimate union is built on mutual commitment and common goals. Your sexuality may express itself as hot or cold, depending on what is going on outside the bedroom. Since you are something of a workaholic, business often comes first. However, when you do make time for lovemaking, you give it your undivided attention, and you need a bed partner who can match your strong desires. Earthy and sensuous, you enjoy pleasing and pampering your lover in bed, but you expect similar attention in return. You regard true intimacy as a profound and deeply emotional experience, and the passion you feel for your beloved is likely to grow stronger through the years.

Tips for Your Ideal Lover

You are attracted to simmering sexual passion, and the bedmate who can provide a bit of spice and the occasional spontaneous moment of unbridled lust turns you on. Since you enjoy comfort and luxury, you find it easier to unwind in well-appointed, sumptuous surroundings.

January 9, *Capricorn 9*

What Makes You Tick

Although a bit old-fashioned and seriously devoted to your loved ones, you are also a romantic idealist. More sensitive and imaginative than you initially appear, you tend to believe in ideals like true love and happily ever after. Of course, you are also highly responsible; when you make a commitment, you keep it. Moreover, unlike some members of your Sun sign, you know when to let your hair down and have fun.

Between the Sheets

You may come off as the strong, silent type at first because of a tendency to hide your restless emotions behind a serene exterior. However, once smitten, you indulge your truly romantic nature. The merging of your sensuality and passion with your natural empathy and creativity makes you an ardent and considerate lover. You're often able to anticipate your partner's needs before he or she is even aware of them. You view sex as a sacred expression of love, and you thrive with a mate who shares your views. A romantic courtship stirs your libido, and play and fantasy enhance your lovemaking. When your mind and imagination are stimulated, your body swiftly follows.

Tips for Your Ideal Lover

Your lusty libido may need some coaxing after a day's work, but once ignited you have stamina to burn. A romantic atmosphere with music and scented candles gets your attention, and slow tantalizing foreplay with lots of touching, stroking, and provocative conversation brings out the sexy beast within.

January 10, *Capricorn 1*

What Makes You Tick

You are dependable and loyal, but also somewhat moody. Consequently, you are not the easiest person to live with. Although cool on the surface, you are a true romantic. Naturally competitive, you view an intimate relationship as a challenge; no matter how much trouble love brings, you never lose your taste for it. When things go wrong, you simply shake off the past and begin again.

Between the Sheets

In your mind, sex, love, and security go together, and casual affairs tend to leave you cold. You may not be easily seduced or caught, but once committed you're in it for the long haul. In the bedroom, you are an amorous lover with a liking for uninhibited fun. Delightfully open to suggestion and experimentation, you have a lusty appetite for slightly naughty sexual adventures. Public displays are not your style; you prefer expressing your devotion in private. However, stolen intimacy in risky places stimulates your desire for lovemaking. When the mood is upon you, you woo your mate with passionate determination. For you, a relationship thrives on trust, and the more risks you take together, the closer you feel to your companion.

Tips for Your Ideal Lover

You blossom with a partner who feeds your ego by complimenting your allure and sexual prowess. You're easily aroused in a luxurious environment, and respond passionately to a daring, adventurous lover who entices you with sweet talk, sex toys, and steamy erotic games.

January 11, *Capricorn 2*

What Makes You Tick

Since love and affection are important to you, you need a relationship that is not only stable and reliable but also romantic and exciting. Your idea of true partnership is a union that functions on all levels. You enjoy engaging in stimulating conversations and sharing common interests with your beloved. Still there is no question that chemistry matters, and your chosen mate must stimulate your body along with your mind.

Between the Sheets

You regard sex as a sacred expression of love, and you do best with a mate who has similar feelings. Lovemaking is typically a highly charged experience for you because you're extremely sensitive to sensual stimulation. You are especially proud of your prowess and the amazing sexual stamina that allows you to go all night long when you feel so inclined. Although you are a romantic idealist when it comes to relationships, your love of pleasure and luxury draws you to a partner who shares your taste for a lavish lifestyle. With your responsible attitude toward love relationships, the idea of a lasting union and growing old with your spouse holds tremendous appeal for you.

Tips for Your Ideal Lover

You like playing out shared sexual fantasies as a means of reaching new heights of ecstasy. Sometimes you enjoy being the aggressor, but at other times you prefer being seduced. A lover with a creative streak turns you on; although you enjoy experimentation, you may have qualms about suggesting it.

January 12, *Capricorn 3*

What Makes You Tick

Always quick with a clever remark or witty reply, you use humor to mask your true nature. As a result, others know how independent you are and how much you like to have fun, but few realize just how loving you can be. Although you believe in true love, you realize that sexual compatibility is an essential dimension to any romantic union. In a secure relationship, you feel totally free to express the passionate intensity you feel for your mate.

Between the Sheets

While you may look in your lover's eyes and get quivery all over, you truly value friendship and companionship in a romantic relationship, and you would never make a serious commitment based on passion alone. You like conversing with your beloved and enjoy sharing common pursuits and interests. Remaining the same doesn't appeal to you, and you could lose interest in a union that doesn't change and grow. Easily bored by routine and repetition, you like to keep your romance fresh and exciting with spicy innovations. You do best with a curious, imaginative, uninhibited bed partner who makes you feel sexy and desirable. Besides, a passionate sex life keeps you feeling happy and rejuvenated.

Tips for Your Ideal Lover

You have a randy, sexually adventurous side, and although you don't flaunt it publicly, pretty much anything goes in private. You are turned on big-time by talking to your lover about your preferences and then exploring them together without embarrassment or reservation.

January 13, *Capricorn 4*

What Makes You Tick

Outwardly you're rather serious and conservative, but in your emotional life you are more adventurous. You thrive in a relationship that gives full range to your sexuality. Family oriented and driven by responsibility, you need a supportive life partner who not only helps you advance in your career, but also understands that in the privacy of the bedroom your lusty sexual appetite makes you a dedicated and passionate bedmate.

Between the Sheets

Not one to engage in casual sex, you prefer to wait for the right partner. In the closeness of a permanent love union, the intensely sensual side of your nature emerges in all its glory. Nevertheless, loss of control frightens you. Even in your most intimate moments, you like being firmly in control of yourself and the situation. It may take you a long time to learn to trust your spouse and even longer to be able to abandon yourself to the moment. You want to be able to take your time when making love, and being rushed or having other things on your mind can get you out of the mood.

Tips for Your Ideal Lover

It may be a closely guarded secret, but you have a very rich fantasy life. Perhaps you imagine being swept off your feet by uncontrollable lust or being ravished by your insatiable lover's unstoppable passion. Whatever your fantasy, you are turned on by the accommodating bed partner who helps fulfill your erotic dreams.

January 14, *Capricorn 5*

What Makes You Tick

More of an individualist than most other goats, you feel little pressure to conform to the status quo. Although you want a stable permanent relationship, it is important for you to be able to maintain a large measure of independence within the structure of a long-term union. Since friends play such an important role in your life, there is a good chance that a close friendship will eventually turn into a lasting love affair.

Between the Sheets

Open-mindedness and variety keep your union strong and growing over the long term. You don't like to be tied down, and you resent it when your mate tells you what to do. For you, an intimate relationship is about both participants encouraging and supporting each other. To your way of thinking, a passionate sex life keeps love fresh and makes the pair of you feel happy and rejuvenated. Playful by nature, you make love with gusto. Behind closed doors, you don't mind a bit of rough-and-tumble lovemaking. In fact, you can be quite adventurous and amorous when you let down your guard and allow your deeper sensuality and lusty appetite for pleasure to emerge.

Tips for Your Ideal Lover

The lover who wants to please you and appeal to your sensuality might give you a full-body massage with aromatic oils. A daring bed partner might engage you in an erotic game of hide-and-seek by candlelight, with the understanding that the one who wins decides what happens next.

January 15, *Capricorn 6*

What Makes You Tick

You are ambitious. Accomplishing something important in life before you settle down is probably high on your list of things to do. Even so, once you find your true love, you tend to put your relationships and family life ahead of career plans. Although you have your choice when it comes to romantic partners, you're quite selective and willing to wait for Mr. or Ms. Right.

Between the Sheets

You are a tender, romantic lover who continues to improve with age and experience. Discriminating by nature, you want it all—passion, intellectual stimulation, and a long-term commitment—in every aspect of your life. If you appear cool and reserved in public, it is just a mask for your earthy sensuality. In private, you have a hearty appetite for physical pleasures, and you need a partner who also enjoys indulging in the good things—fine dining, good wine, and luxurious surroundings. Although you enjoy going out from time to time, you much prefer intimate nights at home where you and your mate can partake of your favorite creature comforts behind closed doors.

Tips for Your Ideal Lover

The lover who knows how to stroke your ego with kind words and help you relax after a busy day scores points with you. Lounging together in a scented spa, or sharing a bathtub surrounded by glowing candles, is a guaranteed turn-on.

January 16, *Capricorn 7*

What Makes You Tick

Although you fall in love slowly, once trust develops and you make the commitment, you are unshakably loyal to your beloved. Even so, you often find it difficult to express your emotions. While the physical side of sex is fine and you have no hesitation when it comes to lusty lovemaking, you may find it easier to show your deep and abiding affection with gifts rather than with words.

Between the Sheets

Outside the bedroom, you place great emphasis on companionship; once inside, however, your lusty physical nature takes over. Beneath your cool public façade pulses a smoldering sensuality that will not be long denied, and when triggered by the right person, your sexual passions burn hot and intense. Deep communication below the surface is quite normal for you, and the psychic bond between you and your mate allows you to tune in to his or her needs and fulfill them. Your ideal mate understands you as well, and you share a common goal of indulging each other's desires in every possible way. You take great pride in your sexual prowess and enjoy basking in the adoration of a contented partner.

Tips for Your Ideal Lover

The fastest way to your heart is through laughter, and a bit of humor can lift you out of your occasional dark, solitary moods. Appealing to your inherent sensuality with lingering kisses and witty, engaging conversation can bring you out of your shell and stimulate your latent desires.

January 17, *Capricorn 8*

What Makes You Tick

You want to be boss, and you can be dictatorial and demanding. However, no one else is as faithful or reliable a mate or lover. You don't jump into a love union without giving it lots of thought, and once you make a commitment, you stick to it. While not outwardly romantic, you are deeply passionate beneath that restrained exterior and very much in need of affection.

Between the Sheets

Emotionally, you may be reserved, but physically, you're filled with desire and very responsive. Highly sexed and swiftly aroused, you use a no-nonsense, direct approach. Whatever you may lack in romance and sweet talk, you more than make up in skill and sexual prowess. Thus the sanctuary of your bedroom becomes the setting for surprisingly sexy intimate encounters. Since endurance is your forte, you probably feel no need to rush things. Careful and methodical in everything you do, you tend to follow an established routine. Once you find something that works, you prefer staying with it rather than exploring new territory. Since you handle all the basics with skill and competence, you probably won't hear many complaints from your bed partner.

Tips for Your Ideal Lover

Spending time outdoors with your beloved gives you a way to recharge your batteries. Cultivating a luxurious, sensual atmosphere at home creates the space to relax and enjoy each other. An erotic massage energizes all the cells in your body and puts you in the mood for lovemaking.

January 18, *Capricorn 9*

What Makes You Tick

Serious and reliable on one hand, but dreamy and starry-eyed on the other, you tend to hide your restless emotions behind a mask of serenity. You want a lasting love union that is dynamic, exciting, stable, and secure. Knowing that you and your mate can count on each other is one of the things that make a loving relationship special and worthwhile.

Between the Sheets

Although you are more tender and romantic than the typical goat, you can be just as controlling and demanding as any other Capricorn. Still, you are prepared to do whatever it takes to make your partner happy, even sacrificing your own interests if you deem it necessary. You're a considerate lover, with almost-psychic instincts about what pleases your significant other, but spontaneity is not your style. You don't particularly care for quickies or unplanned sexual encounters, preferring instead to set up "sex dates" with your lover in advance. Atmosphere has a strong influence on your mood, and you like to make love in a harmonious setting with candlelight and soft music.

Tips for Your Ideal Lover

You respond with enthusiasm to the loving touch of a patient, thoughtful lover. Slow, sensuous foreplay opens all your senses to the erotic experience. Role-playing and fantasy games reveal your creativity and allow you and your bed partner to try new modes of sexual expression.

January 19, *Capricorn 1*

What Makes You Tick

Outwardly cool and restrained, you're not always accessible emotionally, even to those closest to you. Consequently, you find it difficult to share what you're feeling with your significant other. Although you feel things deeply, you don't know how to show it. You're strongly sexed and an ardent lover, but since you're also something of a workaholic, your love life may take a back seat to your career ambitions.

Between the Sheets

Although reserved in public, your earthy sensuality quickly surfaces behind closed doors. You blend eager affection with a straightforward seduction technique. Your need to dominate and control the activity in an intimate union makes you direct and aggressive in bed, and you don't require a great deal of coaxing to become physically aroused. It only takes a little roughhousing in the bedroom to bring out your inner sexy beast. While you have the stamina to keep going all night if you choose, you'd just as soon skip the fancy foreplay and get directly to the main event. Waking you for an encore during the wee hours of the morning makes for sensuous lovemaking.

Tips for Your Ideal Lover

You respond amorously to massage, and your ideal mate knows how to use erotic touch to get you to relax and let down your guard. Since Capricorn rules the knees, gentle stroking behind the knees releases built-up daily tension and starts all your sexual juices flowing.

January 20, *Capricorn 2*

What Makes You Tick

Because of your ability to stay calm when everyone else is upset, you sometimes come across as cool and calculating. Actually, you're quite emotional, but you're not always willing to let your feelings show. A secret romantic, you have a desperate need to be loved and understood. However, you have to trust the other person before you'll commit to an intimate union. When you feel secure, you're the most devoted of partners.

Between the Sheets

Even in intimate situations, you like being in charge. Moreover, you refuse to let anything or anyone distract you from your life goals. As a result, the intensity of your libido rises and falls depending on your workload. Love matters to you, but so does material success. You function better and feel happier with a life partner who understands your shifting moods and shares your interests and ideas. Beneath your restraint bubbles a smoldering sensuality; you crave the affection and emotional reassurance of a caring spouse. In the privacy of the bedroom, you are an ardent, sexy lover. Once your earthy passions are aroused, there is nothing reserved about your physical responses.

Tips for Your Ideal Lover

The ideal lover seduces you from your intense dedication to work and responsibility by appealing to your innate sensuality. Since sex for you is an erotic feast for the senses, you respond amorously to aromatic massage oils, scented candles, decadent edible delicacies, and silky, luxurious fabrics.

January 21, *Aquarius 3*

What Makes You Tick

Although you want passion in an intimate relationship, intellectual companionship attracts you even more. You are loyal to those you love, but you won't tolerate too many restrictions on your freedom. Even with your beloved, sex is not always the first thing on your mind. Nevertheless, when you get around to lovemaking, you're an imaginative lover; variety in sexual expression stirs your desires and keeps your lovemaking fresh.

Between the Sheets

The origins of your passion and sexual impulses tend to be more mental than physical or emotional. Consequently, you value companionship and friendship as much as physical union. Despite being an ardent lover, sex for you is mainly fun and games, and you don't take lovemaking too seriously. In bed and out of it, you have a very low tolerance for boredom or routine. Spicy conversation tends to stimulate your sexual desire in ways that even the most erotic touching may not accomplish. The more you talk about what you like to do or have done to you, the more excited you become. You're quite comfortable discussing your sexuality, yet when it comes to talking about feelings and emotions, you clam up.

Tips for Your Ideal Lover

Just the idea of sexual experimentation ignites your curiosity and stirs your libido. Sensual enhancements such as toys and suggestive attire provide the spice that invariably turns you on. You enjoy engaging in verbal sparring with your lover, and sex talk adds fuel to your erotic fire.

January 22, *Aquarius 4*

What Makes You Tick

On one hand, you're a rugged individualist; on the other, you're a social being who readily identifies with all types of people. Although loyal and devoted to your friends and loved ones, you have difficulty depending on anyone but yourself. As a result, you may come off as emotionally detached, when this is really not the case at all. Still, intimacy is not your strong point, and you avoid wild displays of emotion.

Between the Sheets

Even though you have a strong sex drive, you may try to repress or ignore your physical needs. Simultaneously fascinated and repelled by sexual impulses, you vacillate between strict self-discipline and a desire to throw caution to the wind. Nevertheless, when you stop trying to control and analyze your inclinations, and just give in to your lusty impulses, you make an enthusiastic, sensual lover. For you, physical stimulation begins in the imagination, and one of the most important ingredients in a successful coupling is your ability to share your thoughts and ideas along with your body. While sexual passion may be the best part of lovemaking, it never overshadows your need to establish a mental connection with your lover.

Tips for Your Ideal Lover

The best way to hold your interest is to vary the bedroom routine. Nothing turns you off faster than an unimaginative lover. You enjoy surprising your bedmate and being surprised in return. An erotic massage with aromatic oils is a special treat.

January 23, *Aquarius 5*

What Makes You Tick

Where your emotions are concerned, you often act like someone stumbling around in the dark. You can't quite figure out how to relate to another person in a close alliance without giving up your rights, and you may try substituting intellectual kinship for emotional ties. Still, when you do give your love, you give it wholeheartedly as long as you're able to retain enough personal space to avoid feeling trapped.

Between the Sheets

Even in your most intimate union, your first connection is invariably a mental one. The only thing that's for sure in a close relationship with you is your inclination to view your romantic partner as a friend as well as a lover, and it's virtually impossible to arouse your interest without some type of mind-to-mind contact. You view your bedmate as an individual, not as a sex object. Although sex is important to you, it is rarely uppermost in your mind. The idea of love and sex turns you on almost as much as the act itself. Your deepest need is for a partner who is able to satisfy you intellectually as well as physically.

Tips for Your Ideal Lover

Above all, you enjoy variety and excitement in bed, and if your love life gets really boring, you could decide to leave. Spontaneity and experimentation are the ultimate turn-ons. Naturally adventurous and decidedly unconventional, you like the thrill of trying new positions and discovering unusual places to make love.

January 24, *Aquarius 6*

What Makes You Tick

You are friendly, outgoing, and sensitive. Given all your community activities and hours spent helping with various humanitarian causes, it's a wonder you find time for intimate relationships at all. Consequently, your ideal mate is someone who is as busy and involved as you. When you do take time for your personal life, you're more romantic than the typical Aquarian, and you savor the moments with your beloved.

Between the Sheets

In bed and out of it, you view a relationship as something that helps both people grow, and your partner must be a friend and companion as well as a lover. Above all, you enjoy sharing thoughts and ideas with your mate. Intellectual rapport and easy communication arouse your passions as readily as touching and stroking. Talking during lovemaking is natural to you, and erotic conversation engages your imagination and stimulates your sexual desire. Creating an atmosphere for lovemaking that includes candles and music appeals to your taste for romantic ritual. A skilled and generous bed partner, you merge innovation with tried-and-true techniques to create a satisfying sexual experience for both of you.

Tips for Your Ideal Lover

High-minded and rather serious, you thrive in the world of ideas. An intuitive lover realizes that a bit of lusty lovemaking brings you back to reality where you can enjoy the sensual pleasures that make life worth living. You're turned on by foreplay that includes a soothing erotic massage.

January 25, *Aquarius 7*

What Makes You Tick

Naturally more mystical and idealistic than other members of your Sun sign, your view of love is both tender and romantic. A believer in destiny, you expect to find your soul mate and forge a permanent union. Moreover, you're not likely to settle for less. Commitment and security are important to you; you are seeking a relationship that lasts a lifetime.

Between the Sheets

Good communication with your mate is important because you enjoy intellectual exchanges and clever repartee almost as much as lusty sexual contact. Sharing mutual interests is also necessary to build a happy life with your significant other. Physically, your libido blows hot and cold, and you can be wildly passionate one day, yet seemingly cool and disinterested the next. When you're hot, you are an inventive, imaginative lover who likes to put a fresh spin on romance so that your partner never quite knows what to expect. When the mood is upon you, you enjoy a spontaneous bedroom romp that is as whimsical and romantic as it is erotic and exciting.

Tips for Your Ideal Lover

Your ideal bed partner is articulate and playfully adventurous and knows how to lighten your occasional dark moods with alluring, sexy banter. Always hungry for new experiences and eager to try novel things, you respond passionately to the innovative lover who avoids repetition and dull routine.

January 26, *Aquarius 8*

What Makes You Tick

Although more traditional and conservative than other water bearers, your unconventional nature comes through in your love life. Freedom and independence are important to you, yet with the right person you'll forge a bond that lasts a lifetime. You won't make wild pronouncements about your love for your mate. You'd much rather demonstrate how much you care with considerate acts and gifts than talk about your feelings and emotions.

Between the Sheets

While outwardly cool and controlled, you have a randy side that generally only shows itself behind closed doors. When you stop trying to control and analyze your feelings and give in to your impulses, you're a passionate, enthusiastic lover. Since your sexuality is driven by your intellect, it depends more upon what you think than what you feel. As a result, you are seduced more readily by spicy sexual banter, or a sensual striptease than by actual physical contact. Within the security of a stable union, you feel free to experiment and explore your strong sexual needs, and you prefer a mate who is not afraid to try new things in the bedroom.

Tips for Your Ideal Lover

Since work and responsibility are so important to you, you sometimes get so caught up in the practical considerations of everyday life that you forget about your love life altogether. However, it usually takes only a few sexy suggestions to spark your latent interest and get those juices flowing again.

January 27, *Aquarius 9*

What Makes You Tick

You are a romantic idealist who appears to have your head in the clouds. With your strong humanitarian and spiritual values, you are more inclined to base your relationships on ideals than on practical considerations. As a result, you may see prospective mates as you want them to be instead of as they really are. Slightly quirky, creative individuals hold more appeal for you as lovers than more conventional types.

Between the Sheets

Intimate relationships bring out the contradictory aspects of your romantic nature; your physical inclinations send you one message and your rational mind sends another. You yearn for intimacy, yet you're afraid of entrapment and emotional vulnerability. Your astrological challenge is to find a way to merge the disparate aspects of your character, so that you enjoy love to the fullest. Once you overcome your reservations, you throw yourself into lovemaking with breathtaking intensity. Although you may find emotional demands restricting, you have few such qualms regarding physical demands. A seduction scene, with soft music and sexy apparel, is an effective way to get your motor going.

Tips for Your Ideal Lover

Boredom is an anathema. The idea of exploring your sexual fantasies really appeals to you. You dream of escaping everyday reality through outrageous romantic encounters. As long as your mate or partner is agreeable, you will happily dress up for role-playing games or experiment with outlandish sexual positions.

January 28, *Aquarius 1*

What Makes You Tick

Basically a maverick and a nonconformist, you prefer doing things your way; your life reflects your personal style and originality. Despite your self-sufficiency, you're essentially a "people person," and relationships are vitally important to you. Since you're warmer and more passionate than most other Aquarians, you enjoy a permanent romantic involvement as long as your partner doesn't attempt to restrict your freedom and independence or tell you what to do.

Between the Sheets

Your freewheeling nature may cause you to be rather reckless in intimate unions because you are intrigued by any relationship that offers lots of excitement. You're easily bored in the bedroom and elsewhere. If the lovemaking gets too predictable, you will do whatever you can to shake it up a bit. While your sex drive is strong, you're not particularly romantic. Snuggling by the fireside appeals less to you than traveling or sharing an exciting adventure with your lover. You enjoy being the aggressive force in a game of seduction, and your ideal bedmate is a mental and physical sparring partner who challenges your intellect and stimulates your body.

Tips for Your Ideal Lover

Sex is fun and games for you, and clever, sexual banter ignites the lustier side of your nature. You're not shy about letting your partner know what you like in bed, and since you have no qualms about exploring sexual frontiers, you won't hesitate to satisfy your mate's wildest desires.

January 29, *Aquarius 2*

What Makes You Tick

Your rebellious Aquarian nature requires independence, but the 2 in your numerology chart makes you long for comfort and security. Although most water bearers are uncomfortable with too much intimacy, you want the stability of a close relationship even more than freedom. On a personal level, you're more dependable than the typical member of your airy Sun sign. People respond well to your friendly, gracious manner, and your vibrant personality attracts many friends and admirers.

Between the Sheets

While you may be gregarious and open, you rarely rush into a physical union. Although you can be rather elusive emotionally, your hearty appetite for sensory pleasure quickly overcomes your reservations. Your approach to sex is uncomplicated and direct, and you are energized by the presence of intelligence, cleverness, and wit. In fact, you tend to go back and forth between orgiastic delight in the physical sense and a need to establish a strong mental rapport with your mate. However, this duality in your love nature only adds spice to your union by keeping your lover guessing. You enjoy the delicious tension engendered by tantalizing foreplay, and languid caresses turn you on because your whole body is an erogenous zone.

Tips for Your Ideal Lover

You like to bring fun and spontaneity into the bedroom. Although it doesn't take a lot of frills to excite you, anything new, different, or unusual intrigues you and you would probably enjoy sharing some edible aphrodisiacs that enhance arousal.

January 30, *Aquarius 3*

What Makes You Tick

You're fun loving and sociable, and people are drawn to your charm and wit. Your forte is communication, and you take great pride in your ability to get others to see things from your point of view. In love, your tendency is to view your romantic partner as a friend as well as a lover. Even in an intimate union, it's difficult to arouse your interest without some type of mind-to-mind contact.

Between the Sheets

You love trying new things, and your need for experimentation extends to your sex life. You are not overly concerned with traditional roles or expectations, and your fondness for the unusual coupled with a penchant for sampling the unknown makes you an exciting lover. Emotionally, you can be somewhat detached, but you are extremely sensual and sexual. Alone with your beloved, you make an innovative, inventive bedmate. You have many interests, and you are always eager to hear about anything new and fascinating. You love sharing your ideas and experiences with your significant other; in bed or out of it, the easiest way to get your attention is to show interest in your current pet project.

Tips for Your Ideal Lover

Your sexuality is as unconventional and unusual as you are, and you're usually willing to try just about anything at least once. Your ideal partner shares your open-minded, carefree outlook and sense of adventure, and knows how to tickle your fancy with evocative conversation and erotic physical contact.

January 31, *Aquarius 4*

What Makes You Tick

More disciplined than most other Aquarians, you believe in personal freedom, but you also feel that responsibility and obligation are too important to be ignored. You thrive in an intimate union built on trust and mutual respect, yet you need a witty, outgoing, upbeat partner who provides some balance to your rather serious approach to life. While you enjoy a little intellectual sparring, you want stimulating conversation, not willful battles of opposing ideas.

Between the Sheets

Although outwardly cool, you are anything but detached when it comes to lovemaking. In the bedroom, you are a skillful lover who is always willing to learn new ways to please your mate. Your quicksilver mind leads to original, innovative moves, and relaxed moments open up your languid sensuality. Boldly confident in your sexual prowess and endurance, you feel no need to rush things and your partner can always depend on you to satisfy his or her needs. Typically, your movements are slow and sensual, and you enjoy drawing out the lovemaking in anticipation of a big finish. Even so, too much of the same old thing can be boring, and every once in a while you turn wild and crazy.

Tips for Your Ideal Lover

Your ideal lover knows how to whet your appetite for the pleasures of physical intimacy. Arousal often begins with provocative suggestion and sexy talk. Erotic foreplay and subtle teasing build sexual tension that stimulates your desires and heightens the ecstasy during lovemaking.

February 1, *Aquarius 1*

What Makes You Tick

Brimming with energy and enthusiasm, you conduct your life in a manner that reflects your personal style and originality. As a natural crusader, you're quick to espouse any ideal or cause that catches your fancy. You tackle problems and situations head-on, with little regard for either delicacy or tact. You don't mince words, always saying exactly what you mean, and you expect everyone else to be as plainspoken as you are.

Between the Sheets

Naturally impulsive and rebellious in all life areas, you push the envelope of your ideas to the edge. You don't go by other people's rules, and you don't expect them to follow yours. When choosing a partner, you consider fun and companionship to be as important as sexual compatibility. Like most Aquarians, your thoughts tend to wander off into the stratosphere. During these times your libido may require a wake-up call. Talking about sex spurs you into action, and a well-placed reminder from your mate of what you've been missing is usually all it takes to reignite your sexual fire. Once you get going, your approach in the bedroom is sensual, passionate, and direct.

Tips for Your Ideal Lover

You thoroughly enjoy sex, and your lovemaking is imaginative, innovative, and inventive. Everything begins in the mind for you, and the idea of actually exploring your most outrageous erotic fantasies is really appealing. You'll dress up for role-playing games or experiment with different positions, as long as your bedmate is agreeable.

February 2, *Aquarius 2*

What Makes You Tick

You are a romantic. When you are in an intimate relationship, you are even more idealistic than others of your Sun sign. If you seem emotionally elusive at first, your inherent warmth always shines through. Although a dazzling mind gets your attention, you have a healthy sexual appetite and ultimately it's the physical attraction that seals the deal. You're not the type to play games with another person's heart and you expect the same courtesy in return.

Between the Sheets

Although you consider life incomplete without a mate or partner, your care-free Aquarian spirit is uncomfortable with too much intimacy, and you tend to be cautious regarding long-term unions. As a result, your lovemaking style is full of enigmatic contradictions. More than anything, you bring fun and spontaneity into the bedroom, and the unconventional side of your nature makes you a nimble explorer of erotic pleasures. Friendship and companionship matter to you, and you're most content with a mate you can talk to and who gives you assurance and encouragement in bed and out. While independence is important to you, you can remain happily faithful to the romantic partner who offers versatility and variety along with love and affection.

Tips for Your Ideal Lover

You love to experiment in the kitchen and in the bedroom, and preparing and sharing a meal with your lover enhances your appetite for both food and sex. Using sweet treats to adorn your bodies during lovemaking creates a playfully innovative feast for all the senses.

February 3, *Aquarius 3*

What Makes You Tick

More flexible and versatile than most other members of your Sun sign, you are always on the lookout for exciting new experiences. Although you want a permanent, long-lasting relationship, you dislike being tied down. The person who wants to spend a lifetime with you needs to be able to balance closeness and commitment with freedom and independence. Your best pairing combines intellectual rapport and sexual compatibility.

Between the Sheets

In the bedroom and elsewhere, good times and shared laughter are important to you. However, what really attracts you is mental rapport. In fact, communication and intellectual compatibility may matter more to you than hot sex. Since your mind is your most active erogenous zone, once you have made the mental connection, physical allure and attraction usually follow. Your sexuality is as unconventional as you are, and your curiosity and adventurous nature prompt you to explore all kinds of new territory. You love surprises and novelty, and unpredictability and spontaneity are the spices that keep your juices flowing. Above all, you enjoy lively verbal sparring and sexy talk adds erotic fuel to your inner fire.

Tips for Your Ideal Lover

The best way for your lover to please you is to continuously change your lovemaking routine. As far as you're concerned, even the most exciting approach loses its oomph through repetition. You like doing things that are different and an unexpected romantic rendezvous in an unusual place is a guaranteed turn-on.

February 4, *Aquarius 4*

What Makes You Tick

On the outside, you seem disinterested in intimacy, but you're as much in need of love as anyone. In close relationships, you rarely act the way people expect. Although you dislike having others tell you what to do, you can be quite critical and have little problem telling them what to do. Emotionally, you may fear too much intimacy, but you're open to anything physical that brings pleasure to both parties.

Between the Sheets

You tend to shy away from public displays of affection, but you're warm, witty, and extremely sexy behind closed doors. You require an intellectual connection with your lover in addition to the physical one. Where your mind is engaged, your body naturally follows. Friendship and companionship are very important, and keeping a close relationship on an even keel matters a lot more to you than being involved in a wild, passionate love affair. Rarely effusive yourself, you're uncomfortable when others act out their feelings in a decidedly emotional manner. Yet deep down, you're a genuine romantic. You believe in true love and you want a life partner who shares your ideals.

Tips for Your Ideal Lover

The bright, witty lover who makes you laugh diverts your attention from the responsibilities and concerns of the workaday world. You respond to slow, sensuous foreplay leading to an evening of innovative lovemaking. A skillful erotic massage with aromatic oils relaxes your frayed nerves and puts you in a loving mood.

February 5, *Aquarius 5*

What Makes You Tick

Society's conventions matter little to you, because you march to a different drummer. More idealistic than sentimental, you're more concerned with building a close relationship based on friendship and common interests than on romantic attraction and physical passion. You require lots of freedom and independence, so you're not likely to put up with possessiveness, jealousy, or anyone who is overly dependent on you.

Between the Sheets

As open-minded about sex as about everything else, you enjoy experimentation. You believe that nothing is too far out as long as it pleases both partners. Although you have little problem expressing yourself physically, it's much harder for you to share feelings. Since you tend to rationalize everything, including your emotions, you're not likely to lose control or allow yourself to be swept away by passion. Still, your sex drive is strong and your adventurous spirit and disregard for convention make you a thrilling bed partner. While you're in no hurry to surrender your freedom, once you decide to commit, you're steadfast and not likely to walk away without a good reason.

Tips for Your Ideal Lover

Caresses on the calves and ankles can be highly erotic for you. You like the excitement of trying new positions and finding new places for lovemaking. Imaginative role-playing gives you a chance to experiment with innovative ideas. The romantic atmosphere created by beautiful surroundings helps create an air of romance that turns you on.

February 6, *Aquarius 6*

What Makes You Tick

The combination of the number 6 and your Aquarius Sun sign makes you more partnership-minded than most other water bearers. Not only do you dislike being alone, you actually feel incomplete without a partner to share your life. Even so, you dislike the idea of being restricted in your movements, and you may resist getting seriously involved for quite a while. Your ideal relationship merges romance and passion with friendship and intellectual rapport.

Between the Sheets

In love as in life, you are something of an idealist, yet you can be rather impulsive when someone attracts you. You wouldn't dream of surrendering your cherished independence for a relationship that does not live up to your extremely high standards. However, once involved, you want to please your mate. With a like-minded bed partner, you'll try most anything at least once, yet you pride yourself on your ability to arouse your partner without resorting to any move that is either crude or vulgar. You also like a bit of fun between the sheets, and enjoy being with someone who can amuse and stimulate you both mentally and physically.

Tips for Your Ideal Lover

The preamble to lovemaking is important to you, and a harmonious atmosphere created by beautiful surroundings helps create an air of romance that turns you on. You particularly like being wooed with sensuous foreplay in a romantic setting adorned with flowers and scented candles, while music plays softly in the background.

February 7, *Aquarius 7*

What Makes You Tick

In a close relationship, you tend to blow hot and cold. Moreover, you may feel torn between a love of freedom and the desire for a deeply committed partnership. Your mood swings can be extreme and even those closest to you may not be aware of how you really feel. Since your intimate unions tend to be more idealistic than practical, you may spend more time chasing your dreams than actually settling down to a real-life partnership.

Between the Sheets

There is a secret, mysterious aspect to your character that makes intimacy more difficult than it needs to be. Moreover, feelings of being misunderstood can make you wary of the very commitment you seek. In a love union, you can be wildly passionate one day, yet cool and detached the next. Even though you're an inventive and enthusiastic lover, there are times when you feel conflicted between your intellectual awareness of sex as a purely physical act, and your emotional ideal of lovemaking as a spiritual union. In bed and elsewhere, communication is essential for you, and your mate needs to be able to rouse your mind along with your body.

Tips for Your Ideal Lover

You enjoy the stimulation offered by an uninhibited lover who seduces you out of a dark mood with a combination of humor and daring. Although you're unlikely to be the one to initiate it, bursting through the barriers of sexual propriety and dull routine liberates and excites you.

February 8, *Aquarius 8*

What Makes You Tick

You value your independence, yet you dislike being alone. Although a permanent love relationship may not be at the top of your list of important things, eventually you may have to choose between independence and commitment. Once involved with Mr. or Ms. Right, you make a caring, conscientious, and reliable mate. Although more reserved in public than the average Aquarian, your physical passion and sensuality emerge behind closed doors.

Between the Sheets

Your strong sex drive notwithstanding, you may repress or ignore your physical and emotional needs at times. However, when you stop trying to control and analyze your feelings, and give in to your sexual impulses, you make a passionate, enthusiastic, exceedingly sensual lover. For you, physical stimulation begins in the mind; you can be seduced more readily with words than with caresses. A partner with depth and passion appeals most to you, and caring about the same things keeps your intimate relationship fulfilling and happy. Your ideal bed partner is vocal and responsive and gives you constant encouragement. You particularly like it when your lover tells you exactly what to do to increase his or her pleasure.

Tips for Your Ideal Lover

You thrive in a physical relationship with plenty of experimentation. Since you work and play hard, the rough and tumble of ardent lovemaking with a loving partner can make you feel as if you've had a refreshing vacation away from the responsibilities of your everyday life.

February 9, *Aquarius 9*

What Makes You Tick

You tend to walk around with your head in the clouds and base close relationships on romantic ideals rather than practical realities. Even though your Aquarian Sun sign makes you more independent than most other number 9s, intimate relationships bring out the contradictory aspects of your nature. When you are in love, you feel as if you're involved in a tug-of-war between your intellect and your emotions.

Between the Sheets

Your natural instincts send you one type of message, and your rational mind sends you another. Consequently, you go back and forth between your longing for independence and your desire to establish an intense connection with a soul mate. You yearn for intimacy, yet you are deathly afraid of entrapment and emotional vulnerability. Once you overcome your reservations about intimacy, you're capable of immersing yourself totally in the moment. Romantic fantasy and role-playing games probably play a large part in your love life, and since you are totally uninhibited in bed, anything new or different intrigues you. Unconventional, creative types appeal to you, because you don't want a "one-size-fits-all" relationship.

Tips for Your Ideal Lover

Creating a dreamy atmosphere relaxes you, and a romantic seduction scene, with soft music and sexy apparel, is a very effective way to get you going. During foreplay, sexy eye contact, provocative conversation, and erotic attire all serve as tantalizing aphrodisiacs for your lovemaking.

February 10, *Aquarius 1*

What Makes You Tick

You live your life on your terms. The relationships you find most comfortable involve sharing common interests with your partner, yet also having the freedom to pursue your own projects as well. While you don't want to be joined at the hip to your partner, you are capable of forging a bond that lasts a lifetime with your soul mate.

Between the Sheets

For a person to capture your affection, he or she needs to make you feel as though you can have witty, intelligent conversations along with steamy sexual encounters. Love for you is an adventure, and lovemaking is an opportunity to share exciting new experiences with your bedmate. Easily bored, you may lose interest in a relationship that becomes too secure and routine. In the bedroom, you like to shake things up with innovative ideas, and you enjoy being the aggressive force in games of seduction. Carefree and emotionally detached when it comes to your sexuality, you have few qualms about exploring sexual frontiers or busting through taboos. Your ideal mate helps make your erotic fantasies come true.

Tips for Your Ideal Lover

You like diversity in the bedroom and enjoy exploring the latest in sensual enhancements. Still, cerebral foreplay turns you on as effectively as the physical variety, and words, as well as caresses, serve as aphrodisiacs. The free-spirited lover who can match your sexual imagination ignites a fire in your libido.

February 11, *Aquarius 2*

What Makes You Tick

Your love nature is full of enigmatic contradictions. You yearn for freedom, yet you cling possessively to your beloved. Despite your small regard for society's ideas of proper behavior, you're a genuine romantic. You're also more solid and dependable than other members of your Sun sign, and as long as your partner doesn't impinge on your personal space, you prefer being half of a team to being on your own.

Between the Sheets

Although the emotionally challenged water bearer often runs into difficulty when confronted with too much intimacy, you need a life partner to share your joys and sorrows. Moreover, you understand your own quirks where love is concerned, and your marvelous sense of humor prompts you to joke about your foibles. Up-front and direct about your sexual impulses, you have no compunction about initiating hot sex when the mood is upon you. You particularly enjoy that part of a love affair that involves courting and being courted. However, you need more from your bedmate than just sex. What you actually want is companionship and a mental connection that complements the physical one.

Tips for Your Ideal Lover

You enjoy creating a pleasant atmosphere for your beloved, and you will do whatever you deem necessary to keep the relationship running smoothly both in bed and out of it. You bring fun and spontaneity into the bedroom, and your hearty appetite for tactile pleasure makes you a master of sensual foreplay.

February 12, *Aquarius 3*

What Makes You Tick

Warm and friendly with an offbeat sense of humor, you get along with most people. In fact, you project so much positive energy and enthusiasm that others are naturally drawn to you. Partnership for you needs to be based on shared interests and open dialogue. While you are loyal to your loved ones, you won't tolerate restrictions on your freedom, and you refuse to allow anyone to keep you from doing what you want.

Between the Sheets

You are an exciting, playful, innovative lover, yet you're rarely driven by an overwhelming need for sex and tend to treat it as an enjoyable pastime. Although the physical side of love matters, you don't let it assume major importance in your life. Without companionship, and mental rapport, you quickly lose interest, no matter how hot the sex. When it comes to establishing true intimacy, your intellectual approach and laid-back attitude can be a hindrance. People born on this date are emotionally challenged, so your significant other may not understand why you can't always show how deeply you care. Although you are perfectly comfortable discussing your sex life, you balk when it comes to examining your feelings.

Tips for Your Ideal Lover

You enjoy creative, spontaneous foreplay and trying different positions. You like to experiment and can be so uninhibited that you make your lover blush. Variety in the bedroom is a must; if the sexual relationship becomes boring, you may begin looking elsewhere.

February 13, *Aquarius 4*

What Makes You Tick

In close relationships, you rarely act the way others expect. Since you believe the head should rule the heart, strong emotions make you uncomfortable. Emotionally, you fear too much intimacy, but physically you're open to just about anything that brings pleasure to both parties. Behind closed doors, you're witty and extremely sexy. However, you require an intellectual connection along with the physical one; when your mind is engaged, your body follows.

Between the Sheets

When someone catches your eye, your approach is subtle. You are not likely to broadcast your attentions until you feel certain that you're on firm ground. You are torn between the love of excitement and the unpredictability of your Aquarius Sun sign and number 4's deeper craving for safety and security. Behind closed doors, you're physically passionate yet aloof and reserved emotionally. The wild, unconventional part of you likes to seduce and be seduced in bizarre and unanticipated ways, but another part of you tends to be more traditional and romantic. One moment you are willing to follow your need for sexual fulfillment wherever it leads, and the next you're surprised by your own actions.

Tips for Your Ideal Lover

Your ideal suitor engages your imaginative mind along with your body. Since you see sex as a thrilling adventure, your attitude toward the erotic and exotic is essentially nonjudgmental. Lively sex talk peppered with humor turns you on. In a loving union, you happily make room for the innovative and unexpected.

February 14, *Aquarius 5*

What Makes You Tick

A Valentine's Day birthday means that you may have difficulty figuring out how to relate to others without giving up your own individual rights. As a result, you may substitute intellectual kinship for emotional ties. Even in a close relationship, you need to retain enough breathing space to keep from feeling hemmed in. What you require from a romantic union is both mental and physical satisfaction. When you give your love, it must be on your own terms.

Between the Sheets

In the bedroom, you're naturally low key and may prefer having your partner take the initiative. However, his or her approach needs to be subtle; although you can be seduced, you resist being dominated. Since you are easily bored, you're drawn to the new and unusual. Although your sex drive is not particularly strong, your free-spirited, unconventional nature makes you open to most forms of erotic experimentation. With the right person, you make an uninhibited, passionate, considerate lover, as well as a caring and understanding life partner. While some born on this date seem to prefer casual attachments without commitment, others only enjoy love and sex in a safe, comfortable, long-term partnership.

Tips for Your Ideal Lover

Sexually, you're open to suggestion. In fact, the very idea of sex often serves as a turn-on. Your open mind and unconventional nature could lead you to explore all sorts of exotic pleasures. With your fascination for gadgets and technology, you probably enjoy toys and devices that enhance sensual enjoyment.

February 15, *Aquarius 6*

What Makes You Tick

Generally more partnership oriented than other Aquarians, you feel incomplete without a significant other to share your life. Even so, you wouldn't dream of surrendering your cherished independence for a relationship that doesn't live up to your extremely high standards. Your ideal union combines sex and romance with friendship and mental rapport. In the bedroom, the delicate sophistication of the number 6 adds romance to Aquarius's intellectual style of lovemaking.

Between the Sheets

You're affectionate and caring, yet you project a sense of airy detachment even at the most intimate moments. In love as in life, you are something of an idealist. You hate the thought of being restricted in your movements. Consequently, you may decide to hold off getting seriously involved for quite a while. Still, you can be impulsive when attraction hits you. Once you are involved, the most important thing to you is pleasing your bedmate. With a like-minded partner, you're predisposed to try any position or erotic toy at least once. You also want a bit of fun between the sheets, and you enjoy being with someone who can amuse and stimulate you both mentally and physically.

Tips for Your Ideal Lover

Despite your small regard for society's ideas of behavior, you're something of a romantic. Sexuality is only one of the things you're passionate about, and sometimes your libido requires a wake-up call. Since physical stimulation begins in your active imagination, an elegant seduction scene is a nice way to get your juices flowing.

February 16, *Aquarius 7*

What Makes You Tick

Although you crave sexual fulfillment, you also need a lover with whom you can talk. Moreover, you may feel torn between your love of freedom and your desire for a committed union. Consequently, you blow hot and cold; your moods swings can seem extreme. Since your ideas about intimate relationships tend to be rather idealistic, you may spend more time chasing your dream than actually settling down to a real-life partnership.

Between the Sheets

No matter how close you get to your mate, there's always a part of you that you reserve only for yourself. In the bedroom, you're an innovative, inventive, and enthusiastic lover. Even so, physical lovemaking is not as important to you as mental rapport. Although you regard the sex act as liberating, pleasurable, and fun, you don't necessarily consider it the only basis for a relationship. A long-term union needs to be based on common interests and the sharing of a larger purpose. There are times when you feel conflicted between your intellectual awareness of sex as a purely physical act, and your emotional ideal of lovemaking as a transcendent union symbolizing the spiritual joining of two souls.

Tips for Your Ideal Lover

A dreamy atmosphere in which to enjoy moments of intimacy arouses you and enhances your sensual pleasure. You intuit the most effective way to enchant your lover, and sharing sensual pleasures with your mate sparks your own desires and spurs you on to even more passionate lovemaking.

February 17, *Aquarius 8*

What Makes You Tick

The diverse aspects of your nature combine the mentality of the idealist with the practicality of the realist. Despite number 8's ingrained respect for tradition, your Aquarian Sun sign gives you a freer, more unconventional outlook with regard to intimate relationships. Consequently, half your head is seeking a long-term committed union, while the other half craves unconstrained freedom. Eventually, you must make a decision and choose between independence and commitment.

Between the Sheets

Although you have what it takes to attract anyone you like, you're extremely particular. You're especially likely to rebuff the lover who attempts to control you. Once involved, you crave love and affection, yet you hold back until you feel totally secure—and even then, you rarely surrender to chaotic emotions. Physically, however, you're open-minded and unconventional. When you allow yourself to relax and unwind, your innate passion and sensuality emerge. Still, sometimes you get so caught up in other things that you forget about lovemaking altogether. Usually, it only takes a little reminder and a few sexy suggestions to spark your desire and get your motor going.

Tips for Your Ideal Lover

You may be a bit more conservative than the typical water bearer, but you're also more passionate. The quirky Aquarian in you readily asserts itself behind closed doors, and your attitude toward erotica is nonjudgmental. You believe that nothing is too unconventional, as long as it pleases both partners.

February 18, *Aquarius* 9

What Makes You Tick

There is a part of you that belongs only to yourself. Although you long for intimacy, you may hide your feelings behind a mask of feigned nonchalance in an attempt to protect your cherished independence. Your ideal mate understands your need for some alone time to explore your own interests. You expect more than just sex and romance from a love relationship. What you're really seeking is a psychic link that transcends differences in personality and temperament.

Between the Sheets

Because of a tendency to view relationships through rose-colored glasses, you don't always see yourself or your partner very clearly. With your head in the clouds, you may rush into a relationship based more on fantasy than reality. Then when your more logical side asserts itself, you come back down to terra firma with a thunk. Still, even in your closest relationships, you maintain an air of Aquarian aloofness that is often at odds with the innate emotionality of the number 9. Boredom is an anathema to you inside the bedroom and outside, and romantic fantasy probably plays a large part in your love life.

Tips for Your Ideal Lover

A warm bath or soak in a hot tub with aromatic oils and surrounded by candles relaxes you and your mate, and sexy music adds to the dreamy enchantment. Since you are totally uninhibited in bed, anything new or different intrigues you. Role-playing engages your imagination and inflames your libido.

February 19, *Pisces 1*

What Makes You Tick

Beneath your tender, chameleonlike exterior, you are passionate and adventurous, and you thrive on challenge and excitement in a relationship. A champion of the underdog, you do what you can to help those who cannot help themselves. Unlike others of your Sun sign, you're willing to take risks when it comes to matters of the heart. Even if love disappoints, you refuse to give up on your deep-seated belief that things will get better.

Between the Sheets

In the bedroom, you're a curious combination of sentiment and sensuality and unconventional unpredictability. As a result, you may go back and forth between tender lovemaking and bawdy, outrageous experimentation. By and large, you are demonstrative and straightforward in your affections and extremely considerate of your partner's wishes. Your intuition is highly developed, and you know instinctively what your lover wants and how to provide it. Although you may not always be able to express your own desires in words, your ideal mate understands your need for unconditional love. You particularly appreciate unbounded affection and expressions of love in the form of well-placed words and thoughtful gifts.

Tips for Your Ideal Lover

Tender moments of intimacy in the privacy of your bedroom serve as a wake-up call for your innate sensuality. Alone with your lover, your fantasies find full expression, and your erotic imagination transports you to exotic places. With a little encouragement, love and romance turn swiftly into lust and passion.

February 20, *Pisces 2*

What Makes You Tick

Love is all-important to you, and you tend to dive into a new relationship without much thought as to how it will turn out. A sensitive, caring person, you listen intently to your beloved, and you expect the same kind of understanding and appreciation in return. Because you are psychically sensitive, you often feel what your partner is feeling, and without realizing it, you absorb his or her emotions.

Between the Sheets

Although you may be impulsive when it comes to love, you are the quintessential romantic; once you have given your heart, you're not likely to ask for it back. Since you dislike arguments and disagreements, you act as peacemaker to try to resolve any problems that crop up. Sex is meant to be a communion of both body and soul, and in an intimate union, you need to be able to share your innermost secrets and fantasies with your partner. A feeling of acceptance and belonging is important to you. In your ideal relationship, your significant other is as caring and emotionally involved as you are.

Tips for Your Ideal Lover

A sensualist with a need for a profound connection to your mate, you're turned on by an affectionate partner who is equally ready to make love. Motivated by a strong sex drive and a love of physical pleasure, you're driven over the edge when your lover slowly explores your entire body.

February 21, *Pisces 3*

What Makes You Tick

Although you want the grounding that partnership offers, you fear emotional commitment. Consequently, you may dance around the edges of long-term involvement, while keeping your suitor at arm's length. When you do get involved, however, you make a delightfully romantic partner. Your mind is your most sensitive erogenous zone, and your fluency with playful sexy banter makes you a seductive lover.

Between the Sheets

Sociable, outgoing, and witty, you want a mate who provides intellectual stimulation along with love and companionship. What you're seeking is a psychic link that transcends differences in personality and temperament. Moreover, the dreamy, more idealistic side of your nature also longs for romance. Even though you yearn for the grounding of a stable union, part of you fears commitment. When you love, you love deeply, yet you're uncomfortable with the loss of independence that profound caring engenders. In the bedroom, you are sensual and alluring. A skillful bedmate and compulsive charmer, your technique is a mixture of tenderness and sexual expertise. Since you can feel with your mind as well as your body, verbal communication is as important to you as physical touching.

Tips for Your Ideal Lover

You have few inhibitions, and you dislike having your activities confined to a specific time or place. Boredom is an anathema to you; you find the thought of exploring outrageous sexual fantasies appealing. Sexy talk turns you on, so your idea of great foreplay combines kissing and touching with lively sexual banter.

February 22, *Pisces 4*

What Makes You Tick

You have an idealistic, romantic side, but you try very hard to keep it under wraps. Even so, you crave attention and affection and may not be truly happy without a loving life partner. Although somewhat reclusive, you enjoy the company of a mate who is more outgoing and sociable. In private, your warmth and sexual stamina create many moments of treasured intimacy.

Between the Sheets

Despite a rather serious façade, you have a whimsical, humorous side that makes you a great deal of fun to be with. Behind closed doors, you are a generous, considerate lover. You intuit your partner's unspoken desires and instinctively respond to them. Although ardent and sensual, you are a practical romantic. Your bedroom approach is typically well planned, and your sexual advances are usually carefully orchestrated. You don't much care for unplanned encounters, preferring instead to set up "sex dates" in advance. Especially during foreplay, you tend to follow a set routine. As a lover, your movements are slow and sensuous, and you enjoy drawing out the lovemaking in anticipation of a big finish.

Tips for Your Ideal Lover

Your libido may need a little coaxing after a long workday, but once ignited your passion and physical stamina keep you going through the night. Music and candles create a romantic atmosphere for lovemaking, aromatic massage energizes you, and slow, erotic foreplay draws out your lusty appetite for sensual pleasure.

February 23, *Pisces 5*

What Makes You Tick

Even in your closest relationships, you exude an air of aloofness that is often at odds with the emotionality of your Pisces Sun sign. Love brings out the paradox of your romanticism and your rationality. With your head in the clouds, you rush into a relationship based more on fantasy than reality. Then your more logical side asserts itself, and you come back to reality with a thud.

Between the Sheets

You pour your heart and soul into an intimate union, and your idealistic attitude toward love leads you to expect a lot of give-and-take with your mate. A nurturing, attentive partner brings out the best in you, while a neglectful one makes you want to cut and run. You are an innovative and creative bedmate, particularly with a partner who makes you feel loved and respected. Even so, all by itself, the physical side of love really doesn't do it for you. You admire original thinkers who understand your need to cultivate your own interests, and unless you can experience the closeness of true friendship and companionship, you won't feel totally satisfied.

Tips for Your Ideal Lover

Your ideal partner uses creativity and innovation to devise all sorts of erotic pleasures based on sexual fantasy and role-playing games. Anything new and different intrigues you, and your open-minded, unconventional nature is fascinated by practices that others may consider a bit naughty or beyond the pale.

February 24, *Pisces 6*

What Makes You Tick

Relationships are important to you, and once involved, you identify with your partner's best interests. Since you seek harmony in everything, you may solicit his or her opinions and then reformulate your own thoughts to conform. Your romantic unions are especially intense, because of your tendency to abandon yourself to love. You look at others through rose-colored glasses, so if they turn out to not be everything you'd hoped, you're sorely disappointed.

Between the Sheets

You dislike being alone, and without an intimate relationship in your life, you can feel incomplete. When deeply involved with someone, you're an extraordinarily giving person. Sometimes you become so devoted to pleasing your beloved that you forget the relationship is meant to be an equal partnership. Versatile, and highly skilled in lovemaking, you're as readily aroused by giving pleasure as receiving it. Although you find foreplay a wonderful turn-on, a more direct path to your sensual side is through your intellect and imagination. Although a romantic ambiance with candlelight and soft music puts you in the mood, you really need a lover who knows how to excite your mind along with your body.

Tips for Your Ideal Lover

Erotic play in the privacy of your own home evokes transcendent moments. Nothing delights you more than a warm, aromatic bath with your lover, followed by an intimate massage that engages all your senses. Sharing deep physical pleasures with your beloved re-energizes you spiritually as well as physically.

February 25, *Pisces* 7

What Makes You Tick

In many respects, you're a loner. Although you tend to prefer a relationship that allows you the freedom to do your own thing, you yearn for true intimacy—still it's difficult for you to deal with the demands of such a close union. You sometimes require periods of solitude, but, by and large, you are a romantic. When you find the individual who lights up your soul, you move in pretty quickly.

Between the Sheets

Feeling accepted and appreciated is important to you, and you crave a love connection that nurtures your spiritual, intellectual, and physical self. While you will do just about anything to please your beloved, you need a partner who doesn't expect you to be the only one making sacrifices. You tend to be idealistic regarding love and sex, and you might be tempted to hold back because you're seeking perfection in a mate and in a relationship. However, the intuitive lover knows that your need for companionship outweighs your desire for independence, and with patience, he or she will learn how to release the deep layers of passion hidden beneath your air of aloof mystery.

Tips for Your Ideal Lover

Comfort, beauty, and luxury draw out your romantic ardor, and you respond sensually to gentle caresses and the relaxing pleasure of a foot massage. You have an almost-telepathic sense of how to arouse your bedmate. Once sparked, your libido spurs you on to even more ecstatic lovemaking.

February 26, *Pisces 8*

What Makes You Tick

You have two distinct sides to your character. You are as idealistic as any other fish, yet also serious and practical. In an intimate relationship, you can be dreamy and romantic but also responsible and devoted. While generous and protective of your beloved, your sensitive feelings are easily hurt if you sense that your help is not really wanted or appreciated. Despite the self-sufficiency of the number 8, your Pisces Sun sign craves affection and you may not be happy without it.

Between the Sheets

Starry-eyed and romantic, you can also be completely down to earth. Your ideal lover knows how to charm both sides of your contradictory nature. With the right person, you respond to the magic of the moment; a traditionally romantic courtship stirs your libido. Your seduction style is subtle but powerful, and once you let down your guard, the combination of your sensuous nature and physical passions brings out your strong sexual appetite. In the bedroom, it might take you awhile to let go of the cares of the day, but once you warm up, you are anything but shy and reserved.

Tips for Your Ideal Lover

You don't like to be rushed when making love and a slow-moving, patient lover knows how to ease you into moments of relaxed sensuality. Sweet talk and praise prime you for the erotic experience to come. Once you get going, you welcome a bit of rough-and-tumble sexual play.

February 27, *Pisces 9*

What Makes You Tick

Love for you is the stuff of poetry, dreams, and fairy tales. Your deep feelings are easily engaged—and easily wounded. Because of a tendency to view relationships through rose-colored glasses, you may not see yourself or your partner very clearly. Your gentle, tenderhearted love nature requires tons of affection, encouragement, and emotional support. Yet with your wonderful imagination, you can make even the most ordinary union seem glamorous and exciting.

Between the Sheets

Imaginative and deeply romantic, sex for you is a fanciful escape into an ethereal realm where you connect body, mind, and soul. Fantasy plays a large part in your love life, so candlelight, soft music, and beautiful surroundings add spice to your amorous adventures. Mundane difficulties in your relationship don't matter too much as long as you can enjoy romantically blissful times with your mate. You can create a beautiful mental world that is more real to you than the physical world you inhabit. Your ideal partner shows his or her love and affection in ways that make you feel truly special.

Tips for Your Ideal Lover

Behind closed doors, your passion can be volcanic, and your quiet, submissive nature may become quite demanding and sexually exciting. During foreplay, eye contact, provocative conversation, and erotic attire all enhance your lovemaking. Water is Pisces 9's ultimate aphrodisiac, and swimming or showering with your lover never fails to turn you on.

February 28, *Pisces 1*

What Makes You Tick

Caught between the tenderhearted fish's willingness to help all comers and the "me first" philosophy of the number 1, you often feel conflicted and at odds with yourself. A consummate romantic, you are easily swept off your feet, and since falling in love is a huge experience for you, you tend to view a love match as a binding partnership. However, if the reality of everyday life fails to live up to your idealistic notions, you may be seriously let down.

Between the Sheets

Since you believe that the best defense for susceptible emotions is offensive action, you hide your emotional vulnerability behind a façade of sexual daring, and your aggressive bedroom style places you among the more dynamic of the Pisces lovers. Even so, your romantic side requires a considerable amount of affectionate pampering from your significant other. In return, you are ever cognizant of your partner's wishes and desires and more than happy to fulfill them. However, when disappointments hit your relationship, you may find it easier to make a new start than ride out the emotional storm.

Tips for Your Ideal Lover

There is an adventurous, bawdy side to your love nature that can only be fully expressed in an intimate setting. Even in a long-term relationship, you cling to your fantasies, so role-playing games are always a turn-on. With your wonderfully innovative imagination, you conjure up a sexy, exciting never-never land where passion lives forever and anything that feels good is acceptable.

February 29, *Pisces 2*

What Makes You Tick

You're a romantic, yet you like material comforts and realize you can't live on love alone. Even with your head in the clouds, you manage to keep your feet on the ground. Sensual and affectionate, you're both giving and responsive. A traditionalist in many ways, you enjoy the ritual of courting and being courted. When you settle on the one you consider your soul mate, you're devoted but also possessive.

Between the Sheets

Initially, you may fall in and out of love fairly easily, but once you settle down with Mr. or Ms. Right, you're naturally loyal. As long as you feel secure in the relationship, you make a wonderfully considerate partner. However, when your sensitive feelings are hurt, you become clingy and jealous. Even so, you dislike disagreements and you're usually the first to make up after an argument. For you, lovemaking is a total experience, and you expect the sex act to be physically and emotionally satisfying for both partners. You project an air of mystery that is extremely seductive and alluring, and in the privacy of the bedroom, you are passionate, sensual, and uninhibited.

Tips for Your Ideal Lover

When the lights go out, you turn on. Your sexual impulses are immediate and intense, and once begun, the act of love absorbs you completely. Your imagination and intuition are the keys to establishing a link to your lover, and they play a major role in bringing your erotic fantasies to life.

March 1, *Pisces 1*

What Makes You Tick

You project an air of glamorous excitement that has been known to sweep potential suitors right off their feet. Beneath your calm, easygoing outer façade, there is a passionate sexuality that is best expressed in private. While you may be timid in some life areas, lovemaking is not among them. Consequently, until you meet Mr. or Ms. Right, you can get involved in some pretty tempestuous romantic adventures.

Between the Sheets

Naturally sensuous, with a strong sex drive, you are an ardent, dynamic lover. Although you yearn for the bliss of a perfect union with your soul mate, you may have second thoughts about a long-term relationship once you get it. Although your heart tells you to stay put, your freedom-loving mind may urge you to pull away and reclaim your independence. With your daring love nature and lusty sexuality, you are willing to try just about anything at least once. Since you have few bedroom inhibitions, you enjoy experimenting with new ways of pleasing your partner. Your hot-blooded, passionate side practically guarantees a pleasurable time. However, your sentimental side also enjoys quiet romantic evenings filled with cuddling and kissing.

Tips for Your Ideal Lover

You have a strong libido and a depth to your sexuality that may not be apparent on the surface. Your ideal lover creates a romantic atmosphere for lovemaking, but he or she also understands your fiery sex drive and longing to be carried away on a wave of love and passion.

March 2, *Pisces 2*

What Makes You Tick

The stability of the number 2 helps ground sensitive solar Pisces and provides you with the requisite practicality to turn your dreams into concrete realities. Temperamentally, you're a romantic and an idealist, with a genuine love of beauty. A warm, social being, you have a compassionate heart and a friendly, easygoing manner. In a love union, you're tactful and receptive to the needs and feelings of your significant other.

Between the Sheets

Attentive and caring, you listen closely to your lover's concerns, and you expect similar consideration in return. You need to feel appreciated and to know that you and your mate are working to create a harmonious life together. When things go smoothly, your romantic side emerges and life takes on a deeper meaning. Your well-developed intuition allows you to tune in to the feelings of your bed partner. When you give your heart, you do so 100 percent, so it's important to you that the object of your affection is trustworthy and dependable. Physically passionate, sensual, and affectionate in bed and elsewhere, you have a genuine talent for creating comfortable romantic settings for making love.

Tips for Your Ideal Lover

The pleasures of the bedroom are the glue that ties you to your partner. You enjoy the sexual tension that builds with teasing, tantalizing foreplay. Since your sensuality is sparked by touching and stroking, you are turned on big-time by slow, deliberate exploration of each other's bodies.

March 3, *Pisces 3*

What Makes You Tick

A friendly, talkative fish, you're fascinated by people and interested in everyone you meet. Affectionate and playful, you love romantic wordplay and light-hearted fun, but you need to be careful lest you give the other person the wrong impression. Although you remind yourself to test the waters before you jump into a new relationship, you delight in congenial company and may become seriously involved before you realize what's happening.

Between the Sheets

In bed and out of it, you enjoy trying new things, and you're easily seduced by an invitation to go a bit further than you intended. However, above all else, challenging conversation wins your heart. Intimacy does not come as easily to you as it does to other Pisces natives. Although you want a partner who is a soul mate, you are independent and self-assured and you expect your mate to be the same. Your ideal significant other is adventurous, sexy, fearless, and willing to join you in your exploration of the unknown. Sexually intuitive, you're able to read the unspoken desires of your bedmate and respond as if they had been openly expressed.

Tips for Your Ideal Lover

Your fluency with suggestive banter makes you an extremely sexy, seductive lover, and laughing, talking, and flirting in bed is your idea of exhilarating foreplay. Your own originality and carefree nature give you the courage to try new things, and a creative, innovative bed partner inspires you to push the limit in your sexual encounters.

March 4, *Pisces 4*

What Makes You Tick

Despite a decided romantic side to your nature, you tend to see intimate relationships as serious business and you probably don't give your heart away as readily as others of your Sun sign. However, once you've opened yourself up to another person, you are in for the long haul and unlikely to close back up anytime soon.

Between the Sheets

In bed, you are something of a straight arrow; you are totally honest in your approach to sex. The mate or partner who likes to play emotional games will not get very far with you. Your ideal mate offers sincere affection and quiet admiration. Once you feel safe and secure in a romantic relationship, your lusty passion emerges with little coaxing. You respond with enthusiasm to a classy, romantic atmosphere with music and scented candles. Refined lovemaking can help you communicate the love and caring that you may not be able to express in words. Since endurance is your forte, you find no reason to rush things, and slow, sensual foreplay relaxes you and draws out your deepseated sensuality.

Tips for Your Ideal Lover

You enjoy creature comforts and probably prefer sex in your own bed. While you get off on the simple pleasures of lovemaking, the partner who introduces you to a more exotic erotic sexuality can turn you on in exciting new ways by stirring the red-hot passions bubbling beneath your surface calm.

March 5, *Pisces 5*

What Makes You Tick

An eternal optimist, you believe what people tell you, and at times your idealistic turn of mind can make you seem a bit naive. Even so, you are rather more carefree and independent than other members of your Sun sign. Your ability to keep your problems and difficulties to yourself until you solve them sets you apart from the typical fish and earns you the respect of friends and detractors alike.

Between the Sheets

You expect more than just sex from an intimate union. You respond most readily to a partner who knows how to infuse a touch of romance and a sense of mystery into your relationship. What you are really seeking is a psychic connection that transcends space and time. Since you view love through rose-colored glasses, anything that's coarse or vulgar intrudes into your fantasy world and brings you down with a bang. Although you yearn for intimacy, you're skittish about commitment and somewhat afraid of emotional entrapment. However, once you overcome your reservations, you're capable of throwing yourself into lovemaking with breathtaking intensity; and you can keep going until both you and your lover are totally spent.

Tips for Your Ideal Lover

An ethereal atmosphere with aromatic oils and candles relaxes you, and sexy music turns you on. Your daydreams and erotic fantasies become exciting realities when played out in the bedroom. You like making love near water, especially the ocean, and taking a bath or shower with your lover is a real treat.

March 6, *Pisces 6*

What Makes You Tick

You are the quintessential romantic, yet you're so good at concentrating on other people's needs that romanticism is never the first thing a potential partner notices about you. A deeply sensitive, attentive person, you realize that being with someone requires a lot of adjustment. Although you willingly give your all to your beloved, you like knowing that your kindness is appreciated and you expect no less in return.

Between the Sheets

More than anything, you're attracted to sincerity; depth of emotion matters more to you than sexual technique. Sensual and affectionate, rather than lustful, you crave a love union that nurtures your heart and soul along with your body. A feeling of acceptance and belonging is important to you, and unless you feel a strong emotional connection to your lover, you may not find the lovemaking very fulfilling. Your ultimate desire is to merge sexual pleasure with spiritual union. At times you can be so idealistic where partnership is concerned that it is easy for you to become disappointed or disillusioned. However, you don't give up easily, and when things go wrong, you do everything possible to set them right.

Tips for Your Ideal Lover

In intimate moments, you willingly share your innermost dreams, and playing out your erotic fantasies with your bedmate is your ultimate turn-on. Erotic pleasure evokes transcendent moments, and nothing delights you more than a foot massage or a sensual soak with your partner in a tub strewn with flower petals.

March 7, *Pisces 7*

What Makes You Tick

With your tendency to see the best in everyone, you are genuinely interested in broadening your knowledge of the people around you. You approach romance with an innocent exuberance that makes a potential partner's heart race. However, half the time you live in a dream world. As a result, you can fall hopelessly in love, idealize your significant other, and then give in to despair because he or she cannot live up to your ideal.

Between the Sheets

A caring bed partner, your approach to lovemaking is tender yet subtly seductive. In the bedroom, you intuit the best and most effective way to arouse and enchant your lover. Moreover, sharing sensual pleasures with your mate sparks your own desires and spurs you on to even more passionate lovemaking. However, at times you feel decidedly uncomfortable in a close relationship, and your changeable nature can make you appear shy and hesitant one moment, spontaneous and uninhibited the next. As a lover, you are extremely loyal, generous, and caring but also needy and possessive. Such emotional intensity can lead to frequent mood changes that swing from explosive to brooding and back again.

Tips for Your Ideal Lover

Deep down, you yearn to be swept away on a wave of ecstasy. A dreamy atmosphere in which to share moments of exquisite intimacy arouses you and enhances your sensual pleasure. Imagination plays a huge part in your love life, and you enjoy creating exotic scenarios to act out with your partner.

March 8, *Pisces 8*

What Makes You Tick

Although commitment and responsibility don't frighten you, you're easily hurt by rejection. Even so, you're a secret romantic, and in an intimate union with the right person, you make an ardent lover and a caring and devoted mate. You enjoy nice things and comfortable surroundings. After a hard day's work, you probably prefer spending quiet evenings at home with your significant other to going out on the town.

Between the Sheets

To you, sex and sensuality are part of the entire package that makes up any romantic alliance. Although you crave emotional fulfillment along with sexual gratification, you're more comfortable with physical expressions of love than with discussions about feelings and emotions. In a subtle, unobtrusive way, you usually manage to control and direct much of the bedroom activity. Moreover, you captivate and enchant your bed partner with a unique combination of alluring fantasy and red-hot reality. A mood-setting romantic atmosphere stimulates you and turns you on, and you respond to the loving touch of a considerate lover. Once trust is established, you're capable of letting go completely and losing yourself in the wild expanse of desire generated by your love and passion.

Tips for Your Ideal Lover

You tend to hide both your sensitive emotions and your strong sexual passions behind a serene exterior. Your ideal bed partner is adept at using his or her imagination to invent enchanting erotic fantasies and role-playing games that are as stimulating and exciting as actual adventures.

March 9, *Pisces 9*

What Makes You Tick

Love is one of the few necessities in your life; you probably feel incomplete without it. You are in demand as a romantic companion because you know the secret to making a significant other feel wanted and appreciated. An incurable romantic, you live in your imagination and have wonderful dreams of what love should be. However, when things don't go according to plan, you have trouble letting go of your illusions.

Between the Sheets

Although typically not sexually aggressive, Pisces is one of the most beguiling and seductive Sun signs in the zodiac. When you fall in love, you fall hook, line, and sinker, and this total immersion often proves irresistible to the object of your affections. The mundane aspects of an intimate relationship don't really matter to you. You are happy as long as you can live out your dreams, and enjoy the romantic bliss of being together with your beloved. Love and sexuality are intertwined. With your vivid imagination, you can create a dream world filled with hot sex and old-fashioned romance.

Tips for Your Ideal Lover

The lover who whispers sweet nothings in your ear, scatters rose petals on your coverlet, and makes love to you by candlelight has the edge. Whether it's a romantic cruise, a trip to the beach, or a bath or shower with your mate, nothing turns you on like making love in or near water.

March 10, *Pisces 1*

What Makes You Tick

You send out mixed signals. On the one hand, you're a moody dreamer; on the other hand, you're an aggressive doer. In your passive, poetical mode, you want to watch the world go by. Yet when you're fired up by an idea, your authoritative manner and strong sense of purpose can surprise everyone. In a loving relationship, you're ardent and sympathetic to your partner's desires.

Between the Sheets

Your magnetic sexuality stems from your strong libido and deep-seated need for love and affection. You compensate for your emotional vulnerability by hiding it behind a façade of sexual daring. In the bedroom, your genius is your ability to merge the romantic and passionate elements of your nature in an unforgettable way. You revel in a carnival of the senses; by creating a comfortable love nest with your mate, you set the stage for erotic play to unfold. Sometimes you're filled with bravado, yet your tender side also emerges during lovemaking. Your fiery sex drive is tempered by your romantic idealism, and you're adept at elevating lovemaking to an art form that brings intense pleasure to both partners.

Tips for Your Ideal Lover

A lingering bath with your lover relaxes you and awakens sexual desire. You respond especially well to a sensual foot massage and teasing, fluttery kisses all over your face and body. Bringing music, flowers, and candles into the bedroom adds a seductive touch of romance to the mood of the moment.

March 11, *Pisces 2*

What Makes You Tick

You have an endearing otherworldly quality. Although one part of you is dreamy and romantic, the other part is sensible and down to earth. This ability to combine romance with practicality allows you to enjoy the benefits of both worlds. Physical love alone just doesn't do it for you. You need an intense emotional connection to your beloved in order to feel truly fulfilled.

Between the Sheets

Your idealism means that casual romance has virtually no place in your life. Your sensual nature appreciates the physical side of love, while your idealism engages the spiritual side. When you love someone, you do it with your whole heart, and both your body and your soul get into the act. You refuse to be hurried. In bed or out of it, you like to take the time to explore all the possibilities of sensual pleasure. At times you can be possessive or demanding, but more often you are generous, considerate, and indulgent of your partner's wishes. Despite a yearning for permanence and stability, you fall in love rather easily. However, when you find your "one and only," you are capable of absolute devotion.

Tips for Your Ideal Lover

When you make a genuine connection, you want a partner who knows how to elevate loving to an art form. You particularly adore long, lazy hours of lovemaking, during which you and your mate take the time to explore each other's bodies from head to toe.

March 12, *Pisces 3*

What Makes You Tick

Although you care very deeply in a loving relationship, you dislike the feeling of emotional vulnerability. Moreover, you're afraid of losing your freedom and independence. Sociable, verbal, imaginative number 3 wants friendship and intellectual stimulation, while your idealistic Sun sign craves poetry and romance. As a result, you may be almost as turned on thinking and talking about love as when you're actually having sex.

Between the Sheets

You possess an elusive, ethereal quality that sets you apart. Even in your most intimate moments, you are something of an enigma. You're a sensitive lover capable of extraordinary tenderness, but your bedroom approach is rational and may seem calculated. An unusual mix of romantic dreamer and unconventional thinker, you enjoy trying exotic things in bed as long as they are not crude or vulgar. To a great extent, the intensity of your sex drive depends on your imagination. Although you find physical foreplay a wonderful turn-on, a more direct path to your sensual side is through your intellect and imagination. When your intellect is stimulated by erotic sexual banter with your mate, your physical body quickly follows suit.

Tips for Your Ideal Lover

Your ideal lover excites your mind along with your body. Bewitched by imagination and dreams, you particularly enjoy acting out your erotic fantasies with your bedmate. A master storyteller, you're turned on by a lover with a fantasy life equal to your own.

March 13, *Pisces 4*

What Makes You Tick

Although warm and caring with family and close friends and affectionate in a romantic relationship, you're very private. You keep your own counsel and rarely share you plans with anyone outside your tight circle of acquaintances. When you work, you work hard, but at home you value peace and quiet. A steady relationship provides the secure foundation you need to pursue your ambitious dreams.

Between the Sheets

You depend on your bedmate to help take your mind off work and your responsibilities. An old-fashioned romantic courtship stirs your libido and plays into your erotic fantasies. An air of dignified reserve permeates your love style, but tender touching and stroking reveal the sensitivity you keep well guarded. Although your lusty passion is not on display for the world to see, it readily emerges behind closed doors. The melding of your sensuality and passion gives you a hearty sexual appetite. Your ideal lover is able to charm both the starry-eyed romantic and the serious realist in you. You may need a little coaxing after a workday, but once your ardor is ignited, you have stamina to burn.

Tips for Your Ideal Lover

Your imagination is your major erotic zone. Since you live out your sexy dreams in intimate moments, too much reality in the bedroom can be a downer. You like to take your time in bed and won't rush toward culmination until you've had your fill of tantalizing foreplay.

March 14, *Pisces 5*

What Makes You Tick

You may be torn between romanticism and rationality. You rush into a relationship based on fantasy, then logic reasserts itself and you fall back to earth. In a close relationship, you maintain an air of aloofness that's at odds with the emotionality of your Pisces Sun sign. The mix of warm sympathy and cool-headedness makes you an excellent friend, but it can be puzzling to a lover.

Between the Sheets

Although you long for intimacy, you may try to hide your feelings behind a façade of nonchalance in an attempt to protect your cherished freedom. Your ideal mate understands your need for some time alone to explore your interests. You expect more than sex and romance from a love relationship. What you're really seeking is a psychic link that transcends differences in personality and temperament. Boredom is an anathema to you, inside the bedroom and outside as well. The idea of exploring outrageous sexual fantasies is appealing. You'll dress up for role-playing games or experiment with different positions, as long as your bed partner is agreeable.

Tips for Your Ideal Lover

You're looking for a love that draws you into a mysterious adventure of discovery and excitement. You're turned on by the lover who willingly joins you in sex games and encourages you to act out your wildest fantasies. Creating a dreamy atmosphere with scented candles and sexy music adds to the fun.

March 15, *Pisces 6*

What Makes You Tick

Love is the seminal experience in your life, and once involved, you identify with your partner and his or her best interests. An intensely romantic union can be especially difficult for you, because of a tendency to abandon yourself completely to love. Since you seek harmony and accord in your alliances, you may solicit the other person's opinions rather then formulate your own.

Between the Sheets

Without an intimate relationship in your life, you can feel adrift and incomplete. Yet despite your interest in establishing a committed romantic partnership, your ideas regarding long-term unions are rather unrealistic. When deeply involved with someone, you're an extraordinarily giving person. You look at your lover through rose-colored glasses. Then if he or she turns out not to be everything you hoped, you can be sorely disappointed. Moreover, you are as likely to fall in love with a fantasy as with a real person. Although you find physical foreplay a wonderful turn-on, a more direct path to your sensual side is through your intellect and imagination. You want a mate who knows how to excite your mind along with your body.

Tips for Your Ideal Lover

Since fantasy and imagination play such a large part in your sex life, the person who wants to score points with you in the bedroom devises creative ways to add oomph to your lovemaking. Setting the stage with beautiful things provides an enticing romantic background for your erotic games.

March 16, *Pisces 7*

What Makes You Tick

With your idealistic compassionate nature, you tend to see only the good in others. When you find your special person, you have nothing but high hopes for the ensuing relationship. Although your faith may inspire the other person to be the best that he or she can be, you may be deluding yourself into allowing the object of your affection to take advantage of your essential goodness.

Between the Sheets

Despite your propensity for focusing on otherworldly considerations and a spiritual union with your soul mate, the lusty side of your sexuality quickly emerges in the bedroom. Behind closed doors, you use your colorful imagination to enliven the erotic experience and give it a touch of romantic glamour. While your changeability may be hard for your partner to figure out, your enigmatic aura of mystery is part of your special appeal. Sexually, you are happiest with a mate who offers you variety and introduces you to new ideas and experiences. In addition to exciting lovemaking, you need to be able to engage in stimulating conversation and share interesting ideas with your bedmate.

Tips for Your Ideal Lover

The patient lover knows how to tap the passionate ardor hidden beneath your air of mystery. Erotic pleasures evoke transcendent moments, and nothing delights you more than an intimate massage with scented oils that engages all your senses. Touching and stroking turn you on, and your increased desire spurs you toward ecstatic lovemaking.

March 17, *Pisces 8*

What Makes You Tick

You are romantic without being sentimental. Although something of a loner, you realize that you need a life partner to feel complete. You don't wear your heart on your sleeve like the more typical Pisces Sun native, but once your heart is won, you are one of the most steadfast, loyal partners around. When you love someone, you love very deeply, and it is easier for you to show your love through actions than words.

Between the Sheets

You may be reserved in public, but in the privacy of your own bedroom, you're demonstrative and straightforward in your affections. Sexual chemistry is important to you in a relationship, and you appreciate a partner whose passionate feelings are as strong as your own. While you want a significant other who is a soul companion, you also need to be with someone who shares your worldly values. Coldness and insensitivity are real turn-offs; you appreciate thoughtfulness and consideration. You are fond of traditional courtship rituals, yet you also like innovation and surprise. Your ideal lover is sexy, passionate, and adventurous enough to try new things in bed and elsewhere.

Tips for Your Ideal Lover

You are more than happy to go along with most methods of foreplay, including the use of sex toys that help stoke your engine and fire you up for lovemaking. You revel in spontaneous sexual creativity and your knack for intuiting your lover's needs and desires helps satisfy you both.

March 18, *Pisces 9*

What Makes You Tick

You recognize no boundaries between yourself and your significant other. Given your ability to merge your identity with that of your partner, your sense of self is not strongly developed and you may use close relationships as a measure of defining who you are. When things don't go as expected in an intimate union, you rely on your imagination to help you retreat into a private world of romantic fantasy.

Between the Sheets

You are very much in demand as a loving companion, because you're an expert at making your partner feel wanted and appreciated. Since you know what your lover is thinking and feeling, you are able to intuit his or her sexual needs and desires. You have no desire to dominate in the bedroom, and you're quite happy in a secondary role. Because Neptune rules your Sun sign, you tend to wear your heart on your sleeve, you're easily wounded by even the smallest of slights, and you may need to be constantly reassured of your own worth and importance. Seeking your soul mate could lead to a series of disappointments, but no matter what happens you are not inclined to give up on love and romance.

Tips for Your Ideal Lover

Spontaneous expressions of love turn you on. You adore small gifts of every kind, the more intimate and romantic the better. Being near water soothes your soul, and a surprise getaway weekend near the ocean or a lake delights you and makes you feel loved and appreciated.

March 19, *Pisces 1*

What Makes You Tick

You yearn for a loving union, and when you find it (or think you've found it), you throw yourself into the relationship. Charming and impulsive, you project an air of glamorous excitement. Although you come off as sympathetic and self-sacrificing, you can also be moody and inclined to pull away when things get too intense. While others may not be able to figure you out, the spell you weave can be irresistible.

Between the Sheets

Although a part of you is dreamy and romantic, there is another side that tends to be more sensible and down-to-earth. At times, you can be needy and demanding, but more often you are generous, considerate, and indulgent of your partner's wishes. Your sensual nature appreciates the physical side of love, while your romantic idealism engages the spiritual side. When you make a genuine connection, you long to share all of yourself with your soul mate, thereby elevating your lovemaking to an art form. In bed, your fiery sex drive prompts you to blaze a lusty trail, but you can also be emotionally vulnerable, and if your feelings are hurt, you pull back in hasty retreat.

Tips for Your Ideal Lover

In the bedroom, you don't want too much reality to burst your romantic bubble. The lover who turns you on is the one who shares your erotic fantasies, and role-playing games that enable you to act the part of the storybook hero or heroine excite you both mentally and physically.

March 20, *Pisces 2*

What Makes You Tick

There's an endearing otherworldly quality that emanates from those born on this date, yet even at your most ethereal, you keep your feet close to the ground. Sensual, poetic, and affectionate, you're both giving and responsive as a romantic partner. You fall in love rather easily, and any sign of passion brings out the lover in you. However, when you settle on the one person you consider your soul mate, you're loyal and devoted.

Between the Sheets

Not just sex, but all types of physical contact appeal to you. Since you are somewhat shy, rather than pursuing love, you tend to wait for it to come to you. A stable, loving union provides you with a sense of security, and once you find it, you are not likely to let it go easily. Behind closed doors, you express your affection in a tactile, hands-on manner. You enjoy adding to your sexual repertoire, and with your rich imagination, you have a real talent for setting the stage for lovemaking. You're willing give a great deal to your beloved in bed and elsewhere, but you expect equal consideration in return.

Tips for Your Ideal Lover

A sensualist with a need to establish a profound connection, you require a lot of physical affection. Sexuality begins with touching, and you especially like when you and your lover explore each other's bodies. You revel in a carnival of the senses and sharing the pleasures of sexy foods turns you on.

March 21, *Aries* 3

What Makes You Tick

Although your playful, outgoing personality brings you many romantic opportunities, you can be difficult to pin down, and your restless nature may keep you from sticking with one person for too long. Since you find boredom insufferable, you will stay around as long as your partner offers you plenty of stimulation and excitement. As a result, you try not to get too invested in relationships, and when one ends, you leave without tears.

Between the Sheets

You want everything in your life to be thrilling and spontaneous, including sex, and your ideal mate shares your interest in exploring new erotic territory. Since your intellect is your most sensitive erogenous zone, lovemaking usually begins inside your head. You believe that mental camaraderie creates sexual chemistry, and without it, there is no spark. Where your mind leads, your willing body swiftly follows. Although you enjoy sharing your interests and activities with someone special, you value your freedom and independence so much that a long-term relationship is sometimes difficult for you to sustain. Even in a solid monogamous union, you enjoy the game of love so much that you may continue to look and flirt.

Tips for Your Ideal Lover

Hearing what your lover is thinking and feeling during sex turns you on. You especially like discussing what you like doing or having done to you in bed. If a hint of routine invades your lovemaking, you like to stir things up with fantasy and role-playing.

March 22, *Aries 4*

What Makes You Tick

Meeting your professional and family responsibilities is important to you, and before you cut loose, you like to make sure all your chores are done. When you work, you work hard, but when you play, you want to put aside daily concerns and have some fun. At times, you can come off as headstrong because of your conviction that your way of doing things is best.

Between the Sheets

In bed, you are more ardent than sentimental, and hearts and flowers are rarely as appealing to you as lusty excitement. While you prefer not to rush headlong into romantic entanglements, you possess a robust libido and the passionate side of your nature runs deep and true. As a result, your strongest impulse is to live and love according to the demands of your heart. But sooner or later, you must come to terms with the inner conflicts caused by your yearning for independence and your desire for a committed, stable relationship. Once you develop a sense of trust, you are able to let go and become the truly amorous lover you were meant to be.

Tips for Your Ideal Lover

In the throes of passion, your cool reserve melts into sizzling physical intensity, and you thrive on lusty, high-energy lovemaking. When your mind is otherwise engaged with business and family concerns, your combustible sexual appetite can be swiftly ignited by a provocative look or a playful squeeze.

March 23, *Aries 5*

What Makes You Tick

For you, life's an adventure, and a relationship with you can be a walk on the wild side. In a romantic union, you're a fiery Aries, yet you also possess number 5's cool inner detachment that keeps you from getting truly close on an emotional level. Despite your independent spirit, you're very much a "people person." Although you can be somewhat difficult to live with, you are never dull or boring.

Between the Sheets

Since you need lots of change and stimulation, a quiet, harmonious relationship will probably drive you crazy. In an intimate relationship, friendship and intellectual rapport are as important to you as love and romance. Even so, your lovemaking is likely to be intense and frequent. Although not a particular fan of protracted foreplay, you won't hesitate to experiment with new or different erotic sexual techniques. You simply don't have the patience for sultry drawn-out love scenes. Between the sheets, you prefer slightly bawdy, rough-and-tumble romps to overly sweet and sentimental lovemaking. Since you need plenty of time to explore your own interests, your ideal partner is the person who doesn't expect you to be joined at the hip.

Tips for Your Ideal Lover

Since you have few qualms when it comes to sexuality, your curiosity and search for excitement may lead to exploration and experimentation on the very edges of the sexual frontier. Although you enjoy being the aggressor in the bedroom, you're just as happy being the target of seduction.

March 24, *Aries 6*

What Makes You Tick

You admire those who choose a carefree lifestyle, but you want the companionship of a soul mate more than independence. Your approach to lovemaking is full of contradictions. You enjoy the rituals of courtship; if the spark goes out of your romance, you may begin looking around for new thrills. Your ideal mate understands your enigmatic nature and is capable of switching gears to match your pace and rhythm.

Between the Sheets

Typically less aggressive and impetuous in bed than other Aries lovers, your romantic approach is a reflection of your idealistic nature and appreciation for beauty and harmony. While a part of you may yearn to go crazy and break all the rules, you're more readily aroused by slow, sensual lovemaking. Although happy to take the lead between the sheets, you also enjoy being teased, cajoled, and seduced into sweet submission. You like being enticed into sex with kissing and touching designed to inflame your desires. Even so, you can be slyly seductive about getting what you want. An occasional erotic free-for-all that adds a touch of spice to your bedroom routine may satisfy your most primal urges.

Tips for Your Ideal Lover

You tend to show contrasting sides of your nature in the bedroom. A lusty, uninhibited lover may spark your libido, or you may want sweet, tender caresses in a romantic setting. Either way, you respond ardently to the promise of ecstasy in smoldering hot kisses.

March 25, *Aries 7*

What Makes You Tick

Despite your fiery Aries nature, you feel things very deeply, but your restlessness and adventurous nature make it difficult for you to commit to any situation that might limit your personal freedom. When you do let yourself get intensely involved, you make a romantic, caring, extremely generous spouse or lover. You crave a spiritual connection with your soul mate and can potentially reach levels of intimacy that are beyond most people's comprehension.

Between the Sheets

You tend to come off as spacy and detached in the bedroom, and at times your overanalytical nature can produce an almost-clinical approach to love and sex. Versatility is your strong point, and you are pretty much willing to try anything at least once. However, the physical side of lovemaking alone rarely satisfies you. What you are really seeking is a transcendent experience, leading to a deeper union with your beloved. If your relationship goals are too lofty and unrealistic, you could be prone to disappointment when the union inevitably falls short of your ideal. Your perfect bedmate knows how to stand up to the unpredictable volatility that fuels your libido, without dampening your lusty enthusiasm.

Tips for Your Ideal Lover

Slowing things down during lovemaking can help keep your sexual desire at a steady boil. You particularly enjoy having your lover cover your entire body with erotic touching and stroking, adding soft fluttery kisses around your head and face to wake up your finer sensuality.

March 26, *Aries 8*

What Makes You Tick

You prefer action to emotion. You would much rather be doing something than sitting around talking about life and love. Although outwardly cool and controlled, you're ardent and romantic in the bedroom. You also tend to be moody and, at times, can be difficult to live with. Because you have such high standards, you may get irritable when things don't go as you think they should.

Between the Sheets

Although strongly sexed and sensual, you are quite capable of controlling and directing your passions. Despite your surface reserve, you're a romantic idealist and actually a lot lustier than your outer demeanor suggests. You may have some difficulty expressing your emotions, but you have no such problems when it comes to your libido. Behind closed doors, you make an exciting, passionate, adventurous lover. When you meet someone new, you tend to be careful in your approach, because you can't bear the thought of rejection. Even so, you relish the challenge of the chase, and prefer being the one making the first move. You take your time when choosing a life partner, but once you make the commitment, you do everything possible to secure the relationship.

Tips for Your Ideal Lover

You can be playfully aggressive in intimate moments, and a little roughhousing turns you on. Since you're something of a workaholic, you need a bed partner who knows how to get your attention and bring out the sexy beast with erotic touching and stroking.

March 27, *Aries 9*

What Makes You Tick

Your restless Aries nature is continually at odds with the idealistic notions of love and romance typical of the number 9 vibration. You yearn for an all-encompassing intimate relationship, yet you also want the independence to follow your personal destiny. You fall in love with your entire being, and you probably feel as if no one else has ever loved as you do.

Between the Sheets

Charming, impulsive, and impractical, you can also be totally irresistible. You project an air of glamorous excitement that can easily sweep potential suitors right off their feet. However, beneath your laid-back exterior, there is an adventurous bawdiness that is best expressed in private. With your lusty nature and fiery sex drive, you are willing to try just about anything. You have few inhibitions and enjoy experimenting with new ways of pleasing your mate. The contradictions in your sexual approach can cause you to veer erratically between aggression and passivity. Still, the passionate side of your love nature practically guarantees a great time in bed, while your sentimental side also enjoys quiet romantic evenings with your beloved, just cuddling and kissing.

Tips for Your Ideal Lover

Your vivid imagination can transport you and your lover to exotic places without even leaving home. Music and candlelight add dimension to your role-playing games, and an evening of fantasy and seduction leads to rapturous lovemaking. Better still is a romantic getaway for two, where erotic fantasy actually becomes a reality.

March 28, *Aries 1*

What Makes You Tick

Your affection is easily ignited, and your inclination is to follow your impulses no matter where they lead. Since you are spontaneity personified, your ardor and enthusiasm are likely to die a swift death unless your lover is capable of fanning the flames of passion with novel thrills. You have a fun-loving nature, and you like being with a romantic partner who is a playmate as well as a lover.

Between the Sheets

In bed, you're a force of nature and as headstrong, rash, and impulsive about your sexuality as you are about everything else. Since you enjoy the chase and relish the role of playful pursuer, you don't hesitate to seize the initiative. You're very clear about what turns you off and on, and your energetic style of lovemaking is not for the faint of heart. Even so, it takes more than just sexual attraction to hold your interest. Matching wits with your lover in the bedroom is a potent aphrodisiac; you quickly lose interest in a bedmate who is unable to keep up with you mentally as well as physically.

Tips for Your Ideal Lover

Routine turns you off. You need lots of stimulation, and you are usually eager to try just about any sexual innovation. Sex is a game for you, and your ideal bed partner is open-minded and prepared to join you in an ongoing search for excitement and adventure in and out of bed.

March 29, *Aries 2*

What Makes You Tick

You are a mixture of the directness of your Aries Sun sign and the patience and determination of the number 2. When you want to be with someone, you will pursue the object of your affection with dogged persistence. A dynamic lover, your irresistible mix of bold aggression and languid sensuality attracts potential lovers. However, your heart has more patience then your libido, and you prefer waiting for true love.

Between the Sheets

You like touching and being touched and initiating shared physical pleasures. A slow, steady seduction ignites your powerful sex drive, and pleasing your partner is as important to you as your own pleasure. Turned on by the beauty of nature, you enjoy making passionate love outdoors. Since you want and need stability in your love life, you get off on the closeness of an intimate ongoing relationship. Your ideal mate is both a lover and a friend. Like other Aries natives, you require a great deal of independence. Yet despite your need for personal freedom, you are inherently possessive and not always willing to grant your partner equal space and freedom.

Tips for Your Ideal Lover

Your sensuality extends far beyond the bedroom to other life areas. Sex is as fundamental as eating, and your sensual delight is particularly noticeable in the kitchen. Preparing a romantic meal with your significant other, or playfully feeding each other delectable tidbits, can serve as erotic foreplay for the ecstatic lovemaking that follows.

March 30, *Aries 3*

What Makes You Tick

A spontaneous and creative member of your Aries Sun sign, you refuse to be bound by conventional ways of thinking. Despite your independent nature, you enjoy having someone in your life who complements you emotionally and intellectually. Although you like the thought of sharing intimate moments, you are at times more in love with the idea of a soul mate than the actual fact of the relationship itself.

Between the Sheets

A fun lifestyle is as important to you as a solid, secure life. As a result, you may not be in much of a hurry when it comes to settling down. When you do find your one and only, sharing interests and going exciting places together probably top your to-do list. A penetrating intellectual connection also matters a great deal in a loving union. In the bedroom, your passion burns like a flaming meteor. Seductive suggestion and verbal innuendo inflame your desire and put you in the mood for lovemaking. You like variety; even a hint of routine makes you want to stir things up with innovative moves and spontaneous play or fantasy.

Tips for Your Ideal Lover

Endlessly curious in the bedroom and elsewhere, you thrive with a mate who matches your interest in amorous experimentation. Your mind is your most sensitive erogenous zone, and you're turned on by the partner who describes what he or she wants to do with you and to you.

March 31, *Aries 4*

What Makes You Tick

Although you're careful not to give your heart away too soon, you expect the union with the right person to last a lifetime. Your passion runs deep, and you like to keep your partner close. Betrayal is the one thing you find hard to forgive. However, your standards are so high that sometimes you may have to cope with disappointments in love.

Between the Sheets

You believe in hard work and responsibility, but you also believe in love and romance. Your Aries Sun sign craves a challenging intimate relationship that keeps you on your toes, while still maintaining the traditional roles and values indicated by the number 4 vibration. Your physical needs are strong, and your best romantic pairing includes a dynamic sexual relationship. An invigorating lover, you are anxious to explore all the sensual delights lovemaking has to offer. You like being the one in control, taking charge and setting the tempo for whatever is to happen next. An adventurous partner who is innovative and imaginative sustains your interest, because you require excitement and intensity in the bedroom and elsewhere.

Tips for Your Ideal Lover

After a hard day's work, you appreciate a seductive, aromatic massage. Your ideal mate knows how to use erotic touch to lure out the sexy beast in you. Once relaxed, you can be delightfully aggressive in a game of seduction, and a provocative look or a slow striptease will ignite your lusty libido.

April 1, *Aries 1*

What Makes You Tick

Nothing is hidden in your outgoing personality—what people see is what they get. Generous to a fault, you're loyal to your friends and fair with your adversaries. Rams may be quick to anger, but they're even quicker to forgive and forget. Although you can be difficult to live with, your noble spirit becomes evident when you are met halfway. You demand freedom, but with the right partner you can remain devoted for a lifetime.

Between the Sheets

The typical ram views life as a quest for romance and adventure. Sexually, you're a fireball; once aroused, you can be more passionate than any Sun sign except Scorpio. You prefer being the aggressor, and don't always appreciate being chased by potential lovers. However, once committed, you expect your mate to lavish love and attention upon you. As long as you believe that you've found your soul mate, you'll shower your significant other with tons of affection. Your days together will be full of fun, and your nights will be full of pleasure. For as long as it lasts, the relationship will be close to idyllic. However, if you should decide that it's over, you'll end the affair as quickly and impulsively as you began it.

Tips for Your Ideal Lover

When the thrill begins to fade, your inclination is to leave or at least to start looking elsewhere for fun and excitement. The person who wants to hold your love needs to constantly find new ways to reignite your Aries fire.

April 2, *Aries 2*

What Makes You Tick

Your solar Aries energy and vitality, positive outlook, and leadership capabilities are all well supported by the underlying determination and stability of purpose indicated by the number 2 vibration. However, there may be times when you feel as if you are completely at odds with yourself, especially when your pioneering spirit and go-go energy is being hampered or held back by the need for emotional and material security.

Between the Sheets

Even though you are an independent soul, you love the idea of sharing sensual intimate moments with the person you really care about. While you enjoy the time you spend on your own, you're happiest in a committed relationship. Boredom is an anathema to you; to keep the flames burning, your lover must be playful, imaginative, and adventurous. Your healthy sexual appetite is coupled with a large dose of romanticism, and you are turned on by all the sentimental trappings of sensuous lovemaking like moonlight, scented candles, music, and flowers. Feeding each other delectable tidbits of favorite foods can act as foreplay and heighten the sexual experience.

Tips for Your Ideal Lover

Your own love style is a combination of urgency and slow, steady seduction, and you respond eagerly to a lover with a similar approach. An evening out spent teasing and flirting with your partner can serve as a potent aphrodisiac for ecstatic lovemaking when you get home.

April 3, *Aries 3*

What Makes You Tick

Essentially a romantic, you're in love with the idea of going through life with your soul mate by your side. When you find a solid candidate, you target the object of your affection without hesitation or second thoughts. Unless you get bored or distracted, you make a delightful companion. Despite your passionate nature, sex in a relationship is secondary to mental intimacy and the ability to share ideas.

Between the Sheets

You regard sex as something of a glorious game, and you want a partner who offers more than just physical gratification. To catch and keep your attention a potential lover needs to engage in witty, intelligent conversation. You have a healthy sexual appetite coupled with a very verbal approach to lovemaking, and you particularly enjoy sharing your most intimate thoughts and fantasies with your bedmate. There is nothing worse than boredom; you're anxious to experience all there is in life so you're willing to try anything at least once. You love a challenge, and playful competitiveness in a spirited relationship keeps you hanging around to see what will happen next.

Tips for Your Ideal Lover

You approach lovemaking with enthusiasm and spontaneity, and you rarely plan ahead or attempt to control the action. Routine is like ice water to your libido, and your curiosity may lead you to explore all sorts of new erotic territory. You respond best to an imaginative, open-minded bed partner with few preconceived notions or inhibitions.

April 4, *Aries 4*

What Makes You Tick

A grounded visionary, you take life seriously and you're considerably more controlled than the typical Aries. While you may appear cool on the surface, inwardly you're a true romantic. Although your basic nature is fairly low-key compared to some more colorful rams, your need to win is equally strong. In all life areas, you assume that you are right and generally refuse to take no for an answer.

Between the Sheets

Commitment is not something you take lightly, and your demanding nature makes you rather selective. The screening process you use for a prospective mate is more often ruled by your head than your heart. Nevertheless, once you make your choice, you move ahead with deliberate speed. Your libido is strong and your sexual energy high. In an intimate union, you're a fiery lover with a seduction technique that's straightforward and direct. Although reserved in public, your erotic sensuality quickly surfaces behind closed doors. You don't require a great deal of foreplay to become physically aroused. In fact, you're usually willing to skip most of the appetizers and go straight to the main course.

Tips for Your Ideal Lover

You work hard and play hard, and a sensuous massage can help release pent-up tension. Once you are relaxed, engaging in a little aggressive roughhousing allows you to let off steam and open up to renewed intimacy after a stressful day. Catching you late at night, on the edge of sleep, makes for slow, lingering lovemaking.

April 5, *Aries 5*

What Makes You Tick

You sustain your individuality by following your own course in life, and you fervently resist any attempt to tell you what to do. Despite your independent spirit, you are essentially a "people person," and your magnetic personality attracts others and draws them to you. In love, you seek excitement, but intellectual companionship is as important as physical passion.

Between the Sheets

Inherently romantic and idealistic, you have a penchant for dramatizing and mythologizing every aspect of your life. Thanks to your sunny, fun-loving nature, attracting a lover is rarely a problem. Most people you meet long to get to know you better. In the bedroom, you are an ardent, attentive partner, and boring repetition has no place in your lovemaking. In fact, you rank among the wildest and most inventive of the Aries lovers. Although it doesn't take much to spark your passion, you crave much more than physical satisfaction from an intimate relationship. For you, a love union is a heart-and-soul experience, and your aim is to establish a feeling of oneness with your beloved.

Tips for Your Ideal Lover

You have few qualms when it comes to busting taboos or exploring the edges of the sexual frontier. Your innate curiosity may lead you to experiment with various techniques, including erotic fantasy games and sex toys. Your ideal lover is a verbal sparring partner who stimulates your mind along with your body.

April 6, *Aries 6*

What Makes You Tick

Although more tactful than the typical ram, you're just as ardent. While you admire individuals who live a carefree lifestyle, you want the companionship of a fulfilling union more than your independence. Since passion is not as important to you as intellectual rapport, you don't expect the initial sexual fireworks to last forever. However, if the romantic spark fades, you may begin searching for a new soul mate.

Between the Sheets

Less aggressive in bed than other Aries lovers, you thoroughly enjoy the romance of courting and being courted. In fact, you relish the steps leading to the sex act almost as much as the thrill of fulfillment. You prefer making love in a pleasant atmosphere with beautiful surroundings, where you and your lover can merge as a harmonious unit. For you, lovemaking is seduction in its highest expression. Equally turned on as seducer or the one being seduced, you respond to the slow, sensuous dance of erotic temptation. Sexy attire, smoldering looks, romantic words, sensuous food and drink, soft music, scented candles, luxurious bedding, and moonlight all put you in the mood for love.

Tips for Your Ideal Lover

You enjoy being enticed into sex with kissing and touching designed to inflame your desire. You love the feeling of being pursued and having your lover wear down your resistance. Whether it's a game of strip poker or a sensuous strip-tease, watching your partner undress for you is a sure-fire turn-on.

April 7, *Aries 7*

What Makes You Tick

You have your own ideas of what a loving relationship should be. You're looking for a partner who accepts you as you are, despite your changing moods. At times you may require periods of solitude, but never when your mate feels like making love. You don't favor casual alliances, and your romances are likely to be serious. Given your high expectations, you may be severely disappointed if real life doesn't conform to your ideals.

Between the Sheets

In the bedroom, you're imaginative and inventive, with a spontaneous, enthusiastic approach to lovemaking. You regard sex as the highest expression of love, and you enjoy adding touches of the erotic and experimental to the mix. However, to experience true fulfillment, you need to establish a bond with your partner that is spiritual as well as physical. You require a certain amount of pampering from your mate or lover. In return, you are sympathetic to your partner's wants and needs and more than willing to gratify them. You tend to be cautious about making the first move, because you loathe rejection, yet you're impulsive and direct when you know that your feelings are returned.

Tips for Your Ideal Lover

Considerably more sensitive and insecure than you let on, you like having your ego massaged along with your body. Your smoldering sexuality bursts into flames when your lover tells you how wonderful you are while he or she is touching your hair, rubbing your temples, caressing your face, or playing with your ears.

April 8, *Aries 8*

What Makes You Tick

While you can't bear the thought of rejection, you relish the challenge and excitement of the chase. In love, you like to make the first move, and you may not respond positively to romantic attention you do not seek. Although you take your time when choosing a life partner, you'll do everything possible to secure the relationship.

Between the Sheets

Your cool, self-contained exterior masks a lusty sexual being. You tend to be more careful in your approach to love than other Aries natives, yet beneath your seemingly businesslike attitude toward love, you're a fireball. You possess a strong libido that promises and delivers dynamic bedroom encounters. Although you may need to be reminded to take time out for lovemaking, there is absolutely no stopping you once you get going. A powerhouse of sexual energy, you rely on stamina to carry you and your partner to the heights of pleasure. You can come across as rather domineering, but you're also fair and considerate. Moreover, you're as involved in gratifying your bedmate's desires as your own.

Tips for Your Ideal Lover

You dream of a blissful escapade on a deserted island, where you and your mate make love endlessly with no interruptions. Since getting away for a long vacation isn't always possible, the next best thing is to whisk your beloved off for a romantic weekend in a lovely, very private hideaway.

April 9, *Aries 9*

What Makes You Tick

Your restless, impulsive Aries nature is continually at odds with the ideal-istic notions of love and romance typical of the number 9 vibration. While you yearn for an all-encompassing intimate relationship, you also want the freedom and independence to follow your destiny. Your true soul mate either matches your frenetic pace or is willing to keep the home fires burning while you explore the world.

Between the Sheets

You may be controlled in public, but you are quite the lusty ram behind closed doors. A sensualist and an idealist, you believe that strong sexual chemistry is the essential component of a romantic union. While you may crave the spiri-tual ecstasy of a transcendental sexual experience, you also need to satisfy your lusty physical desires. Lurking beneath your sweet exterior is a bawdy, adventurous love nature that comes alive only in the bedroom. An ardent and seductive lover, you enjoy catering to your partner's whims and desires. How-ever, you expect your bedmate to consider your wishes as well. You want a loving physical relationship, where you and your lover feel free to act on your most intimate sexual fantasies.

Tips for Your Ideal Lover

Some of your most erotic dreams may take place on a beach. Even if you don't have an ocean nearby, a bath or shower with your lover can be a fairly good substitute. Try sharing a glass of wine, caressing and soaping each other, and then making passionate love in the water.

April 10, *Aries 1*

What Makes You Tick

An impulsive romantic, you plunge headlong into a new love relationship without a thought as to where it may lead. If you're dumped, your pride may suffer, yet you'll dust yourself off, get back up on your horse, and gallop off in search of another soul mate. Although you cherish your freedom and independence, when you find the right partner you're capable of settling down and remaining devoted for a lifetime.

Between the Sheets

Your Sun sign, Aries, is one of the most passionate in the zodiac. You set such a lively pace in the bedroom and elsewhere that it takes a dynamic person to keep up with you. You don't mind a spirited disagreement from time to time. In fact, you thrive on arguments that shake things up a bit. The one thing you can't abide is boredom. If your mate's approach to lovemaking becomes too repetitious, you can lose interest. Although you're happy to gratify your partner's desires, you rarely think to ask what they might be. Since you're open and upfront about your own needs, you expect your lover to be the same.

Tips for Your Ideal Lover

Although you can be ultraromantic when it suits your mood, what you really enjoy is a bawdy, uncomplicated romp in the hay. Your idea of a total turn-on is a physically exhilarating lover who challenges you mentally as well. While emotional games are a no-no in your world, you absolutely adore sexy physical ones.

April 11, *Aries 2*

What Makes You Tick

Although you yearn for action and excitement, you need roots and security. Your biggest challenge is to find a way to combine your desire for independence and adventure with a comfortable home life. While you can be romantic, you're too sensible to be fanciful. The things you want most from an intimate relationship are affection, emotional security, and good sex, which means an exciting but basically uncomplicated physical relationship.

Between the Sheets

You enjoy exploring life's erotic delights, and you like being the innovator. Your approach to lovemaking swings between playful and relaxed and urgent and intense, and you dazzle your partner with an irresistible mix of languid sensuality and audacious aggressiveness. However, your physical and emotional needs are so closely intertwined that you need a lover you can connect with in a meaningful way. When making love, you know how to walk the fine line between arousal and consummation. Unlike some rams, you're a patient lover. Intent on pleasing yourself and your partner, you take your time and savor every moment.

Tips for Your Ideal Lover

You have a marvelously tactile nature. You like touching and caressing and being touched and stroked, until both you and your partner are absolutely shivering with delight and anticipation. Following this petting session, you will be ready to abandon yourself to unimagined erotic delights and sensual pleasures.

April 12, *Aries 3*

What Makes You Tick

Generous, warm, and loving, you like interacting with people in social gatherings and one-on-one situations. However, your go-go personality and tendency to scatter your energies in a number of different directions make you hard to pin down and even harder to hold on to. Although you enjoy sharing your ideas and interests with someone special, you value your freedom and independence so much that you could have difficulty maintaining a long-term intimate relationship.

Between the Sheets

You want everything in life, including sex, to be spontaneous and exciting. With your action-oriented, restless nature, you're continually seeking fresh physical and mental sensations. The ability to mix words with actions is your specialty. In bed, you know what you want and you're not afraid to ask for it. Your joyful enthusiasm and powers of persuasion virtually guarantee that your every wish will be gratified. Your aversion to boredom is legendary, and the idea of exploring new sexual territory fascinates you. Words get you going, and your urge to communicate encourages frequent verbal exchanges with your bedmate. Since your major erotic zone is in your brain, hearing what your lover is thinking and feeling during lovemaking sparks your desires.

Tips for Your Ideal Lover

Your carefree lifestyle shows that you don't like wasting time in planning and preparation; you want to be swept off your feet. Your idea of a great turn-on is witty, fast-paced verbal sparring accompanied by exciting and innovative sexual moves leading to ultimate culmination.

April 13, *Aries 4*

What Makes You Tick

In school, you probably didn't receive high marks in "plays well with others." Typically you rush into a situation, assume the lead, and expect everyone else to follow. In a love union, you're an assertive, caring, and protective partner. Although strongly sexed and ardent, you're not one for cuddling and exchanging intimate little secrets, and you can be quite demanding.

Between the Sheets

Your sunny vitality is most likely to surface in the bedroom, so it's not surprising that it is where you shine. You make a truly exciting lover, combining passion and sensuality with physical stamina and just a touch of flamboyance. You crave physical release and really love any sort of challenge. You also have a playful, daring side. Although your approach to lovemaking is forthright and not particularly romantic, your feelings are profound when you feel a strong connection between yourself and your bed partner. A naturally generous lover, you explore your mate's sexual preferences along with your own. You enjoy variety in bed, and you will try just about anything.

Tips for Your Ideal Lover

The aggressive side of your Aries character likes to lead and control. You're turned on by sexual games that involve challenge and conquest. A wild bedroom romp that turns into a jousting match or a competition for sexual dominance is practically guaranteed to ignite your passion.

April 14, *Aries 5*

What Makes You Tick

You possess an inner emotional detachment that keeps you from clinging too tightly to friends and lovers. An independent spirit, you need a relaxed mate who allows you to be yourself. In your search for exciting new experiences, you may shock people by thwarting social convention or changing partners frequently. However, once you find Mr. or Ms. Right, you're not averse to the idea of a permanent romantic union.

Between the Sheets

You value your freedom and the companionship of shared interests above all else; intellectual rapport is as important to you as romantic love. Where your sexuality is concerned, you are innovative and adventurous. You have few qualms when it comes to exploring sexual frontiers or taboo territory. Mentally restless and easily bored, you can lose interest in a partner who is unable to challenge you intellectually. Although you enjoy playing the aggressor in a seduction scenario, you are also capable of tender moments. Sex is a carefree, ever-changing game to you, and you engage in it with joyful enthusiasm.

Tips for Your Ideal Lover

You live as much in your mind as in your body, and it takes a lover who emits mental sparks to ignite your physical passion. You're turned on by the idea of experimenting with your most erotic fantasies. Just talking about what you would like to do to each other puts you in the mood to do it.

April 15, *Aries 6*

What Makes You Tick

Daring and adventurous, you view life as a romantic quest for idyllic love. You give yourself to love totally and unconditionally and refuse to let past disillusions impinge on your idealistic dreams. When you think you've found your soul mate, you expect your days to be filled with fun and your nights with pleasure. Since you value committed partnership more than a frivolous love affair, you expect the union to last forever.

Between the Sheets

In social settings, you come off as an easygoing, fun-loving charmer who revels in the challenge of a new romance. In the bedroom, you are affectionate and more passive than the other members of your Sun sign, and you enjoy the courtly rituals of romance almost as much as the lusty passions of sexual love. Your approach to lovemaking is a reflection of your vibrant imagination and deep-seated appreciation for beauty and harmony. Flirtatious and seductive in a very un-Aries-like manner, you can lure your bed partner into your arms with little more than a come-hither smile. Moreover, you prefer allurement and guile to the blatant sexual pursuit practiced by other rams.

Tips for Your Ideal Lover

Your sexual desires are aroused by carefully staged and sensually perfumed romantic settings, with indirect lighting, and music playing in the background. Where love and sex are concerned, you're holding on to a lifelong fantasy of courtship and seduction. Nothing turns you on more readily than feeling your youthful dreams come to life.

April 16, *Aries 7*

What Makes You Tick

You are naturally caring, and your compassion and interest draw people to you. Even so, you're basically independent, and intimate relationships can be difficult. A romantic idealist, you fall in love with the idea of love. Yet your capacity for enduring boredom is low, and you stick around only as long as your partner holds your attention. If the excitement leaves, you could follow it out the door.

Between the Sheets

You exude an aura of mystery that your lovers find intriguing. Subject to a variety of moods, you seem to change a little bit each time you're with your mate. Nevertheless, once you overcome your moods and insecurities, you make a sensual, ardent, and perceptive lover. You believe that strong sexual chemistry is the essential component in an intimate union. Lurking beneath your sweet exterior, there is a bawdy, adventurous, and sensuous love nature that comes alive in the bedroom. During lovemaking, you tend to alternate between bold assertiveness and gentle tenderness. Since you are such a challenging, exciting bedmate, you expect no less in return.

Tips for Your Ideal Lover

A lusty ram, you long for love that is wildly romantic and ardently sexual. You value a partner who is passionately interested in the arts, especially music and dance. A slow, sexy dance with a lover who sings to you or woos you gently with sweet words and poetic language is a sure-fire turn-on.

April 17, *Aries 8*

What Makes You Tick

Although you are less impulsive than other members of your Sun sign, you are a romantic idealist at heart. Something of a workaholic, you're often willing to put your desires on the back burner in favor of your ambitious career plans. It is important for you to realize that love and achievement are not mutually exclusive. Actually, it is the other way around. When you are relaxed and content in your personal life, you function better at work.

Between the Sheets

Romantic gestures are simply not part of your agenda, and neither is sharing your most intimate feelings with your mate or partner. Physically, you're strongly sexed and sensuous yet capable of controlling and directing your passions. You may come off as somewhat impersonal in public situations, but you're a very exciting, adventurous lover. Although you have great difficulty expressing your deepest feelings and emotions, you have no such problems when it comes to your active libido. Physically, you are passionate, energetic, and demonstrative. Your style of lovemaking is forthright and direct. You need to feel safe and secure in an intimate relationship, but when you do, just about anything goes.

Tips for Your Ideal Lover

A long soak in a tub or spa, followed by an aromatic massage that combines muscle manipulation with a search for your "hot buttons" can do the trick. You particularly like it when your partner asks what turns you on and then carries out your wishes.

April 18, *Aries 9*

What Makes You Tick

You need a loving relationship in your life, yet you also want the freedom to follow your destiny. You probably like having it both ways. The dual aspects of your personality make you both a homebody and a gregarious, enthusiastic partier. While you enjoy dashing around town and meeting new people, you also like retreating into the private space that you only share with your significant other.

Between the Sheets

You may be shy in some life areas, but the bedroom isn't one of them. With your playful, adventurous love nature and fiery sex drive, you're willing to try just about anything. You probably enjoy acting out your romantic fantasies, many of which may include dashing heroes, fair ladies, and dangerous rescues from fire-breathing dragons. Unlike some rams, your style of lovemaking is neither pushy nor aggressive. Moreover, you have few inhibitions and you like experimenting with imaginative, innovative ways of pleasing your partner. Although you believe that strong sexual chemistry is the essential component in a romantic union, you tend to alternate between bold assertiveness and gentle tenderness.

Tips for Your Ideal Lover

Sex is a game for you, and you play it with gusto. The hot-blooded, passionate side of your nature practically guarantees a good deal of sexual pleasure. However, your sentimental side also enjoys spending peaceful hours alone with your beloved, just cuddling, drinking wine, watching films on TV, or listening to music.

April 19, *Aries 1*

What Makes You Tick

In a love union, you are romantic, passionate, and idealistic. A life partner is important to you, yet you won't sacrifice everything to have one. You thrive on change, and a relationship that becomes routine quickly loses its attraction. When life goes too smoothly, you get antsy and try to generate fresh excitement. More often than not, you get the sparks flying again by deliberately creating conflict.

Between the Sheets

Sensation-oriented and hot-blooded, your sexual approach is straightforward and uncomplicated. You refuse to play games in the bedroom. Since you don't act coy or send mixed messages, the art of subtle seduction is totally wasted on you. You prefer open and direct communication. You know what you want, and you don't like being teased or put off. You're not afraid to come right out and ask for what you want, and you expect your mate to do the same. Since you are so open to trying new things, no request is too outrageous to consider. There is no subtlety in your nature. When asked a direct question, you respond with the truth as you see it.

Tips for Your Ideal Lover

Given your need for constant stimulation, a lover who is able to surprise you with something new or different will continue to hold your interest for a long time. You're fond of little presents, especially if the gifts are enticing garments or toys specifically designed to increase sexual excitement and pleasure.

April 20, *Taurus 2*

What Makes You Tick

You are loving and romantic yet sensible and practical. Ultimately, security and stability in a relationship matter more to you than thrills and excitement. Your tastes in love and sex are straightforward, and you don't need a lot of frills to entice you. Your ideal mate is someone with whom you can share the many creature comforts you cherish.

Between the Sheets

In an intimate union, you're passionate and generous. Good sex ranks high on your list of life's priorities, and your approach to lovemaking is sensual and erotic. Physical intimacy energizes your body and nourishes your inner being. Although you enjoy experimenting with a variety of sexual positions and techniques, it is actually the warmth of close contact and shared affection that you find most satisfying. Your dream lover shares your appreciation for the sensuous comfort of luxurious surroundings. Most of the time, you are relaxed and full of fun. However, sometimes you show your jealous and demanding side. You crave safety and security in life and love, and you become rather difficult when your emotional stability is threatened.

Tips for Your Ideal Lover

You're an exceedingly tactile person, and you are turned on by a bed partner who enjoys touching and being touched as much you do. All types of physical contact appeal to you, from long hugs and lingering kisses to sensual massages with essential oils and scented lotions.

April 21, *Taurus 3*

What Makes You Tick

While you enjoy the stability of a serious relationship, too much togetherness makes you uncomfortable. Despite your need for love, you blow hot and cold where long-term commitment is concerned. Part of you wants to be unencumbered, the other part longs to settle down. Although you relish the physical pleasures that love offers, there is also a mental component to your sexuality that longs to establish intellectual rapport.

Between the Sheets

As a lover, you're affectionate, sensual, and exciting. When you close the bedroom door, you try to leave everything that's disagreeable or unpleasant on the other side. Less conservative than the typical Taurus bedmate, you're always on the lookout for innovative ways of spicing up your lovemaking. Delightfully verbal as well as physical, you have a knack for turning subtle innuendo and clever quips into masterful tools of seduction. Spicy sexual banter allows you to share whatever you are thinking and feeling with your bed partner. However, lusty conversation is only part of the package. The lover who shows how much he or she truly cares is the one who will get your juices flowing.

Tips for Your Ideal Lover

You channel a great deal of your energy into verbal communication, and one of your favorite topics of conversation is sex. In fact, you enjoy bantering with your partner almost as much as making love. You particularly enjoy discussing what you are going to do with your lover once talk turns into action.

April 22, *Taurus 4*

What Makes You Tick

Security is important to you, and a loving union is the natural foundation of a lasting romantic relationship. Aware that actions speak louder than words, you show your love in tangible ways. You need a close partnership to give meaning to your life, and casual love affairs have no place in your plans. Once you make a commitment, your mate can always rely on you.

Between the Sheets

Although you may not express yourself with fireworks, your consideration and ardent sensuality make you an exceptional lover. Wild fantasy and theatrics are not your style. You crave the transcendent but uncomplicated lovemaking of an enduring union that serves as an anchor for a comfortable, ordered life. A sentimental and generous lover, you'll do whatever you can to keep romance fresh and alive throughout the relationship. You may be somewhat reserved in public, but once you close the door on the outside world you make love with abandon. A powerhouse of sexual vitality, you rely on an unbeatable combination of patience and physical stamina to build slowly to a peak of ecstasy.

Tips for Your Ideal Lover

You respond readily to the mate who arouses you with passionate kisses and intimate caresses. Thrilled by the idea of forbidden fruit, you can develop a taste for bawdy sexual antics if they're not too outrageous. Although not bold enough to suggest innovation, you welcome it from a more adventurous bed partner.

April 23, *Taurus 5*

What Makes You Tick

You can be stubborn and set in your ways, yet you're also prone to occasional spurts of unconventionality. While one part of your head is mired in traditional values, another part is somewhat rebellious and eccentric. Outgoing and sociable, you enjoy parties and joining friends for a few drinks and a meal. When it comes to your sex life, you're open-minded and willing to explore all sorts of erotic pleasures.

Between the Sheets

You like the security of a stable relationship, yet your independent spirit fears an excess of intimacy. Eventually, however, your need for consistency overcomes your reservations. Until you find your soul mate, you're perfectly capable of enjoying an agreeable romantic alliance that's free of fetters. Earthy, sensual, and innovative, you like experimenting with various positions during lovemaking. You bring the joy of discovery to everything you do, and appreciate a bed partner who shares your uninhibited approach to sexuality. A playful lover, you like being a bit quirky in the bedroom. Although the joy of sensate pleasure may draw you in, it takes a more meaningful connection to hold your interest for a lifetime.

Tips for Your Ideal Lover

A generous, considerate bedmate, you're concerned with pleasing your partner, and you're happy to cater to his or her wishes as long as you receive the same type of treatment in return. Tactile by nature, you regard lovemaking as a carnival of the senses where you enjoy each and every ride.

April 24, *Taurus 6*

What Makes You Tick

You dislike solitude and cannot imagine being without a close companion for very long. Since you strive to remain calm and relaxed at all times, the peace and serenity of harmonious surroundings are as important to your well-being as food and drink. Sentimentality may propel you into various romantic escapades, but once you find your soul mate you make a devoted and steadfast life partner.

Between the Sheets

Since you are both an idealist and a hedonist, romance and sex are intertwined in your mind; you crave both passion and romance in the bedroom. One of the best things about an intimate relationship is the shared experience of exploring the world of the physical senses through sexual contact. Your gift for using words and touch to engage both the mind and body of your lover can lead to extraordinarily sensual, exciting lovemaking. When you find Mr. or Ms. Right, you are more than capable of remaining loyal and committed to the end. However, if you expect a paradise of harmony and contentment, you are bound to be disappointed when your lives together are less than perfect.

Tips for Your Ideal Lover

You respond to an elegant erotic courtship that builds toward a peak in desire, and you shiver in anticipation during a slow, sensuous exploration of your body. A romantic ambiance with luxurious linens, scented candles, soft music, affectionate gestures, and loving words all help put you in the mood.

April 25, *Taurus 7*

What Makes You Tick

You may feel as if you are being pulled in opposite directions where your love life is concerned. While the restless side of your nature can make it difficult for you to commit, your Taurus Sun sign makes you yearn for the safety of a loving union. Although emotional and mental compatibility rank very high in your estimation, you also crave the electric intensity of sexual chemistry and strong physical passion.

Between the Sheets

You're not likely to be content with superficial sexual encounters. You want to share yourself with your lover completely: physically, emotionally, mentally, and spiritually. At times, you can be boldly direct about sexual matters; however, you can also be lighthearted and full of fun in bed, and laughing together can be as fulfilling for you as deeper intimacies. Your ideal mate appreciates your willingness to explore new ways to enhance pleasure in the bedroom and elsewhere. However, romance and sensuality are only part of the package for you. You want to be appreciated for who you are, and you need a partner who truly understands you and puts up with your occasional moods.

Tips for Your Ideal Lover

Sex makes you come alive, and rapturous foreplay brings your richly layered sensuality to the surface. You don't need a lot of frills, but a lover with a keen intuition inflames your earthy libido with soulful kisses, erotic touches, and teasing indications of the delights to follow.

April 26, *Taurus 8*

What Makes You Tick

You are a secret romantic, yet when you meet someone new, you are inherently cautious. Despite a desire to be loved, you need to develop trust before you will commit to an intimate relationship. When you feel safe and secure in a loving union, you make the staunchest and most reliable of partners. You have a lot to offer the right person, and you expect no less in return.

Between the Sheets

Simmering just below your calm exterior is a sensuous nature that emerges behind closed doors. Careful in your approach, you keep your powerful sexual urges under control outside the bedroom. In private, however, you let loose your considerable passion and deep sensuality. You're a considerate mate, and a master at creative lovemaking. An earthy Taurus lover, you like to take your time, making sure that both you and your partner enjoy every delightful moment together. Naturally you want to have your own needs met, but you will also go to any lengths necessary to keep your partner happy. There is virtually nothing you won't try in bed, as long as you and your lover are on the same page.

Tips for Your Ideal Lover

The sensual pleasures of the bedroom can provide the glue that binds you to your lover. Typically, you prefer a spicier, more innovative brand of erotic expression than other Taurus 8s, and you respond most readily to a sexy partner's simmering sparks of physical passion.

April 27, *Taurus 9*

What Makes You Tick

You have an endearing otherworldly quality. Although part of you is dreamy and romantic, the other part is more sensible and down to earth. When you love someone, both your body and your soul get into the act. Physical love alone just doesn't do it for you. You need to establish an intense emotional connection with your significant other to feel truly fulfilled.

Between the Sheets

You have the rare ability to combine the romantic with the practical, the passionate with the spiritual. Despite a yearning for permanence and stability, you fall in love rather easily. However, once you find true love, you are capable of absolute devotion. When you make a genuine connection, you long to share all of yourself with your beloved, and you know how to elevate lovemaking to an art form. You refuse to be hurried, either in bed or out of it. You like to take your time exploring all the possibilities of sensual pleasure. You can be possessive, demanding, or clingy, but more often you are generous, considerate, and indulgent of your partner's wishes.

Tips for Your Ideal Lover

Displays of love and affection make you come alive, and your innate gift for relaxation allows you to enjoy each intimate moment in private with your lover. You especially adore long, lazy hours of lovemaking, during which you and your bedmate take the time to explore each other from head to toe.

April 28, *Taurus 1*

What Makes You Tick

You have a zest for all the good things in life including love. More easygoing than other bulls, you find it hard to understand why some people seem to go through so many ups and downs in their relationships. What you want most from an intimate union is affection, emotional security, and lots of good sex. When you find someone you like, you jump right in with a compelling mix of aggressiveness and sensuality.

Between the Sheets

Your approach to lovemaking combines urgent sexual intensity with earthy sensuality, and you prefer forthright, uncomplicated bedroom encounters that are ardent and exciting. While you can be somewhat demanding in the bedroom and elsewhere, you are also exceedingly generous, good-natured, and caring. You enjoy making love, and your physical stamina enhances the sexual experience. Moreover, you are willing to invest a great deal of energy in making the act gratifying for both you and your partner. A sucker for old-fashioned romance, you get off on being wooed and having sweet nothings whispered in your ear. But ultimately, you are not the most patient of Taurus lovers. Once aroused, you want action, not talk.

Tips for Your Ideal Lover

Although you enjoy being pursued, you also like being the playful pursuer and either role is actually a turn-on. Your libido stands open and ready day and night. While a slow seductive approach with lots of touching and stroking inflames your desires, fast and furious lovemaking keeps you energized.

April 29, *Taurus 2*

What Makes You Tick

You know how to unwind and enjoy the many pleasures the world has to offer. Although you're able to find joy in these delights on your own, you enjoy them even more with a loving partner. In an intimate union, you can be stubborn, demanding, and possessive. However, your devotion to your beloved is rock-solid, and your kindness and generosity are beyond question.

Between the Sheets

In the bedroom and elsewhere, you are capable of focusing totally on whatever you're doing, and you take the time to do it right. Your cheerful nature and legendary staying power make you an excellent lover, and your bed partner is all but guaranteed a satisfying lovemaking experience. You're naturally sensual and seductive, and you know just what to do to set the stage for romance. Once your powerful libido is let loose, you are capable of depths of passion that can leave your lover gasping for breath and begging for more. Since few Sun signs appreciate sensory pleasures as much as Taurus, you usually go along with anything that feels good and makes your partner happy.

Tips for Your Ideal Lover

Basically a homebody, you're happy spending a cozy evening on the sofa watching movies, or curled up together in the love seat listening to music and feeding each other sinfully rich candies and pastries. The right mate satisfies your need for tactile sensuality and affection with tender touching and long, lingering kisses.

April 30, *Taurus 3*

What Makes You Tick

Sociable and articulate, you have a facility for conveying your thoughts and ideas to others. Your typical response to new people and situations is swifter and more open than that of other bulls. As a romantic partner, you are affectionate and sensual. Emotionally, you flip back and forth between cool logic and intense feelings. You want life to be safe and serene, yet you also crave change and diversity.

Between the Sheets

As a connoisseur of physical pleasure, you believe in making the most of each bedroom encounter. A playful, inventive lover, you're considerably more drawn to sexual experimentation than other members of your Sun sign. Although happy to engage in languid sex when time allows, you relish the excitement of an occasional impulsive quickie. With your earthy, practical approach to lovemaking, you won't hesitate to consult a sex manual or video, if you think it will help improve your overall technique. You enjoy perusing lavishly illustrated books of erotic art, in tandem with a willing bed partner, and you like it when your lover describes his or her desires and plans for gratifying yours.

Tips for Your Ideal Lover

You have a powerful libido and lovemaking is one of your favorite ways to have fun. You're turned on by the idea of acting out your secret fantasies. Perhaps it's frolicking with your lover in a joyous sexual romp through the woods or re-enacting a scene from a bordello with satin sheets and plush velvet pillows.

May 1, *Taurus 1*

What Makes You Tick

In an intimate union, you are warm, sensual, and passionate. At times you show a side of your nature that is possessive and demanding, yet at other times you are easygoing, relaxed, and full of fun. Since you crave safety and security, you can be rather difficult when your emotional stability is threatened. However, once you are sure that you have found the right person, you're happy to make a long-term commitment.

Between the Sheets

Enamored of all the earthly pleasures, your lovemaking approach is a combination of languid sensuality and bold aggressive action. You don't like being hurried or rushed, either in bed or out of it, and you much prefer a slow, steady seduction to fast, furious lovemaking. Outside the bedroom, your magnetic personality gives off subtle hints of the ardor simmering beneath your surface reserve. In the throes of passion, your reserve melts away, and in the sizzling intensity of the moment, you respond with total abandon. Your physical prowess and sensuality enhance the sexual experience, and you are willing to invest a lot of energy in making the sex act gratifying for both you and your bed partner.

Tips for Your Ideal Lover

You would like to be able to make love whenever the mood hits you. Since this is rarely possible in everyday life, nothing turns you on like the prospect of a secluded romantic getaway. Freed from daily concerns, you and your lover bask in an atmosphere of unfettered sensuality and passion.

May 2, *Taurus 2*

What Makes You Tick

Reliability is your trademark, and your quiet strength inspires trust in others. Your natural inclination is to find Mr. or Ms. Right and settle into a routine of domestic bliss. Although you may tread cautiously at first, once you fall in love, you expect it to last forever. You view broken promises as betrayals and threats to your security, and you don't take kindly to betrayal.

Between the Sheets

Although deeply passionate, Taurus is somewhat shy and reserved. Much of what you feel takes place beneath the surface, and your romantic style is typically more passive than aggressive. You prefer waiting for others to come to you. When you decide to make the first move, you are subtle in your approach. Beneath your tranquil exterior, you harbor strong desires and deep enduring passions. There is a delicious intensity to your lovemaking that can be quite thrilling. You have an uncomplicated approach to sexuality that is gratifying but not particularly imaginative. When you find something that works for you, you like to stick with it. Even so, your sensuality, passionate nature, and legendary staying power make you an excellent lover.

Tips for Your Ideal Lover

Your fantasies almost always involve sensual pleasures. From delicacies such as whipped cream to the pampered luxury of a neck rub or a full-body massage, you want to be catered to and indulged. You love being touched, stroked, kissed, and told over and over how desirable you are.

May 3, *Taurus 3*

What Makes You Tick

Your sociability makes you popular, and people are captivated by your charming sense of humor. Although you may seem flirtatious at times, you are actually gregarious and just like being with people. While your friendly manner attracts admirers, you remain devoted to your beloved. You prize the stability of a committed union, and when you find true love you're not likely to sacrifice it for personal freedom.

Between the Sheets

You are a thoughtful lover with lots of sexual stamina. Despite your tactile sensuality, your mind is as sensitive and erogenous as your body. Unlike the typical placid Taurus native, you possess a considerable amount of nervous energy. This energy finds its best expression through communication, and you consider the ability to talk with your lover at least as important as physical lovemaking. Since your robust libido is as likely to be turned on by words as by caresses, verbal enticements have a big impact on you. Provocative conversations are a big turn-on, and spicy sexual banter and fantasizing allow you to share what you are thinking and feeling with your bedmate.

Tips for Your Ideal Lover

Naturally inquisitive, you love hearing stories about the amorous exploits of others, including all the salacious details of their intimate lives. You also enjoy reading and sharing erotic books, especially the illustrated ones. You particularly like having your lover describe his or her secret wishes and desires and plans for gratifying your sexual needs.

May 4, *Taurus 4*

What Makes You Tick

You want a stable home life, but it takes more than devotion to hold your interest. You crave the intensity of strong sexual chemistry. Although mental compatibility ranks high in your estimation, you consider it less important than the spark of electricity generated by physical passion. Your ideal lover is proper and respectable in public, but once you close the door on the outside world, he or she makes love with total abandon.

Between the Sheets

You may be reserved in public, but you are quite demonstrative in the bedroom. A powerhouse of sexual vitality, you rely on a combination of patience and physical stamina to build slowly toward the peak of pleasure. You appreciate a lover who enjoys pleasing you as much as you like pleasing him or her. Although typically the one in control, you're generous and as eager to gratify your mate's desires as your own. Moreover, you don't mind when your partner decides to take charge and lead the way. In fact, you welcome it. While you may not be bold enough to suggest erotic innovations, you welcome a partner who takes you to unfamiliar sexual territory.

Tips for Your Ideal Lover

You respond readily to a lover who arouses your senses with passionate kisses and intimate caresses. While your bedmate is stroking and kissing your body, especially your neck, you like having words of love and devotion whispered in your ear. Erotic pillow talk in luxurious surroundings adds to your pleasure.

May 5, *Taurus 5*

What Makes You Tick

A part of you adores the idea of a committed romantic relationship, but the adventurer inside your head dreams of independence. As a result, you can be difficult to pin down and even harder to hold. Eventually, however, your inner bull demands the safety and security of a permanent union. Since finding a genuine soul mate takes some time, you may indulge in a few unconventional alliances while you're waiting.

Between the Sheets

An uninhibited lover, you enjoy exploring various avenues of intimate experience. The physical part of your amorous nature yearns to relax into complete sensuality in a luxurious atmosphere. However, you quickly dismiss this idea as boringly conventional. Your mind plays as much a part in your lovemaking as your body, and words and pictures tend to rouse your passions. Since arousal begins in your head, you like engaging in witty banter before and during lovemaking. You appreciate a partner who shares your open attitude to bedroom experimentation. Spontaneity and surprise thrill you, and you get off on the idea of engaging in sexual activity in improbable places and at odd times.

Tips for Your Ideal Lover

Your fantasy life is rich with ideas for erotic encounters that you act out with your lover. You get a charge out of seductive suggestions in songs, films, TV, or whispered by your bed partner. The rebel in you also likes the idea of naughty activities in situations with a risk of discovery.

May 6, *Taurus* 6

What Makes You Tick

You are naturally sociable and enjoy a little flirting from time to time, but what you want more than anything is the safety and security of an ongoing intimate union. When you find the mate who suits you, you are prepared to love him or her passionately and with total commitment. You can be quite lavish in expressing your feelings through gifts, words, and physical displays of affection.

Between the Sheets

You want both passion and romance. One of the best things about making love is the shared experience of exploring the physical senses through sexual contact. However, the setting must be just right to appeal to your love of comfort and luxury. You recognize the value of give-and-take and compromise in all areas of life, and it gives you great pleasure to gratify your partner's desires. When it comes to making love, quality and mutual gratification are much more important to you than quantity. Although you can be quite inventive when necessary to keep your lover happy, you probably prefer old-fashioned lovemaking to kinky sexual innovation.

Tips for Your Ideal Lover

Experiencing all the good things in life with your significant other makes you feel cherished and appreciated. You come alive during a romantic evening out at a restaurant, the theater, or a concert. Witty conversation, delectable gourmet food, beautiful surroundings, tenderness, and passionate sensuality are the things that turn you on.

May 7, *Taurus 7*

What Makes You Tick

You are generous and devoted to those you love, yet living with you can be a roller coaster ride. Although ardent and affectionate, you're also moody and often feel unappreciated or misunderstood. You possess a deep reservoir of wisdom, yet when your emotions come into play, reason falls by the wayside. Your ideal romantic partner understands the duality of your nature.

Between the Sheets

When you close the bedroom door, you leave everything disagreeable or unpleasant on the other side. Warm-hearted and affectionate, you're naturally tactile, with a love of sensual pleasure. You particularly like touching and being touched by your lover. Less conservative than the typical bull, you can be quite spontaneous, especially when acting out your sexual fantasies. Moreover, you won't hesitate to contribute fresh, innovative ideas for spicing up lovemaking. However, romance and sensuality are only part of the package; you want a partner who truly understands you. At times, you radiate so much magnetic sex appeal that would-be suitors find themselves mesmerized by it. At other times, you give the impression of wanting nothing more than to be left alone.

Tips for Your Ideal Lover

Imagine a luxurious late-night picnic, outdoors in a beautiful, secluded spot, sharing delicious gourmet food and drink with your lover. Follow the tasty meal with a sensual massage and the result is a dream come true. Then, top the evening off by making love under the stars.

May 8, *Taurus 8*

What Makes You Tick

Personal magnetism and a warm, sociable nature add charm and charisma to your powerful personality. The affable, easygoing image you project conceals a practical inner nature; your persistence and diligence practically guarantee success in all your undertakings. Yet despite your obvious self-sufficiency, your need for emotional security requires the support of friends and family, without which you never feel truly content.

Between the Sheets

You know how to keep your powerful sexuality under control outside the bedroom. However, simmering just beneath your calm exterior is a strong sex drive and warm sensuality that emerges behind closed doors. When you feel secure in a loving union, you delight in physical love, and once you get going, you're virtually unstoppable in the sack. Skilled at satisfying your partner, you prefer taking things slowly, postponing the ultimate payoff for as long as possible. A considerate lover, you pride yourself on your ability to control and direct your passion. Wild fantasy and theatrics between the sheets, or elsewhere, are just not your style. You crave the transcendent and uncomplicated lovemaking of an enduring union that serves as an anchor for an ordered life.

Tips for Your Ideal Lover

You respond readily to the lover who arouses your senses with passionate kisses and intimate caresses. Although typically not bold enough to suggest erotic innovation, you welcome a more adventurous bedmate and you can easily develop a taste for bawdy sexual antics, as long as they're not too outrageous.

May 9, *Taurus 9*

What Makes You Tick

In an intimate union, you are the consummate romantic. Tenderhearted and sincerely devoted to your beloved, you're prepared to make sacrifices if you deem it necessary. Despite a yearning for permanence and stability, you fall in love rather easily. Since what you are seeking is a fairy-tale romance, you are just as easily disappointed if things go wrong.

Between the Sheets

You're one of the most open-hearted lovers in the zodiac, and there is a delicacy and sensitivity to your bedroom approach that is quite irresistible. Dreamy and romantic yet practical and earthy, your smoldering magnetism brings a feeling of enchantment to your bedroom activities. You refuse to be rushed, taking all the time you need to discover what pleases both you and your partner. Tantalizing foreplay is your specialty—lots of cuddling; long, luxurious caresses; and deep, lingering kisses. You particularly enjoy slowly exploring your lover's body until the two of you are shivering with anticipation. Even on occasions when the sex act is not fully consummated, you still cherish the snuggling and petting.

Tips for Your Ideal Lover

You have an enviable knack for knowing how to relax and enjoy each moment. You respond sensually to the combination of water and your lover's caresses, and making love in a bath or shower sparks your passion. Afterward, you might dry each other off, and then indulge in a few drinks and gourmet snacks.

May 10, *Taurus 1*

What Makes You Tick

Extremely openhanded, you enjoy spending your money on comforts and luxuries for yourself and your loved ones. When attracted to someone new, you charge right in and overwhelm your target with sweet words and romantic gifts. You don't just fall in love; you fling yourself into it without hesitation. You may be slow to settle down, but once you do, you're quite capable of remaining loyal for a lifetime.

Between the Sheets

More action-oriented than other bulls, you are predisposed to making exciting things happen, and your energy and enthusiasm extend to your love life. In the bedroom, you swiftly take charge and steer the activities in the direction you wish them to go. While passionate and somewhat demanding, you are also good-natured, considerate, and caring. You enjoy making love and you will do everything possible to make sure your bedmate enjoys it, too. Your lusty libido cries out for an active, exciting sex life, but you also like a good helping of love and romance with your passionate encounters. Your approach to lovemaking is uncomplicated and direct, and your physical prowess and earthy sensuality enhance the sexual experience.

Tips for Your Ideal Lover

A sucker for romance, you get off on having sweet nothings whispered in your ear. But ultimately, you want action, not talk, and once aroused, you are ready to get down and dirty with your lover. Your ardor is increased by tactile sensations, and indulging all your senses stirs your physical desires.

May 11, *Taurus 2*

What Makes You Tick

A large circle of family and friends gives you a sense of security and fulfillment, yet too much togetherness can make you feel claustrophobic. Although you're loyal and truly enjoy the stability of a committed union, you crave change and diversity almost as much as safety. You need to find a mate who stimulates you both mentally and physically, or you may lose interest and begin looking elsewhere.

Between the Sheets

In relationships, you can be somewhat difficult to fathom. As a romantic partner, you're affectionate, sensuous, and exciting. A good-humored, enthusiastic lover, your tactile sensuality makes you eager to explore new ways of heightening ecstasy. You believe that lovemaking is meant to be relaxed, comfortable, and fun. Even so, your bedroom style depends on your changing moods and can run the gamut from light and playful to hot and heavy. There is also a changeable aspect to your sexual nature that is turned on by the unexpected. The bedmate who aims to please you will entice you with fresh erotic moves or previously untried seductive approaches.

Tips for Your Ideal Lover

Deeply sensual by nature, you enjoy touch of all kinds, and an erotic massage with lots of stroking and kissing is a genuine turn-on. Whether making love or being made love to, you like to take your time. Once started, your motor does not stop in a hurry and you prefer lovemaking sessions that last.

May 12, *Taurus 3*

What Makes You Tick

You're bright and articulate, with a wonderful facility for conveying your thoughts and ideas. Emotionally, however, you flip back and forth. At times, you're logical and detached, yet when your feelings are called into play, you can become remarkably emotional, determined, and obstinate. As a romantic partner, you are affectionate, sensual, and exciting. You like safety and serenity, yet you crave change and diversity.

Between the Sheets

A true connoisseur of physical pleasures, you believe in making the most of each bedroom encounter, and you're considerably more drawn to sexual experimentation than other members of your Sun sign. Unlike the typical placid bull, you possess an excess of nervous energy that finds its best expression through communication. You're sensual and truly relish the physical pleasures love has to offer, yet there is also a mental component to your sexuality that yearns for intellectual rapport. Sexy banter and verbal fantasizing allow you to share what you are thinking and feeling with your bedmate. In fact, you get off on the very idea of acting out your sexual fantasies with your lover.

Tips for Your Ideal Lover

Turned on by building excitement between you and your partner, you favor a saucy style of lovemaking that makes you feel a bit naughty. The fires of your passion will begin stirring if your lover first blows in your ear and then starts to whisper the salacious details of the sexual indulgences he or she has planned.

May 13, *Taurus 4*

What Makes You Tick

You know what you're looking for in a life partner, and you're not likely to settle for less. More than anything, you need a calm, stable home life, with the kind of closeness that comes from a permanent union. While you can be demanding and possessive, you are also loyal, dependable, and responsive to your partner's desires. Generous by nature, you're genuinely concerned about your loved ones and like being involved in their lives.

Between the Sheets

When you work, you work hard, but when you play, you want to relax and enjoy yourself. You have a sensual, earthy nature and a deep appreciation for the physical side of love. As a lover, you are warm, affectionate, and responsive; you want mutual pleasure more than variety and excitement, and you enjoy lingering over sex in an elegant atmosphere. You like getting to know your lover in every possible way, and you'll go to great lengths to gratify his or her desires along with your own. However, your need for safety and security can make you oversensitive, and you are easily bruised by slights or insults, either real or imagined.

Tips for Your Ideal Lover

You respond eagerly to any kind of seductive technique that is deliberately slow and sensuous. Your idea of a guaranteed turn-on is for you and your bed partner to explore each other by touching, stroking, kissing, and probing all the secret places.

May 14, *Taurus 5*

What Makes You Tick

You want the security of a close relationship, yet your independent spirit fears too much intimacy and togetherness. Once you decide to commit to another person, you do it with your whole heart. However, until you find your soul mate, you're perfectly capable of enjoying an agreeable romantic alliance that is free of demands and commitment.

Between the Sheets

A playful lover, you think it is fun to be a bit unconventional and outrageous in the privacy of the bedroom. Earthy, sensual, and innovative, you like experimenting with different positions during lovemaking. You particularly enjoy exploring various avenues of intimate experience, and a lover who is open-minded and uninhibited really turns you on. You bring the joy of discovery to everything you do, including your sexual experiences. Since your mind plays as much a part in your lovemaking as your body, words and pictures can rouse your passions, and you get an erotic charge out of seductive suggestions, whether in a song, a film, on TV, or whispered in your ear by your bed partner.

Tips for Your Ideal Lover

You are turned on by tactile, sensory pleasures, so you enjoy spontaneous play that consists of equal parts fun and sexual arousal. Silky fabrics, soft feathers, edible erotic delicacies, and flavored oils all enhance your pleasure and anticipation. Languid caresses from head to toe electrify your senses, because your entire body is an erogenous zone.

May 15, *Taurus 6*

What Makes You Tick

You are not a loner and cannot imagine being without a mate or partner for very long. Since you truly enjoy the physical side of love, you are perfectly at home in the warmth of a committed, loving union. Although you actually prefer being seduced, you will summon your more assertive primal instincts if necessary. Even so, you never pounce. Why drag your partner off to a dank cave when you can stay at home and make love in lavish comfort?

Between the Sheets

You are a true romantic, and love and sex are forever intertwined in your mind. You like nice things and the beauty and serenity of harmonious surroundings are almost as important to your well-being as food and drink. Your lovemaking style is attentive but relaxed. In bed and out, you dislike being rushed, preferring to build slowly toward the peak of desire. In the bedroom, your gift for using words and touch to engage the mind and body of your lover can lead to extraordinarily sensual, exciting lovemaking. Sentimentality may propel you into various romantic escapades, but once you find your soul mate, you make a steadfast and devoted life partner.

Tips for Your Ideal Lover

Nothing turns you on like sharing a few gourmet nibbles with your partner before or even during lovemaking. However, you view love as a feast for all five senses. You get off on the touch of silken fabrics, the sound of soft music, and the sight of beautiful furnishings.

May 16, *Taurus 7*

What Makes You Tick

In an intimate union, you want emotional security, and your affectionate nature compels you to find a permanent love relationship. Yet despite your need for roots and structure, a part of you yearns for freedom and independence. As a result, you may become bored and restless if you stick close to home for too long. Your ideal mate understands your occasional solitary moods and accepts you as you are.

Between the Sheets

In the bedroom and elsewhere, you project a mysterious quality that is at once earthy and ethereal. Less emotional than the typical members of your Sun sign, you may have difficulty sharing your innermost thoughts with another person, no matter how close. Moreover, there may be times when you just want to be alone. However, there is also a side to you that knows instantly when Mr. or Ms. Right crosses your path. That is when the sensual, deeply passionate part of your personality emerges. You're not likely to be content with superficial sexual encounters; you yearn to share yourself totally with your lover.

Tips for Your Ideal Lover

Just being with a lover who has an attitude toward love and sexuality that is as enthusiastic as yours is a guaranteed turn-on. You also enjoy injecting an element of romance and mystery into your lovemaking. Passion can overtake you quite suddenly, so you appreciate a partner who responds to sexual overtures made at unlikely times.

May 17, *Taurus 8*

What Makes You Tick

Your need for structure prompts you to seek a stable, long-term romantic relationship. Since your approach to love is cautious, it may take a while before you feel ready to share your heart, home, and bank account with another person. You are as warm-hearted as other bulls, just less comfortable about letting your feelings show. However, once involved you make an affectionate lover and a generous, dependable mate.

Between the Sheets

Despite your desire to be loved and understood, you need to be sure that you can trust the other person before you will commit to an intimate relationship. Passionate and sensual by nature, you need physical affection and the emotional reassurance that comes from a caring and devoted spouse. Earthy and sensual, you love to touch and be touched. You delight in the physical expression of love, and you are quite skilled at satisfying your bedmate's desires. Despite your powerful sex drive, you pride yourself on your ability to control and direct your passion. You want to gratify your sexual appetite, but you refuse to let it make you either physically or emotionally dependent on another person.

Tips for Your Ideal Lover

Nothing turns you on as readily as the beauty and comfort of an ultraluxurious setting. Although you know that money can't buy happiness, it sure can buy a lot of goodies. Even if you can't afford champagne and caviar, you still appreciate a suitor who knows how to create a sumptuous atmosphere for lovemaking.

May 18, *Taurus 9*

What Makes You Tick

While you may be idealistic about relationships, you are practical enough to know that lovers cannot live on love alone. You are more than willing to share everything you have with your beloved, and you make sure there is plenty to go around. Once you find your true love, you are completely devoted. However, you have a rather possessive nature, and expect absolute loyalty in return.

Between the Sheets

Caring and affectionate, you're both giving and responsive as a mate or partner. You enjoy all the stylized rituals of courting and being courted. You know how to elevate lovemaking to an art form. When you make a genuine connection, you want to share all of yourself with your significant other. You will unite body and soul with the right person. You respond to all the sensual pleasures, and your idea of true intimacy is to shut out the world and concentrate on your bedmate. Pleasing your partner and yourself is paramount in your mind. Your leisurely approach is slow and deliberate. Gently and steadily, you stoke the flames of desire until they erupt into a raging fire.

Tips for Your Ideal Lover

Enjoying a scented bubble bath with your lover provides the perfect prelude to an evening of rapturous lovemaking. You revel in the sensuous delights of a late-night gourmet supper that ends with feeding each other delectable tidbits, such as fruit dipped in melted chocolate, alternating with sips of wine or champagne.

May 19, *Taurus 1*

What Makes You Tick

In an intimate union, you're warm, sensual, and passionate. Easygoing, friendly, and upbeat, you don't understand why others go through so many ups and downs in their relationships. Your tendency is to look for the best in your significant other, and you usually find it. Although you like the idea of freedom and independence, you're likely to make a long-term commitment with the right person.

Between the Sheets

Your approach to lovemaking is sensuous and erotic. You like being with a bed partner who appreciates luxury and creature comforts as much as you do. A dynamic lover, you have a strong sex drive and a taste for adventure. Physical intimacy energizes you and nourishes your inner being. Although you enjoy experimenting with various techniques and positions, the warmth of close physical contact and sharing affection satisfies you the most. Sometimes you are possessive and demanding, yet you can be relaxed and full of fun. Since you need stability, you may be rather difficult when your emotional security is threatened.

Tips for Your Ideal Lover

Indulging all your senses stirs your physical desires. Your ardor is increased by tactile sensations. Trailing a feather or a bit of silk along your skin is a great source of titillation. Since each part of you is an erogenous zone, a fragrant full-body massage inflames your libido while providing immediate pleasure.

May 20, *Taurus 2*

What Makes You Tick

Although you are both passionate and romantic, your relationship considerations tend to be as practical as they are affectionate. Security and stability are important, and you are not likely to sacrifice either on the altar of wild romance. You want a life partner who enjoys creature comforts as much as you do. A loyal mate, you give a great deal to your beloved, but you expect equal devotion in return.

Between the Sheets

You appreciate all the sensory pleasures in life. In bed or elsewhere, whatever feels good is usually okay with you. For you, sex is as natural and necessary as eating, and your earthy nature provides you with a direct approach regarding physical pleasure. Your desire for touch makes you hungry for sensual contact, and your ideal mate knows how to satisfy your need for tactile sexuality. Because you have few sexual hang-ups, you can be a marvelous lover. Your lovemaking tastes are straightforward, and you probably don't need a lot of fills to entice you. You easily make up for any lack of imagination in the bedroom with sexual prowess and all-night endurance.

Tips for Your Ideal Lover

Enjoying a gourmet meal or an evening of music or theater out on the town with your beloved puts you in the mood for love. However, sharing the comforts of home in a private sanctuary filled with flowers and lighted with scented candles can also be a major turn-on.

May 21, *Gemini 3*

What Makes You Tick

You enchant others with your breezy charm, and your inquisitive nature can lead to experiments with various lovers before you settle down. Good communication is as important to you as sex, and you want a mate who is a friend and confidant. As far as you're concerned, no amount of physical attraction can make up for a lack of shared interests or the inability to talk things over with your partner.

Between the Sheets

You can be restless and unpredictable in close relationships. Solicitous of your partner's needs one moment, you go off on some tangent of your own the next. Effusive feelings scare you, and sometimes you're so mistrustful of your own emotions that you try to rationalize them out of existence. To hold your attention, your mate needs to find a way to engage your intellect along with your emotions. Your brain is your most prominent sex organ, and you enjoy sharing your thoughts and ideas as well with your lover. Clever verbal foreplay is your forte, and your silver-tongued seduction technique is witty and amusing rather than sweetly romantic.

Tips for Your Ideal Lover

Sex is mainly fun and games, and you don't take it too seriously. Verbal enticements have a big impact on your libido, and erotic sexual banter turns you on almost as swiftly as physical contact. You particularly like having your bedmate describe what he or she likes to do in great detail.

May 22, *Gemini 4*

What Makes You Tick

Although part of you longs for a long-term relationship, another part prefers to skim happily along the surface of love. Bright, lively, witty conversations stimulate you almost as much as sexual encounters, and the lover who can make you laugh is the one most likely to steal your heart. Ultimately, you would rather be single than stuck in a relationship with someone who isn't clever enough to hold your interest.

Between the Sheets

While you may appear reserved in public, you're ardent and sensual behind closed doors, and you want a lover who knows how to unleash your simmering passions. Although caring and affectionate, you're unlikely to forgo compatibility in favor of romance. Talking about ideas and sharing information makes you feel closer to your significant other. Without mental affinity, you quickly become bored and start losing interest in the relationship. Your libido is sparked by images of what you plan to do, and you find verbal stimulation as exciting as physical foreplay. While you may come off as shy in public, you're liable to try just about anything behind closed doors with the right partner.

Tips for Your Ideal Lover

You respond best to an inventive bed partner who infuses a spirit of discovery and a sense of fun into your lovemaking. You particularly enjoy spicy pillow talk, and exchanging verbal banter and sharing erotic fantasies with your bedmate charges the very air around you with sexual anticipation.

May 23, *Gemini 5*

What Makes You Tick

You're charming, quick-witted, sociable, and easygoing, and you have a knack for getting along with all kinds of people. While you may crave the intensity of a close relationship, you are wary of any situation that makes you feel emotionally vulnerable. Companionship and mutual understanding attract you more readily than passion and romance, and a partner who shares your many interests is a must.

Between the Sheets

You are open-minded and prepared to try almost anything once. As an innovative, inventive lover, you are always open to novel ideas. Once you get going, you are skillful and considerate and intent on heightening the pleasure for both you and your partner. Sensual enhancements such as sexy toys keep you interested and add variety and spice to your lovemaking. However, it takes more than sex to hold your attention. If your lover is unable to have an intelligent conversation, you swiftly lose interest. When involved in a committed union, you're loyal to your beloved as long as he or she respects your need for some personal space.

Tips for Your Ideal Lover

Taking the time to relax with your lover opens the door to sensual pleasure. Focusing on your body with a shared shower, aromatic massage, or teasing foreplay arouses you and gives your frenetic mind a minivacation. Provocative verbal exchanges spark your libido as they add fuel to the erotic fire.

May 24, *Gemini 6*

What Makes You Tick

Your idea of a loving union does not always include lots of passion. What you want most is companionship and a true meeting of the minds. Even in your most intimate moments, you prefer keeping things light and playful. Since words are your forte, language is your most powerful tool of arousal and seduction. Beauty and comfort gratify your refined sensibilities, and a tasteful décor adds to your sensual pleasure.

Between the Sheets

You are a romantic, and relationships mean a lot to you. Yet you may find yourself torn between the contradictory messages coming from your head and your heart. Although you are not comfortable discussing your feelings and emotions, you can be totally uninhibited physically. An adventurous bedmate, you aim to please and be pleased. If you don't know what your partner likes in bed, you ask. Since your mind is your major erogenous zone, just the thought of making love can trigger your desire. You enjoy engaging in verbal banter with your significant other, and when you can't be together physically, you like to keep in touch via telephone, text messaging, or e-mail.

Tips for Your Ideal Lover

Easily bored, you thrive on change and variety in your sexual routine. Since you cannot quite separate romance and sensuality, you long to be swept off your feet in high style. Elegant rituals of courtship that include music, soft lighting, and a romantic ambiance turn you on.

May 25, *Gemini 7*

What Makes You Tick

Romantic partnership works best for you when it is rooted in companionship and intellectual rapport. While one part of you longs for a committed, long-term union, the other part prefers to skim happily along love's surface without actually taking the plunge. Ultimately you're something of a romantic gypsy, and if intimacy becomes too cloying, you may suddenly decide to search for a less restrictive relationship.

Between the Sheets

Your paradoxical nature may puzzle even those closest to you. You yearn for the emotional fulfillment of a deep and transforming union, while you crave variety and change in your love life and enjoy playing the field. As much of a chameleon in the bedroom as elsewhere, you are an odd combination of passion and intellect, and it generally takes both physical and mental stimulation to kindle and hold your interest. Sometimes you come off as playful and lighthearted, and on other nights nothing seems to matter except your desire for physical gratification. Either way, no partner of yours is ever likely to be bored in bed.

Tips for Your Ideal Lover

Totally convinced that variety is the spice of life, you are constantly on the lookout for exciting new experiences and challenges. Playful fantasy keeps your imagination engaged, and the uninhibited lover who employs innovation and spontaneity in the bedroom has the best chance of holding your interest over the long term.

May 26, *Gemini 8*

What Makes You Tick

You have an outgoing, genial manner and a way with words that draws others to your side. Playful one moment and serious the next, your changeability may perplex potential suitors. Where romance is concerned, you analyze everything about a person before you get involved. The need to examine all possibilities in advance stems from your fear that intimacy could complicate your life and prevent you from achieving your personal goals.

Between the Sheets

You usually shy away from overt displays of public affection. However, the privacy of the bedroom allows you to drop your reserve and reveal your lusty sensuality. With your ideal mate, any hesitation you may feel swiftly departs and you enjoy experimenting with new ways of increasing sensual pleasure. You like to initiate spontaneous encounters with sexy words and steamy passionate touching. Although you want a physical relationship that will take you and your lover to the heights of passion, your mind needs to be stimulated along with your body. As a result, you prefer a partner with something fascinating to say to a great-looking, empty-headed sexual athlete.

Tips for Your Ideal Lover

Variety in sexual expression turns you on, and you respond amorously to role-playing games and exotic stories of spicy romantic adventurers. In advance of lovemaking, a calming bath with aromatic oils settles your nerves, and a clever bedmate relaxes you with soothing conversation and lots of erotic touching and stroking.

May 27, *Gemini 9*

What Makes You Tick

In an intimate relationship, you care deeply but dislike the feeling of emotional vulnerability. Although you want the grounding of a long-term partnership, you fear losing your freedom and independence. Your sociable, chatty side needs friendship, conversation, and intellectual stimulation, while the romantic part of you craves poetry, moonlight, and roses. As a result, you are almost as happy thinking and talking about lovemaking as when actually engaged in the sex act.

Between the Sheets

You possess an elusive, ethereal quality that sets you apart from other members of your Gemini Sun sign. Even in the bedroom, you are something of an enigma. On the one hand, you're a sensitive, alluring lover capable of extraordinary tenderness. On the other hand, your sexual approach is so rational at times that it may seem calculated. Either way you thrive in an atmosphere of fun and creativity, and when your intellect is stimulated by erotic sexual banter, your physical body quickly follows suit. An unusual mixture of romantic dreamer and unconventional thinker, you enjoy trying exotic new things in bed as long as they are neither crude nor vulgar.

Tips for Your Ideal Lover

Bewitched by imagination and dreams, you enjoy acting out your erotic fantasies with your ideal bedmate. To a great extent, the intensity of your sex drive depends on your vibrant imagination and you are turned on by a lover with a fantasy life equal to your own.

May 28, *Gemini 1*

What Makes You Tick

You are such a delightful, fun-loving companion that you cannot help attracting friends and admirers. Your approach to love is enthusiastic; when you see someone you like, you jump right in without worrying about consequences. However, it takes both physical attraction and intellectual rapport to capture your heart. Unless there is some depth to your love connection, you may lose interest and begin searching for new romantic territory.

Between the Sheets

Intensely passionate, idealistic, and romantic, you fall in and out of love rather easily. You cherish your independence, and your mercurial nature rarely allows you to stay put long enough for anyone to pin you down. Moreover, your preference for adventure over security makes it difficult for you to stay with one person forever. Being friends with your lover is really important, as is sharing your most intimate thoughts and ideas. On a physical level, you're more ardent than most other Gemini natives. You view lovemaking as a fun-filled game, and you manage to avoid bedroom boredom by employing a broad range of sexual techniques.

Tips for Your Ideal Lover

Your need for lots of variety makes you eager to try just about anything new or different. If even a hint of routine invades your boudoir, you quickly stir things up with spontaneous play or wild fantasy. Your ideal bed partner turns you on by employing a spicy combination of erotic talk and action.

May 29, *Gemini 2*

What Makes You Tick

Among the most sensual of Gemini lovers, your appreciation for the joys of the flesh makes you a very desirable bed partner. Lovemaking for you is a total experience, and you're careful to see that neither body nor mind gets short-changed. Although you get off on sharing erotic thoughts and ideas with your mate, you are adept at expressing your lusty sexuality through both word and deed.

Between the Sheets

Despite your lighthearted, easygoing approach to life, you have a decidedly sensitive, romantic side where love is concerned. Although partnership and sharing are vital to your happiness, too much intimacy makes you uncomfortable. Naturally more touchy-feely than most other twins, you enjoy foreplay that includes protracted periods of kissing and stroking. As a sophisticated lover, you know how to tantalize your mate with an elegant courtship that builds slowly to a peak of pleasure. You see sex as a wonderful way to communicate with your significant other. In the bedroom, you like to feel that you are the center of your lover's world, and you delight in knowing that he or she is turned on by you.

Tips for Your Ideal Lover

Both sensuous and curious, you are always eager to explore new ways to induce, prolong, and heighten the shared ecstasy. You are particularly delighted when your bedmate comes up with innovative ways to enhance your lovemaking with verbal and physical enticements that have a huge impact on your libido.

May 30, *Gemini 3*

What Makes You Tick

Moody and unpredictable in relationships, you can be responsive to your partner's needs physically at one moment, and off on some tangent the next. Effusive emotions scare you, and you're so mistrustful of your own feelings that you may try to rationalize them away. You intellectualize everything, and your ideal mate is the one who finds a way to engage your mind along with your body.

Between the Sheets

Clever and quick thinking, you live inside your head most of the time, and no amount of romantic passion causes you to lose emotional control. It's unlikely that you'll ever experience the ecstasy of being swept away by love. Since your brain is your most active sex organ, you view communication as the most important ingredient in an intimate union. You have the ability to "feel" with your mind and enjoy sharing thoughts and ideas with your lover. However, when a relationship progresses to the point of commitment, your inclination is to hit the panic button and run off into the night.

Tips for Your Ideal Lover

You are turned on by a rollicking session of lovemaking that includes lots of laughter and erotic experimentation. Flirtatious banter comes easily to you, and spicy verbal repartee always makes you smile. When the sex talk turns really hot and heavy, you like to amaze your lover with impromptu plans for an evening of passion.

May 31, *Gemini 4*

What Makes You Tick

On the outside, you appear high-spirited, easygoing, and lighthearted. Given your flirtatious manner and roving eye, others may assume that you are not really serious about settling down. However, you are more stable and responsible than most people realize, especially in a romantic relationship. You may be somewhat unsure where love is concerned, but you actually long for the safety of long-term commitment.

Between the Sheets

You truly believe that love and romance make the world go around, and you have an idealized notion of what an intimate union should be. You alternate between cool detachment and lusty ardor, depending upon your mood. Although you crave the variety sought by other members of your Sun sign, you can be rather shy in the bedroom, and you like having a bold lover who knows how to melt your inhibitions. Even more important, you want to be able to talk to your partner. Once you feel comfortable with your mate, there is no limit to what you will do to keep him or her happy.

Tips for Your Ideal Lover

In public, you may insist on reserved expressions of love and affection, but when you're alone with your partner, you like to initiate steamy encounters. Behind closed doors, you want to be seduced by a lover who knows how to unleash pent-up passion and soothe your simmering sexual tension.

June 1, *Gemini 1*

What Makes You Tick

There's never a dull moment when you're around, but your friends and lovers may have a hard time keeping up with you, because you think and act with lightning speed. Although you delight in the idea of love, you could have difficulty staying in one place long enough to cement a relationship. You excel at the rituals of courtship, and your silver-tongued patter endears you to prospective partners.

Between the Sheets

Always on the lookout for new experiences, you're attracted to the suitor who teaches you things in bed. A nimble, innovative lover, you get off on sharing what you know with your lover. However, you need to be able to communicate verbally as well as physically. You enjoy talking about what feels good to you, and you want to be told which moves gratify your mate. When you make a promise, you expect to keep it—and you do, just as long as nothing comes along to divert your attention. Routine bores you to tears. You enjoy activities that are exciting, unusual, or dangerous inside the bedroom or outside of it.

Tips for Your Ideal Lover

You respond readily to a gentle touch, accompanied by seductive verbal enticements. Playful flights of fancy keep your imagination engaged while you indulge in physical pleasure. You might try crafting a tale of torrid sexual adventurers with your lover and then acting out the story you've created.

June 2, *Gemini 2*

What Makes You Tick

You prefer sharing your life with another person to going it alone. You need a significant other with whom you have a mental affinity as well as a physical one. Less adventurous than other members of your Sun sign, you like it best when life is reasonably serene. Even so, there is an independent side to your character that yearns for diversity and the freedom to pursue your goals.

Between the Sheets

Your innate sensuality makes you eager to explore new ways to prolong and heighten the shared sexual ecstasy. A sophisticated lover with refined sensibilities, you lure your partner with an elegant courtship that builds slowly toward a peak of pleasure. You like to tantalize your mate with whispered promises of unimagined delights, and the duality of your nature prompts you to keep your lover guessing as lighthearted verbal teasing turns to smoldering physical passion. However, there are some incompatible elements in the way you relate to your partner in an intimate union. Although physical closeness presents no difficulty, you are considerably less accessible emotionally.

Tips for Your Ideal Lover

Both sensual and curious, you are turned on by sexual experimentation. You're particularly delighted when your partner comes up with novel tricks and innovative ways to enhance your lovemaking. The very idea of trying out an aphrodisiac or searching through a book of erotica for inspiration appeals to your craving for change and variety.

June 3, *Gemini 3*

What Makes You Tick

You love to party, socialize, and flirt, but in a close alliance you're rather changeable and moody. You probably have an active sex life, yet you're somewhat ambivalent regarding intimate relationships. Although you love both the sex and the sensation of being in love, romance is rarely the most important thing in your life. While you find physical intimacy pleasurable, you desire it more for the experience than because of emotional or physical needs.

Between the Sheets

At times, the idea of lovemaking attracts you more than the act itself. Yet when you're in the mood, you will make love just about anywhere, and you're glib enough to talk your partner into going along with virtually anything. You're often in too much of a hurry to bother with courting rituals, but when you do take the time to sweet-talk your beloved, you say whatever you think he or she most wants to hear. Moreover, you mean whatever you say, even if only for the moment. Fidelity is foreign to the Gemini temperament. However, you will usually stick with a basically good relationship, unless it becomes hopelessly dull and boring.

Tips for Your Ideal Lover

You have a wonderful way with words. Pillow talk turns you on, and you can banter, joke, and play little sex games all night long. You enjoy stories about other people's scandalous exploits almost as much as sharing the details of your own secret desires.

June 4, *Gemini 4*

What Makes You Tick

Relationships matter a great deal to you, and having a large circle of friends gives you a sense of belonging and fulfillment. Romantically, you are considerably more ardent and less flirtatious than most other members of your Sun sign. Even though you crave security, you resist surrendering your freedom to achieve it. Your ideal mate realizes that it may be a lot easier to catch you than to hold you.

Between the Sheets

Your adaptable nature helps you deal with diverse situations in and out of the bedroom. Although generally lighthearted and easygoing, you have a romantic side where love is concerned. You like to feel that you are the person at the center of your lover's world. Exploring the mysteries of your partner's feelings provides you with endless fascination. You appreciate a vocal bedmate who openly expresses sexual preferences and pleasures. Since you believe variety makes life more interesting, the more innovative the moves and ideas, the happier you are likely to be. You need a partner who stimulates you mentally as well as physically. Otherwise, you could lose interest and start looking elsewhere.

Tips for Your Ideal Lover

More sensual and touchy-feely than the typical Gemini native, you get off on protracted periods of foreplay involving a fair amount of kissing and stroking. However, nonverbal communication alone just doesn't do it for you. Spicy sexual fantasies fueled by steamy erotic conversation add adventure and excitement to your lovemaking.

June 5, *Gemini 5*

What Makes You Tick

Quick-witted and gregarious, you possess a breezy personality and a great sense of humor. Everyone wants to be your friend, because you have an instinct for getting along with people. You may crave the intensity of a close union, but you're exceedingly wary of emotional vulnerability. Mutual understanding attracts you more than passion and romance. Although you're loyal, you won't tolerate restrictions on your movements.

Between the Sheets

As one of the most innovative lovers in the zodiac, you thrive on diversity, change, and versatility. An inventive bed partner with unlimited curiosity, you're always open to novel ideas for sexual experimentation. Emotionally, however, there is a discernable coolness in your nature that causes you to intellectualize and analyze your own erotic experiences. Adaptable and suggestible, you are never boring either between the sheets or elsewhere. However, your inner world is composed of thoughts and ideas that are, in many ways, more real to you than the world outside. As a result, you get almost as much pleasure from thinking and talking about the sex act, as from doing it.

Tips for Your Ideal Lover

Since your obsession with words transfers to the bedroom, you are turned on by anything sexual that involves verbal expression, and you need a partner who can share your vibrant and changeable fantasy life. From whispering sweet nothings, to talking about intimate desires in the most explicit language, you like discussing it all with your lover.

June 6, *Gemini 6*

What Makes You Tick

Your definition of true love does not necessarily include a lot of sex. What you are really looking for is companionship. You like being connected to another person and you feel incomplete without an intimate relationship in your life. Although you yearn for a permanent life partner, your freewheeling Gemini nature gives you a fondness for playing the field. As a result, you may go through a string of romances before settling down.

Between the Sheets

You are not much given to emotional intimacy, because your inclination is to share your deepest feelings only with your twin self. The key to your heart (and your body) is communication, and a spirited conversation can be as stimulating to you as a passionate sexual encounter. You regard lovemaking as a meeting of the minds and as a means of exchanging thoughts and ideas. On a physical level, however, you can be totally uninhibited. An adventurous lover, you aim to please and be pleased. If you don't know what your partner wants, you ask. If he or she doesn't know what you like, you are prepared to describe your preferences in graphic detail.

Tips for Your Ideal Lover

Fantasy and role-playing games turn you on. The right combination of imagination and reality can send shivers up and down your spine. You are more sexual than sensual, so the slow, languid approach doesn't really do it for you. You prefer being seduced with deep eye contact, dazzlingly sexy dialogue, and not-so-subtle hints of impending erotic delights.

June 7, *Gemini 7*

What Makes You Tick

Your paradoxical nature is a puzzle, and at times you appear moody and solitary. You often find yourself torn between contradictory messages from your head and your heart. On a physical level, you're passionate and sexy. However, it takes both intellectual and physical stimulation to hold your interest. You fervently resist any attempt to box you in, and an excess of emotion may scare you off.

Between the Sheets

The duality of your nature is most pronounced in the bedroom. Convinced that variety is the spice of life, you're constantly on the lookout for fresh challenges and adventures and your sexual needs and wishes are as varied as all your other interests. Sometimes you seem physically aloof and more concerned with making conversation than making love. At other times, you assume the role of the lighthearted, devilishly charming lover who equates sex with fun and games. Then there are the nights of intense passion and single-minded devotion to erotic pleasure. Your fondness for the unusual makes you a tantalizing bed partner, and your ideal mate enjoys spicing things up by interjecting a touch of fantasy.

Tips for Your Ideal Lover

You need an innovative lover, someone capable of keeping your interest alive with new ideas for sparking your libido. The bed partner who turns you on is the one whose curiosity equals your own. You always enjoy trying new things, and sexual experimentation is at the top of the list of things you like to do.

June 8, *Gemini 8*

What Makes You Tick

Your geniality and disarming charm mask a controlled inner self. Inclined to distance yourself from your emotions, you are not even aware of what you're feeling half of the time. Settling down may not be at the top of your agenda, yet once your success in life is assured, you may begin thinking about a long-term love relationship. Until then, the highly sexed lover inside you must continue competing for time with the workaholic.

Between the Sheets

Initially, your overworked psyche may resist surrendering to the delicious sensations of freely expressed passion. However, once you put work and responsibility aside, your reactions to sexual stimuli are strong and immediate. The lover who stirs your imagination also inflames your libido. Restless and curious, you enjoy experimenting with various sexual techniques and positions. Despite the serious edge to your character, you don't want a life that is all work and no play. When you get going, you're quite a lusty playmate, and a fun-filled bedroom romp brings out your uninhibited sexuality. You channel lots of energy into communication, and since you consider mental compatibility as essential as physical compatibility, you need a mate you can talk to.

Tips for Your Ideal Lover

Sex play is exactly what you need to help you relax. Soaking in a warm bath, prior to lovemaking, calms you down and soothes your jangled nerves. A slow, erotic massage releases you from worldly cares. Your ideal lover initiates spontaneous encounters with sexy words and passionate touches.

June 9, *Gemini 9*

What Makes You Tick

You have an elusive quality that makes you appear remote from the real world. Your paradoxical nature puzzles friends and lovers alike. In an intimate union, you are a romantic, delightful lover. You are sincerely devoted to your beloved and even prepared to make sacrifices if necessary. Although you care deeply, you are emotionally vulnerable and easily disillusioned. When things get rough, you could be tempted to move on to another idealized partner.

Between the Sheets

Even in the bedroom, you are a charming enigma. On the one hand, you are a sensitive, alluring lover, capable of extraordinary tenderness. On the other hand, your sexual approach is so rational that, at times, it may seem calculated. Either way, you thrive in an atmosphere of fun and creativity. An unusual mixture of romantic dreamer and unconventional thinker, you enjoy trying new things, in bed and elsewhere, as long as they are not crude or vulgar. Your amorous performances can take place indoors, or outside, under the stars. While you crave the grounding that a permanent partnership can offer, you fear commitment and may go through several steamy affairs before settling down with the right one.

Tips for Your Ideal Lover

A great storyteller, you spin your own fantasies with little or no trouble. The bedmate who turns you enchants you with erotic fantasies created and staged just for you. You may dress up in a costume or undress at your partner's direction.

June 10, *Gemini 1*

What Makes You Tick

Youthful in mind and body, you believe in always having a rollicking good time. Routine bores you. You prefer going to exotic places, meeting interesting people, and trying unusual things. Exploring fresh romantic territory fascinates you, and your restless nature may cause you to shy away from cozy domestic situations. Still, when you find someone exciting enough to hold your interest, you will make a commitment.

Between the Sheets

Typically, your approach to intimacy is spontaneous and full of ideas for introducing variety into your lovemaking. You have a mischievous sense of humor and delight in the fun and adventure of sexy role-playing games. When your mind is aroused, your body follows. Words that engage your vivid imagination will inflame your sexual desire; you respond amorously to erotic banter and other verbal enticements. By the time innuendo changes to an explicit discussion of what you're going to do to each other, your passion meter shoots up from zero to 100 percent. Your high-strung, go-go-go personality requires the calming influence of a partner who is capable of holding on loosely, without letting go entirely.

Tips for Your Ideal Lover

Your mind is your most sensitive erogenous zone, and when your steamy thoughts and ideas meet up with reality, you relax readily into a deep sensuality. Spontaneity turns you on, and you enjoy a lover who wakes you up with all-over kisses and erotic touches that inflame your passion.

June 11, *Gemini 2*

What Makes You Tick

You like surrounding yourself with friends, and you're happiest in social situations where you can swap ideas with various kinds of people. Although you crave the closeness of an intimate union, you dislike sacrificing your independence to get it. Your ideal partner understands this and loves you without holding on too tightly. Since you want a friend as well as a lover, you need to share your thoughts as well as your body.

Between the Sheets

Inherently easygoing and open to suggestion, you're inclined to "go with the flow" between the sheets and elsewhere. You delight in knowing that your bedmate is turned on by you, no matter how long you two have been together. Because you thrive on variety, you try to keep your love fresh and alive by having sex in diverse or unusual settings. You particularly get off on the idea of exploring the erotic possibilities of romantic venues other than your own bed. Delightfully verbal, you're adept at turning subtle innuendo into a means of seduction. You appreciate a mate who tantalizes you with promises of the unexpected, and the occasional quickie gratifies your restless nature.

Tips for Your Ideal Lover

You're turned on by hours of languorous sex. Since it's difficult for you to stay in one place for long, you like to make love for a time and then take a break. When you've shaken off your nervous energy, you get back to your lover with renewed desire.

June 12, *Gemini 3*

What Makes You Tick

Fun loving, flirtatious, and popular, you're a social being who loves to party and can usually be found where the action is. More at home with thoughts than feelings, your demeanor turns from charming to cool indifference when faced with emotional demands or personal restrictions. The lover who wants to stay close to you will give you plenty of breathing room and never attempt to control you.

Between the Sheets

You view a positive sexual connection as just another way to communicate with your mate or partner. Although you crave tenderness and devotion, you are really turned on by the person who is your intellectual equal and interested in sharing your thoughts and ideas. Imaginative lovemaking that is full of surprises stimulates both your body and mind. You enjoy learning new things and sharing what you've learned with your significant other, so being with you is never boring. With your clever, agile mind, you are able to come up with lively, innovative ways of making love that keep your union fresh and exciting. With the right person, you can be a generous, warm, and loving partner.

Tips for Your Ideal Lover

You consider pillow talk and exchanging intimacies and secrets a sexy form of verbal foreplay. It arouses you to hear the details of what your partner is thinking and feeling during all the stages of lovemaking. You particularly enjoy spending time laughing and frolicking with your lover, either in the bedroom or elsewhere.

June 13, *Gemini 4*

What Makes You Tick

Your friendly, easygoing manner effectively conceals a single-minded pursuit of worldly success. Unlike most other twins, when you want something (or someone), you absolutely refuse to give up until you have achieved your objective. A charming flatterer and engaging storyteller, you are something of a throwback to the troubadours of a bygone era. Somehow you manage to be totally in love with the idea of being in love, yet completely sincere in your affections.

Between the Sheets

In the bedroom, you have a playful approach to sexuality that can cause your lover to forget that you actually take making love very seriously. Alone with your beloved, you shower him or her with affection and freely exhibit the lustier side of your nature. Lighthearted fun and a quirky sense of humor bring out your uninhibited, tactile sensuality. You enjoy expressing your sexual desires verbally. Witty banter with your mate spurs you on and sets the stage for shared passion. A forward-looking curiosity permeates everything you do, and you consider innovation and variety the most important ingredients in lovemaking. Moreover, you are willing to try virtually anything to spice things up a bit.

Tips for Your Ideal Lover

You respond amorously to being teased with a feather or gently massaged with scented oils. However, nothing holds your attention quite like wit and charm, and you're turned on by erotic word games. Exchanging evocative quips with your partner during foreplay creates a steamy atmosphere that heats up your libido.

June 14, *Gemini 5*

What Makes You Tick

In social situations, your breezy personality makes people long to get to know you better. In an intimate union, you make a loving partner, despite being protective of your independence. You thrive when paired with someone who understands your need for your own space. Although you can take romance or leave it alone, you need intellectual companionship and a mate who is tolerant of your many and varied interests.

Between the Sheets

Where love and sex are concerned, you tend to be more than a little absent-minded. Sometimes you get so immersed in your intellect that you all but forget about your body. However, all it usually takes to ignite your desire is a small reminder of what you have been missing. The right suitor knows that a combination of gentle touches and spicy verbal banter quickly eases you into the mood for making love. Once you get going, you are a considerate, skillful lover, intent on heightening the pleasure for yourself and your partner. Your endless curiosity prompts you to consider a variety of erotic pleasures and practices, and taking time to relax with your bedmate opens the door to further exploration.

Tips for Your Ideal Lover

Your already restless nature is quickly bored by repetition. It is not unusual for you to try to intensify the eroticism of your sexual experiences through aphrodisiacs and other sensual enhancements. Sex toys and suggestive attire get your juices flowing and add spice and creativity to your lovemaking.

June 15, *Gemini 6*

What Makes You Tick

In an intimate union, you're tender and considerate, and friendship and companionship are as vital to you as love. Basically partnership oriented, you prefer a committed relationship. Even so, you can be fickle in your attachments, and it may take a while before you decide to settle down with Mr. or Ms. Right. Idealistic where your love life is concerned, you need to be able to admire your partner and respect his or her intelligence.

Between the Sheets

Since you prefer being the one pursued, you rarely make the first move. You rely instead on your innate ability to attract and inspire your lover. The poet in you enjoys all the charming rituals of old-fashioned courtship. Highly civilized by nature with delicate sensibilities, you tend to avoid discord whenever possible and you are easily offended by crudeness and vulgarity. You respond enthusiastically to a beautiful and harmonious bedroom ambiance that includes flowers, candlelight, and soft music. After a glamorous evening of social and cultural happenings, you like to unwind with your lover in a secluded hideaway where you can enjoy the intimacy of a private supper before making love.

Tips for Your Ideal Lover

You long to be swept off your feet in a romantic fantasy. Beauty, luxury, and comfort gratify your senses and put you in the mood for lovemaking. Since your mind is your number-one erogenous zone, you're extremely susceptible to verbal enticements. Seductive glances and other spontaneous romantic gestures trigger your sexual impulses.

June 16, *Gemini 7*

What Makes You Tick

Although you can be temperamental, people are attracted by your magnetic personality. While shared interests are important to you in an intimate union, you believe there should also be room for separate activities. Even after you find true love, you require some alone time to follow your intellectual pursuits. You want to be with someone who accepts you as you are; knowing your partner loves you for yourself means a lot.

Between the Sheets

Your restless Gemini nature abhors inactivity; sometimes you need to be seduced away from the thoughts and ideas swirling around in your mind. Although it may take a while for you to warm up, when the mood seizes you, you forget everything else. You tend to alternate between freewheeling playfulness and serious passion. Since you regard the brain as the sexiest organ in the body, you particularly enjoy inventing and acting out sexual fantasies with your bedmate. Convinced that variety is the spice of life, you're continually on the lookout for new challenges and adventures in the bedroom and elsewhere.

Tips for Your Ideal Lover

The lover who makes you feel sexy and desirable fuels your passion. You're quite intuitive about the other person's needs, and you expect to receive similar consideration in return. Since you are initially shy, you need a lusty, encouraging partner to spark your libido and melt your innate reserve.

June 17, *Gemini 8*

What Makes You Tick

Despite your obvious social skills, you're careful where love is concerned, and you approach intimate relationships with caution, at least until you are sure that your feelings are reciprocated. It may take quite a while for you to make the ultimate commitment, but when you do, you're in it for the long haul. Once you feel secure and confident, you are able to reveal your true passion and sensuality.

Between the Sheets

One of the more ardent of the Gemini lovers, you enjoy sex a great deal. Nevertheless, you sometimes feel intellectually removed from the demands of your body. Even at your most abandoned, you maintain control and refuse to allow the physical act of love to gain precedence over the power of your mind. As much a creature of the intellect as of the body, you need a partner with whom you can share a good conversation. Your ideal mate is sexy and affectionate and, above all, never boring. Given your great sense of humor, you want a serious partner who is also fun loving and able to lighten things up when they begin to drag.

Tips for Your Ideal Lover

Mental stimulation acts as foreplay for you, and you get a considerable amount of pleasure anticipating your next bedroom encounter with your beloved. You get off on a sense of ongoing excitement between yourself and your bedmate, and you respond passionately to sexy talk and whispered sweet nothings in your ear.

June 18, *Gemini 9*

What Makes You Tick

You're a romantic idealist, given to wild flights of fancy; stability in an intimate relationship is not one of your top priorities. Although you enjoy the emotional security a permanent union offers, you fear commitment. Since you are extremely social, the freedom to come and go as you please is more important than the relative safety of a long-term liaison. Moreover, when a relationship begins to lose its sparkle, you could decide to move on to something more exciting.

Between the Sheets

A poet at heart, you tend to view true love as something magical but elusive. Your sexual interests lie as much in the realm of the romantic and otherworldly as the physical. To a great extent, the intensity of your sex drive depends upon your vibrant imagination. The slightest flirtatious erotic suggestion can trigger torrid mental images. When your intellect is stimulated by steamy thoughts, your body quickly follows suit. With your imagination invoked, the sexy scenarios of shared fantasy create a feeling of deeply felt sensuality that envelops both you and your bed partner, transporting you to exotic, unknown times and places, without ever leaving the bedroom.

Tips for Your Ideal Lover

Your fluency with sexy language makes you a very seductive lover, and you are turned on by a bed partner with a fantasy life equal to your own. Together you create fabulous, unforgettable tales of lusty romance, excitement, and adventure that merge the sacred with the profane.

June 19, *Gemini 1*

What Makes You Tick

You may be carefree and independent, but you are also extremely sociable. You realize that no one is an island, and you want someone special in your life to complement you intellectually and complete you physically and emotionally. Since you prefer adventure to security, fidelity is not your strongest suit. You'll stay in a relationship only as long it remains fun and interesting. When the excitement leaves, so do you.

Between the Sheets

An unabashed optimist, your eternally youthful outlook can be contagious, and you possess tons of charm and a bubbling personality that exude sparks of life. You're such a delightful companion that you just can't help attracting many potential suitors. On a sexual level, you are considerably more ardent and sensual than other Gemini natives. An innovative lover, you avoid routine and repetition by employing a broad range of sexual techniques. Physical lovemaking, however, is secondary for you; ideas turn you on, and you love sharing your most intimate thoughts with your lover. The person who hopes to catch and keep you must hold your attention intellectually as well as physically.

Tips for Your Ideal Lover

Sex is a game for you. Your spontaneous, impulsive nature responds playfully to titillation at wildly inappropriate moments. A passionate kiss behind the boss's back, an erotic suggestion whispered during the opera, or a look of naked desire flashed at a family dinner are all it takes to turn you on for a night of lovemaking.

June 20, *Gemini 2*

What Makes You Tick

A loving relationship matters a great deal to you, because it provides you with feelings of intimacy, belonging, and fulfillment. Romantically, you are considerably more ardent and less flirtatious than most other twins. Even though you crave security, you will resist surrendering your freedom in order to achieve it. Moreover, you need a partner who stimulates you mentally as well as physically. Otherwise, you may lose interest and start looking elsewhere.

Between the Sheets

You have a sensitive, romantic side where love is concerned. Although your approach to sex is as cool-headed as other members of your Sun sign, you have a genuine appreciation for the joys of the flesh. You like a vocal bedmate who openly expresses sexual preferences and pleasures. You need to know that you are at the center of your partner's world, especially in the bedroom. Since you believe variety makes life more interesting, exploring the mysteries of your mate's feelings provides you with endless fascination. The more innovative your lover's moves and ideas, the happier you're likely to be. Your ideal mate realizes that it may be a lot easier to catch you than to hold you.

Tips for Your Ideal Lover

More sensual and touchy-feely than the typical Gemini native, you get off on protracted periods of foreplay involving a generous amount of kissing, touching, and stroking. You are turned on by raunchy sexual fantasies, fueled by steamy erotic conversation that adds adventure and excitement to your lovemaking.

June 21, *Cancer 3*

What Makes You Tick

The sensitive, imaginative, intuitive crab experiences the world through feelings and emotions, whereas rational number 3 dwells mainly on a mental plane of words and ideas. This dichotomy in your love nature makes you a fascinating, dynamic, multifaceted, if somewhat difficult to understand, romantic partner. Although your significant other may sometimes tire of dealing with your shifting moods, he or she will never be indifferent or bored while you're around.

Between the Sheets

In an intimate union, you are romantic but not starry-eyed. You think twice before exchanging the easy atmosphere of friendship and companionship for a serious, long-term love relationship. Sometimes it is difficult to reconcile your lighthearted, flirtatious side with your deep emotional need for the security of a permanent love union. However, with the two sides of your character working in sync, you dazzle your mate with your unique mix of witty sexual banter and heightened sensuality. You get off talking about your own thoughts and feelings, and with your seductive aura and sensitivity to your partner's moods and desires, you can be absolutely irresistible in the bedroom.

Tips for Your Ideal Lover

At times you may seem a little distracted, but your bedroom radar actually picks up every nuance of your lover's body language. Sexy communication turns you on, and unlike so many others of your Sun sign, you enjoy expressing your lusty desires with spicy erotic talk as well as sensuous touching and stroking.

June 22, *Cancer 4*

What Makes You Tick

Thoughtful and generous with those you love, you're also extremely sensitive and self-protective. Easily hurt by slights to your dignity, you may be tempted to crawl into your crab's shell whenever things don't go your way. You can be a bit shy and may prefer keeping your true emotions hidden until you're sure that your partner shares your feelings. Once involved, however, you make a caring and affectionate lover.

Between the Sheets

In love, you may sometimes feel as if you're being pulled in two directions at the same time. You don't like to appear vulnerable; even in your most intimate moments you need to feel in control. However, once your confidence has been won, you'll remain devoted forever. Casual sex just doesn't do it for you. You're no prude, but you like to establish strong connections to your partner before embarking on a physical relationship. In bed, you prefer taking your time and building slowly to an all-encompassing passion. An idealist, you want a lover who meets your expectations, yet you may resent being held to the same high standard.

Tips for Your Ideal Lover

A romantic courtship with elegant dinners suits you, but you also enjoy cozy nights at home with your beloved. Your ideal lover creates a romantic atmosphere of soothing tranquility. Although you prefer the straightforward pleasure of lovemaking to more exotic moves, a bedmate who introduces thrilling change into your routine stirs your passions.

June 23, *Cancer 5*

What Makes You Tick

At times your emotions are so contradictory that you don't even know what you want. As a result, intimate relationships can be difficult. One part of you is conservative and domestic and longs to settle down, while your more rebellious side is carefree and independent. The patient suitor who is willing to make allowances for your mood swings is most likely to win your heart.

Between the Sheets

Playfully innovative, you enjoy spontaneity and thrive with a sensual, romantic lover who can get you to forget everything and surrender to the moment. Feelings of closeness inflame your desire and increase your appetite for physical intimacy. Your ability to combine subtle seduction with a bit of fun and games keeps your lovemaking fresh and exciting. A part of you wants friendship and intellectual companionship almost as much as romance and emotional fulfillment, and that part may be attracted to lifestyles that are somewhat less conventional. In a secure, loving union, you may willingly make room for a little experimentation and variety in your sex life.

Tips for Your Ideal Lover

The mate who engages your mind and imagination has the edge, and your appetite for physical pleasure grows along with your trust in your partner. You get off on talking about your own thoughts and feelings, and you find a seductive, sensitive lover who understands your moods and desires absolutely irresistible.

June 24, *Cancer 6*

What Makes You Tick

You think in "twosomes" and feel incomplete without a partner to share your life. However, your desire for the perfect romance prompts you to do everything possible to make your relationship conform to your idea of what love ought to be. All you really want is make your significant other happy, but your determination to place him or her at the center of your world may be smothering.

Between the Sheets

You're a romantic idealist, and likely to hold off making a serious commitment until you are reasonably sure you've found Mr. or Ms. Right. Once involved, you make a wonderfully nurturing, thoughtful lover. Romance and sex are closely intertwined in your mind, and your sensual desires are heightened by feelings of a strong intuitive connection to your partner. Without that strong emotional bond, the initial attraction may begin to lose its luster. Although your lovemaking tends toward the traditional, you're willing to put your inclinations aside to please your bedmate. When you make your lover happy, you feel happy, too. Your desires are heightened by luxurious surroundings in a romantic setting.

Tips for Your Ideal Lover

Your ideal lover intuits your fluctuating moods and unlocks your passion by slowly exploring your deeper sensuality. Time spent in or near water brings out your languid sexuality; once relaxed, you sink into the passionate rhythms of lovemaking. Long hugs and lingering kisses become foreplay that builds to a dramatic climax.

June 25, *Cancer 7*

What Makes You Tick

You crave love, yet you are fearful of exposing your emotional vulnerability. Sensitive and basically passive, you are often tempted to stand aside and let your partner call all the shots. Because you are so nurturing and giving, people may take advantage of you. When you're happy, no one is nicer or more generous, but when you're upset, you retreat to a solitary corner to brood.

Between the Sheets

High ideals dictate your actions. Casual love affairs hold little temptation for you because you regard a sexual relationship as a genuine partnership. You like to bask in the erotic pleasures of sensual lovemaking in the comfort of luxurious surroundings. Although your sex drive is strong, it can be somewhat erratic. Boredom is an anathema to you, but spontaneity and fun can turn you on as readily as the most ardent foreplay. Despite your seemingly traditional attitude toward sexuality, you long to be swept away on a wave of passionate, ecstatic lovemaking. Your ideal bedmate understands your paradoxical nature and appeases your thrill-seeking side by lovingly luring you into uncharted sexual territory within a committed relationship.

Tips for Your Ideal Lover

The intuitive bedmate whose lack of inhibitions behind closed doors matches your own knows what to do to satisfy your fantasies and secret cravings. You shine in relaxed, unhurried moments with your lover, and you respond ardently to aphrodisiacs and sharing sexy edible treats in bed.

June 26, *Cancer 8*

What Makes You Tick

An air of dignified reserve permeates your love nature. While you are unlikely to gush or be unduly demonstrative in public, you keep your beloved close to your heart. You thrive on domesticity and probably want a traditional marriage and family life. Beneath the covers, your tenderness and sensuality reveal an emotional sensitivity that you keep well guarded outside the bedroom.

Between the Sheets

While a close, loving relationship is central to your life, you want more from an intimate union than just good times and sexual gratification. Lovemaking should be part of a lifestyle that includes all the elements of a committed, stable pairing. In your public life, you seek recognition and success. In private, however, your well-defined domestic side craves the comfort and security of home and family. A genuine romantic, you like to touch, stroke, hug, kiss, and cuddle your significant other, and you enjoy surprising him or her with sentimental gifts. When you find the love and acceptance you seek, you make a sexy, responsive lover and a practical, dependable life partner.

Tips for Your Ideal Lover

You cannot be rushed, in the bedroom or anywhere else. Romantic evenings of slow, sensual seduction turn you on. Endurance is your forte, and you are proud of your bedroom prowess. Your randy side emerges behind closed doors, and you revel in steamy bedroom romps with an imaginative partner.

June 27, *Cancer 9*

What Makes You Tick

Because of your powerful need for closeness, you tend to view an intimate union as a partnership in which you and your mate share absolutely everything. A true romantic, you are either in love, looking for love, or fantasizing about finding your soul mate. When you do find him or her, you are intensely nurturing and blessed with a tremendous capacity for pleasing your beloved.

Between the Sheets

You're motivated more by your emotions than your body. Lovemaking is not just a physical act but rather a total intimacy involving body, mind, and soul. Mutual give-and-take is important to you—in the bedroom and elsewhere. Once involved with someone, you soak up his or her feelings and desires like a psychic sponge. Sometimes you have difficulty separating your thoughts and feelings from what you're picking up from your bedmate. A dedicated sensualist, you enjoy engaging in verbal and physical teasing, murmuring sweet nothings one moment and touching and stroking the next. You like being wooed and seduced in return, and your ultimate desire is to be swept away on a tidal wave of romantic passion.

Tips for Your Ideal Lover

Love is your ultimate turn-on, and you get off on all the trappings of old-fashioned romance. The suitor who appeals to your sentimental side with thoughtful gifts and spontaneous surprises has it made. An evening of lovemaking that includes a fragrant bath with your partner also rates extremely high in your book.

June 28, *Cancer 1*

What Makes You Tick

The impetuosity of the number 1 is continually at odds with the moody apprehension of your Cancer Sun sign. Although you possess a subtle power to charm that accounts for your smoldering charisma, your doubts and insecurities keep you from making bold moves unless you are sure they will be welcomed. Since your pride is easily wounded, you could be subject to fits of depression when your actions are challenged.

Between the Sheets

You may consider yourself daring and independent, but you actually crave the comfort of a committed, long-term union. Despite your desire for intimacy, you are basically moody and shift back and forth between a need for security and a yearning for personal freedom. Although nurturing, generous, and loyal in a close relationship, you can also be temperamental, demanding, and possessive. In the bedroom, however, you combine tenderness and consideration with intense passion and erotic excitement. Between the sheets, your only aim is to please and be pleased. Trying new things excites you and keeps your lovemaking fresh and interesting. If you sense love and approval from your lover, you will not hesitate to venture into previously untried sexual territory.

Tips for Your Ideal Lover

Your red-hot libido may be quick on the trigger, yet your deepest feelings often remain a carefully guarded secret. Consequently, you are happiest with an intuitive partner who can sense the fluctuations in your emotional rhythms and is capable of soothing your daily stresses with joyful, exuberant lovemaking.

June 29, *Cancer 2*

What Makes You Tick

Comfort and security are what matter most to you in an intimate union. More than anything, you appreciate sensory delights, and you're happiest when you can combine two or more—such as good food, good drink, and good sex. You're responsive to the other person's needs and desires, and when you find Mr. or Ms. Right, you have little hesitation about settling down to an idyllic life together.

Between the Sheets

You long for a calm, stable home life and the closeness of a permanent union. When you commit to someone, you do it with your whole heart, and you continue to nurture the relationship with lots of tender loving care. A passionate lover, you revel in the sensual pleasures of lovemaking. You take great pleasure in lavishing love and affection on your partner, both inside and outside the bedroom, and you expect the same kind of thoughtfulness and consideration in return. Emotional bonding is as important to you as physical union, and you need to know that you both are always on the same page where your relationship is concerned.

Tips for Your Ideal Lover

You're a born romantic, and hugging and kissing and all the traditional rituals of courtship are important to you. You are more likely to be moved by your lover's actions than by his or her words. You enjoy sharing creature comforts, and preparing a special meal and eating it together turns you on.

June 30, *Cancer 3*

What Makes You Tick

It's difficult for you to reconcile your lighthearted, flirtatious nature with your deep-seated need for a permanent love relationship. The coolness of your intellectuality is continually at odds with the intensity of your emotions. Although cheerful and lots of fun, you are quite touchy and your sensitive feelings are easily hurt. When this happens, your typical reaction is to internalize your anger and slip into a dark mood.

Between the Sheets

With your sexy aura and sensitivity to your partner's feelings, you can be truly irresistible in the bedroom. Your approach to sex is generally less conservative than most other Cancer natives, and you don't always play it safe where love is concerned. You actually prefer acting spontaneously, following your heart rather than your head. You think that lovemaking is meant to be fun, and you fully expect to have a good time under the covers. Good communication is important to you in an intimate relationship. You enjoy expressing your lusty desires verbally and also less directly with seductive looks and gestures. The lover who picks up on your sexual signals and responds in kind has a definite edge.

Tips for Your Ideal Lover

Both your heart and mind need fulfillment, and you require depth as well as breadth in an intimate union. In bed and elsewhere, you need to be able to talk to your lover. Spicy language and inventive imaginative moves turn you on.

July 1, *Cancer 1*

What Makes You Tick

Your emotional life resembles a roller coaster. At times you may feel as if you are being pulled between a desire for continuity and your love of freedom and independence. As a result, you can be sensitive and nurturing one moment, explosive and demanding the next. When you feel insecure in a love relationship, you become moody and apprehensive. First, jealousy rears its ugly head, and then you turn clingy and possessive.

Between the Sheets

A true romantic with the soul of an adventurer, you radiate a type of sexual magnetism that makes you much sought after as a lover. Considerably bolder than other Cancer natives, you have a flair for the theatrical that adds drama and humor to your bedroom activities. Your charm and charisma are extremely seductive. When you feel comfortable with your bed partner, you let down your guard and reveal a surprisingly sensitive side to your love nature. Time spent near water brings out your languid sensuality, and once relaxed, you glory in the rich, passionate rhythms of lovemaking. You are at your best with an intuitive mate who is tuned in to your wavelength.

Tips for Your Ideal Lover

The lover who turns you on can walk the fine line between passionate lovemaking one night and tender sensuality the next. Sexual spontaneity can provide you with endless thrills, and a clever bed partner will keep your relationship fresh and exciting by initiating impromptu moments of playful eroticism.

July 2, *Cancer 2*

What Makes You Tick

You know exactly what you are looking for in a loving union, and you won't settle for less. You want a calm, stable home and the closeness of a committed relationship. A genuine romantic, you make a caring and thoughtful lover. Innately generous and concerned about your beloved, you like being totally involved in his or her life. However, problems may arise if your mate views your nurturing as possessiveness.

Between the Sheets

A hedonist where sex is concerned, you view lovemaking as the pursuit of pure pleasure. Generous in bed and out, you willingly lavish your significant other with attention and affection. Even so, you are inclined to temper your passions with a dose of caution. You don't rush into intimate situations, and you avoid many of the emotional extremes that often plague other Cancer natives. Ever sensitive to your partner's wishes and desires, you know the best ways to please your beloved. Your favorite sexual fantasy probably includes good food and great sex, and feeding each other delectable little snacks in bed can turn into an erotic free-for-all.

Tips for Your Ideal Lover

The right mate senses your need for tender touches and emotional bonding, and sharing the comforts of home sets the stage for the pleasures of the bedroom. You appreciate every kind of sensory delight. Preparing and eating a luscious feast with your lover evokes an atmosphere of voluptuous indulgence that turns you on.

July 3, *Cancer 3*

What Makes You Tick

Naturally loving and affectionate, you want and need a stable romantic alliance in your life, and you are looking for someone who shares your numerous interests. Despite your inherent loyalty, however, if you tire of a romantic union, you could decide to give up and move on. Your mate may grow weary of your emotional peaks and valleys, but the relationship will never be dull or boring.

Between the Sheets

A sensitive lover, you have a powerful need to establish a strong emotional link with your mate. Initially, you may approach a prospective partner cautiously, at least until you are sure your feelings are returned. When your feelings and intellect work together, each balances the other, but your frequent mood swings and mind changes make it difficult for you to decide when to follow your head and when to follow your heart. Along with wit and sparkling conversation, you bring tenderness, warmth, and generosity to your bedroom frolics. Although you are passionate and sensual, you're also fun loving. You enjoy sex, and you are as interested in having a good time in bed as everywhere else.

Tips for Your Ideal Lover

Nothing turns you on like a romantic getaway. You prefer intimate and charming to elegant and luxurious. You're happiest in a picturesque country inn or quaint bed and breakfast. Although you enjoy walks in the country, the sensual lovemaking in the cozy old-fashioned bed really gets your juices flowing.

July 4, *Cancer 4*

What Makes You Tick

Basically generous, loving, and nurturing, you can also be jealous and possessive. Like most crabs, you're extremely touchy and have a terrific sense of humor about everything except your own foibles. In the blink of an eye, you can change from outgoing and protective to withdrawn and self-protective. When your feelings are hurt, you retreat into your shell and may refuse to come out until your bad mood passes.

Between the Sheets

Passionate, affectionate, and tender, you're enough of a sexual athlete to gratify your partner completely. A genuine romantic, you don't give your heart away easily, and you prefer keeping your feelings under wraps until certain they are reciprocated. Consequently, you may require a little extra encouragement to help overcome your fear of rejection. Where lovemaking is concerned, you cannot be rushed or coerced, and you need to be wooed before you are won. You enjoy romantic movies, candlelit dinners, holding hands in the rain, dreamy evenings on the beach, and nights of lovemaking in front of a blazing fireplace.

Tips for Your Ideal Lover

Inherently traditional and conventional, you're not really comfortable with kinky bedroom moves or extreme sexual experimentation. Instead, you are a wonderfully sensual, old-fashioned sweetheart who likes to kiss and cuddle. Hugging and touching and other preliminaries are important to you, as is a comfortable romantic atmosphere in which to make love.

July 5, *Cancer 5*

What Makes You Tick

Your emotional needs are contradictory, and you don't always know what you want from an intimate union. Basically a traditionalist, you are home and family oriented. Yet you often feel conflicted between your desire for roots and commitment, and a yearning for freedom and independence. Moreover, a part of you craves intellectual companionship as much as love and is attracted by less-than-conventional lifestyles.

Between the Sheets

You like to take your time, before exposing your deepest feelings. Sometimes you are tender and loving, sometimes cool and distant. Although you want warmth and nurturing, you're afraid of the emotional vulnerability that intense feelings can reveal. You do best with a sensitive, caring partner who is able to love you without attempting to smother or cage you. In the right situation, with the right lover, you'll throw yourself into sensual pleasure with complete abandon. Behind closed doors, detached coolness turns into smoldering passion as you indulge in erotic foreplay, or spin out a torrid fantasy before moving on to a superb night of spontaneous and uninhibited lovemaking.

Tips for Your Ideal Lover

The lover who engages your mind and imagination with humorous stories and lively conversation also enlivens your spirits and inflames your libido. Expressing your sexual desires verbally turns you on, and you enjoy exchanging provocative pillow talk with your bedmate. With a little encouragement, you might enjoy experimenting with various kinds of sex toys and gadgets.

July 6, *Cancer 6*

What Makes You Tick

Relationships matter to you, and your idyllic vision of love has you imagining the ultimate in romantic bliss. When things don't turn out as you planned, you may withdraw into your crab shell. However, you don't stay there long, because companionship is as vital to you as breathing. Since you refuse to accept halfway measures, your high expectations might make your lover think twice before making a lifelong commitment.

Between the Sheets

In love with the idea of love as well as the actuality, you're as likely to fall for a romantic ideal as a real person. Since you bring elegance and refinement to your sexual desires, you prefer making love in a congenial, harmonious, luxurious atmosphere. In the bedroom, as elsewhere, your aim is to please as much as to be pleased. When you make your lover happy, you feel happy, too. By creating a sensuous, comfortable place to be together, you demonstrate your love and affection. Romance is your middle name. Music, flowers, and aromatic massages get you in the mood for lovemaking.

Tips for Your Ideal Lover

You enjoy the preliminaries leading up to sex almost as much as the act itself. Words of love and promises of intimacy delight you and spark the lusty side of your ardent nature. Your ideal lover wines and dines you in a romantic ambiance before attempting to sweep you away on a wave of passion.

July 7, *Cancer 7*

What Makes You Tick

Socially, you're friendly, outgoing, and flirtatious. In an intimate union, however, you're more cautious and, like most crabs, subject to emotional swings. When life doesn't live up to your romantic view of how things ought to be, you have a tendency to become despondent. While you recognize the importance of togetherness, you believe each partner needs some alone time to follow his or her own interests.

Between the Sheets

Sexually, you're something of a free spirit, and you enjoy making love whenever and wherever the desire seizes you. Since you can't abide the idea of a love life that falls into predictable patterns, you are happiest with a partner who knows how to go with the flow. On occasion, you may become withdrawn and disinterested in sex. When this happens, it's best to leave you alone until you come out of your funk. Once the clouds pass, you'll make up for lost time. You're turned on by the promise of the unexpected, and you enjoy dancing around the edges of danger and adventure. You may not actually do anything naughty, but you like contemplating the possibility.

Tips for Your Ideal Lover

Your sensitive, emotional side craves lots of romance and affection with sex. Your appetite for erotic pleasure grows along with your trust in your partner. In addition to creating a romantic ambiance for lovemaking, your ideal mate intuits your shifting moods and woos you accordingly with fiery passion or tender caresses.

July 8, *Cancer 8*

What Makes You Tick

Although you work harder and are more serious than most members of the zodiac, you are also more emotional. In your public life, you want recognition and success. In your personal life, you crave love and understanding. The domestic side of your nature longs for the comforts of home, and when you find the love and acceptance you seek, you make a caring, responsive lover and a dependable life partner.

Between the Sheets

In the bedroom, you show yourself for the passionate lover you are. More interested in doing than talking, you rarely gush about your deepest feelings. Instead you demonstrate your affection through the generosity and creativity of your lovemaking. Your tender touch and consideration for your bedmate reveal an innate sensitivity that you usually keep hidden. Endurance is your forte, and you like to take the time to savor every sensuous moment. A night of romantic seduction stirs your passion and inflames your lusty libido. When you go out on the town, your idea of a fine evening includes sophisticated entertainment. However, at home, you allow your sentimental side to show with spontaneous hugs and long, languid kisses.

Tips for Your Ideal Lover

Sexual tension builds with an intuitive lover who picks up your nonverbal clues. Your ideal mate is gifted at soothing daily stresses; a slow, erotic massage releases you from worldly concerns. Although you usually prefer the simple, straightforward pleasures of lovemaking, you welcome the occasional innovation of an adventurous bedmate.

July 9, *Cancer 9*

What Makes You Tick

In matters of the heart, you are a genuine romantic, and relationships are never far from your thoughts. You are either in love, looking for love, or involved in a rich fantasy life where love rules. Once smitten, you are cautious and a little hesitant but also extraordinarily loving and giving. You thrive when all goes well, but if your significant other doesn't live up to your expectations you can feel totally shattered.

Between the Sheets

The intensity of your emotions makes it impossible for you to have a sexual alliance based on physical attraction alone. For you, sex is about the joining and melding of two souls. When you love someone, you long to devote yourself to the needs and wants of your beloved. However, you expect similar consideration and devotion in return. In bed, you like being coaxed and wooed, and the more seductive the approach, the more readily you respond to it. You are extremely sensual and capable of intense physical passion. Although you long to be swept away on a tidal wave of romantic love, it generally takes a bit of enticing to truly inflame your lusty libido.

Tips for Your Ideal Lover

Love may be the ultimate turn-on for you, but a beautiful romantic ambiance helps awaken your passion and increase your pleasure. Your ideal lover knows that fantasy plays a large part in your love life, and devises role-playing games and other fanciful activities to enhance your shared sexual experience.

July 10, *Cancer 1*

What Makes You Tick

Despite a longing for emotional intimacy, your shifting moods take you back and forth between a need for love and a desire for freedom. Although you consider yourself independent, too much time alone can make you feel restless and depressed. The thought of taking risks never fails to thrill you, yet you fear having your heart broken. What you actually want from a close relationship is commitment and continuity.

Between the Sheets

At once ardent and romantic, you tend to view lovemaking as a totally sensual experience. In the bedroom, you are intensely serious and wickedly humorous by turns. You have a way of making the most ordinary pleasures sparkle with fun and excitement. Your sexually complex nature gives rise to an intimate association that is a blend of drama and passion interwoven with tenderness and sensitivity. Although you are turned on by the thought of doing something shocking in bed, your emotional insecurities make you hesitant. While nurturing, generous, and giving, you can also be demanding, temperamental, and rather jealous in a close relationship. In your ideal union, you share everything with your lover, without sacrificing your individuality.

Tips for Your Ideal Lover

Although somewhat moody, with a lover you trust, you are able to relax and follow wherever your lusty libido leads you. Acting out erotic fantasies through role-playing games allows you to indulge your more outrageous sexual desires without feeling emotionally vulnerable.

July 11, *Cancer 2*

What Makes You Tick

In an intimate union, you're sensual, passionate, generous, caring, and responsive. You truly enjoy the dance of courtship and romance. Yet you long for the safety and security of a committed partnership and settled home life. You believe happiness comes from being with the person who is right for you. Nevertheless, you would rather be alone than spend your life in an unhappy relationship.

Between the Sheets

You are an ardent bed partner who revels in the physical pleasure of making love. However, emotional bonding is also important, and you like knowing that you and your partner are on the same page in your relationship. You really don't need a lot of erotic thrills to entice you. In sharing the comforts of home, you set the stage for love and romance. Your sensitivity to tactile, sensory pleasures allows you to communicate through touch. You shiver with rapturous anticipation during a slow exploration of your lover's body, and giving or receiving a massage with warm herbal oils, or a relaxing neck rub, helps put you in the mood for love and sex.

Tips for Your Ideal Lover

Your lusty libido emerges only after trust has been fully established. You prefer subtlety and romance to flashy courtship rituals. There are times when all you really want to do is kiss and cuddle, and your ideal mate understands your sensitive nature and senses your need for tenderness and understanding in the bedroom and elsewhere.

July 12, *Cancer 3*

What Makes You Tick

Your freewheeling personality and chatty intellectuality are often at odds with the intensity of your emotions. It's difficult for you to reconcile the carefree side of your nature with your need for security and a permanent relationship. Although cheerful and a great deal of fun, you can be touchy and sensitive; your feelings are easily hurt. When this happens, you may internalize your anger and slip into a dark mood.

Between the Sheets

Because of an inner restlessness, you require more variety in your sex life than other crabs. In the bedroom, you much prefer spontaneously following your heart rather than your head. Good communication is very important in an intimate relationship. You like talking about your feelings, and you encourage others to share their emotions with you. You especially enjoy expressing your lusty desires with spicy sexual banter and flirty words and less directly with seductive looks and gestures. The lover who picks up on your various sexual signals and responds to them in kind is the one who can turn you on.

Tips for Your Ideal Lover

You believe lovemaking should be fun, and you expect a good time beneath the covers. Although you value safety in some life areas, your overall approach to sex is generally less conservative than others of your Sun sign. You're turned on by being able to tell your lover exactly what you like and having him or her do the same.

July 13, *Cancer 4*

What Makes You Tick

Outwardly sociable and gregarious, you live your life with zest and enthusiasm. Within yourself, however, your deepest feelings often remain a carefully guarded secret. You believe love makes the world go around, and in an intimate union, you are romantic and affectionate. Even so, you're slow to make a serious commitment; once you commit, you are in for the long haul and you make an exceedingly loyal and devoted mate.

Between the Sheets

In the bedroom and elsewhere, you are a thoughtful, considerate, and generous partner. You enjoy the sensual pleasures of lovemaking and like experiencing them in a luxurious, romantic ambiance. You may not show it, but you want to be admired and adored by your lover. In return, you are prepared to do whatever it takes to gratify your mate's desires. Your love nature is ardent but also playful and fun loving. Romantic evenings of slow, sensual seduction stir your passions, and soaking in a hot tub with your beloved evokes a blissful mood of cozy togetherness. You can't be rushed where love is concerned, and you shine in unhurried moments, drawing out the lovemaking in anticipation of an exciting finish.

Tips for Your Ideal Lover

You are turned on by glamorous and sophisticated bedroom attire, and erotic novelties such as enticing sex toys and amusing, suggestive edibles. In acting out your secret fantasies, you engage your entire being in a game of seduction, while adding spice and excitement to your love life.

July 14, *Cancer 5*

What Makes You Tick

Potential suitors are attracted by your charming personality, and your aura of concerned compassion makes you popular. However, you often feel a conflict between your desire for independence and your need for stability. Although devoted to your significant other, you want a partnership that features an equal give-and-take. Typically, once you find what you are looking for, you overcome any reluctance you feel about entering into a permanent relationship.

Between the Sheets

An innovative lover, you want a physical relationship that is as spontaneous and inventive as it is sensual and romantic. You can be totally serious and absurdly funny by turns, and beneath the covers, your ability to combine subtle seduction with a bit of outrageous fun keeps your lovemaking fresh and exciting. Naturally intuitive, you are able to pick up on your partner's wishes by tuning into his or her private thoughts. Both inside the bedroom and outside, compromise and sharing are extremely important. You don't like to appear emotionally vulnerable and prefer dropping hints about what you like, rather than coming right out and asking.

Tips for Your Ideal Lover

The suitor who engages your mind and imagination has an edge. Anything new or different intrigues you, and you thrive with a lover who takes advantage of spontaneous moments of passion to provide the unexpected instead of slipping into routine lovemaking. Experimenting with your bedmate increases your lusty appetite for physical intimacy.

July 15, *Cancer 6*

What Makes You Tick

You are oriented toward other people and feel incomplete without a loving partner. Even so, you will hold off on making a commitment until you're sure your feelings are reciprocated. Once the commitment is made, you believe the two of you will live in a blissful state of harmony and cooperation. If this best-of-all-possible realities fails to manifest, you may be hurt and inclined to blame your disappointment on your mate.

Between the Sheets

A tender, gentle, considerate lover, you desperately want intimacy, but the ingrained suspicion of your self-protective Cancer Sun sign makes it difficult to trust completely. You tend to put your partner's needs before your own, and you do whatever it takes to accommodate his or her desires. Although rather shy about expressing your own wants, you usually manage to communicate your likes and dislikes in the bedroom. More sensual and romantic than passionate, you're content to be wrapped in your lover's arms. You're seeking an emotional connection, not wildly acrobatic sex. Soft lights, romantic music, flowers, and candles all add to your pleasure.

Tips for Your Ideal Lover

You enjoy being wined and dined in a fine restaurant with lovely décor and a pleasant atmosphere, but the real turn-on is the intimate conversation and sexual banter that you exchange with your lover over dinner. Even holding hands in a darkened theater can evoke as much closeness as a rapturous sexual encounter.

July 16, *Cancer 7*

What Makes You Tick

Your charming personality attracts people, and your air of glamour and mystery draws them in. Caring, affectionate, and responsive, you need a partner who makes you feel cherished and appreciated. In a close relationship, shared interests are extremely important, yet you also believe that there should be room for separate activities. Even after you find your true love, you continue to require private time to follow mental and spiritual pursuits.

Between the Sheets

You want to be with someone who accepts you as you are; just knowing that your partner loves you for yourself means a great deal. In bed, you can be bold and carefree one moment and urgently serious the next. With a little bit of encouragement from your mate, your ardor ignites with rapid intensity. There is nothing dull, boring, or routine in your approach to lovemaking. You're always ready to try new things, either between the sheets or elsewhere. You have a rather goofy sense of humor, and making love in unusual places gives you an added thrill. You are unpredictable, and you prefer an imaginative bedmate who keeps you on your toes.

Tips for Your Ideal Lover

You're most likely to be turned on by a far-out idea, such as a sexy game of hide-and-seek. A clever lover will leave clues, leading to a torrid tryst in a secret place protected from prying eyes and frequent interruptions.

July 17, *Cancer 8*

What Makes You Tick

A close, loving relationship is central to your life, and you thrive in a secure union with your true love. Because you work hard, you may be away from home a lot. However, you are happiest when you know that the one you love is there, awaiting your return. Love and trust don't come easily to you, but once your confidence is won, you remain loyal forever.

Between the Sheets

You want more from your love life than mere sexual gratification. Lovemaking is part of a lifestyle that includes all the elements of a committed relationship. In the bedroom, you are a passionate, yet controlled lover. Despite the depth of your feelings and the strength of your desires, you rarely allow yourself to be swept away by your emotions. Proud of your sexual prowess and expertise, you take pleasure in your ability to satisfy your bed partner. It doesn't take flashy theatrics or elaborate fantasies to turn you on. You get off on the simple feelings than come from the real thing, and all that is required to awaken your ardor is affection and a touch of romance.

Tips for Your Ideal Lover

A slow, sensuous aromatherapy massage releases you from the stress of everyday concerns, stimulates your sexual desires, and connects you to your earthy physicality. Once you warm up, you are anything but shy, and in your careful, methodical manner, you lead the way to new heights of erotic pleasure.

July 18, *Cancer 9*

What Makes You Tick

You have a sympathetic, compassionate nature, and you go out of your way not to offend anyone. People are drawn to you because of your gracious affability and delightful sense of humor. Vulnerable in matters of love and romance, you need to be aware of a tendency toward self-deception. You are capable of an enormous amount of affection, yet you hold back until you feel comfortable and accepted by your lover.

Between the Sheets

Once committed, you thrive in an atmosphere of intimacy, especially with a confident partner who makes you feel safe and secure. Sex for you is all about your intense emotions. You fall in love quite easily, once your romantic imagination is brought into play. When making love, a bedroom atmosphere replete with soft music and scented candles and oils appeals to your romantic soul. You soak up your companion's feelings and desires like a psychic sponge. Sometimes you can't tell which emotions are yours and which you're picking up from your lover. In a good relationship, this can lead to a sensation of having a total union with your lover. In a bad relationship, it could present a huge problem.

Tips for Your Ideal Lover

A romantic outing to the seaside, where you can hear the pounding of the surf as you make love is a guaranteed turn-on. If a trip to the shore is not possible, a sound machine that plays recorded ocean sounds will evoke many of the same feelings.

July 19, *Cancer 1*

What Makes You Tick

You probably think of yourself as adventurous, but where love is concerned, you are self-protective and fearful of being hurt. These traits prompt you to seek the comfort of a permanent relationship, even though you may be longing for freedom and independence. To be truly happy, you need the love and support of Mr. or Ms. Right; without it, moodiness and anxiety can cause you to act in a passive-aggressive manner.

Between the Sheets

In bed, you can be bold and carefree one moment and urgently serious the next. Inherently passionate and sexually vigorous, the physical side of love with spontaneous gestures of affection and lots of hugging, kissing, and touching is important to you. However, keeping romance alive is also high on your list of priorities. Openness to change makes you more willing to break with convention than other Cancer natives. Trying new things excites you, and helps you keep your lovemaking fresh and interesting. You long to be swept away by passion, but it takes a person you trust completely to make it happen. Once awakened, your lusty libido carries you to heights of ecstatic pleasure.

Tips for Your Ideal Lover

You respond eagerly to a mix of languid sensuality and bold aggression. Although you enjoy experimenting and taking risks in bed, it generally requires some encouragement from your partner to get you started. The skilled lover who can overcome your initial shyness and inhibitions is the one most likely to turn you on.

July 20, *Cancer 2*

What Makes You Tick

You are sensual, affectionate, and devoted. In love, you're extremely loyal and responsive to the other person's needs and desires. Sensitive and deeply emotional, you are more likely to be moved by deeds than words. Romance and the rituals of courtship are important. However, you want a partner who is not only your soul mate but who is also willing to commit to a long-lasting relationship.

Between the Sheets

Both material and emotional security play important roles in a close relationship. Just knowing that your partner is there for you means more than anything else. You possess an innate sensuality that shows itself in the bedroom, but is also evident in your thoughtful attentiveness throughout the house. In sharing the comforts of home, you set the stage for love and romance. Physical contact is as natural to you as breathing, and you like touching, hugging, and kissing your lover wherever and whenever the mood strikes you. You take great pleasure in lavishing love and affection on your significant other, and you expect the same type of attention in return.

Tips for Your Ideal Lover

You need a mate who helps you escape from the world and all its stresses. Just being together, where no one else is allowed to intrude, turns you on. Soft music, wine, and tender words of love, accompanied by an intimate supper, set the stage for an evening of languid sexuality.

July 21, *Cancer 3*

What Makes You Tick

Yours is a rather quirky, creative nature that can make you seem different from others of your Sun sign. Although caring and nurturing and desirous of a home and family, you're also more independent and less possessive than the typical Cancer native. You want a loving relationship where each partner supports the other and, in addition to shared activities, each has time to explore his or her hobbies and interests.

Between the Sheets

Despite your need for emotional security, you are less intense in intimate situations than other crabs, and you place greater emphasis on the fun-and-games aspect of lovemaking. You prefer acting spontaneously in bed and fully expect to have a good time between the sheets. Your heightened sensuality and ability to tune in to your partner's thoughts and feelings make you a sensitive, intuitive, skilled bedmate. Your ideal partner is not only sexy but also smart and interesting. An exchange of witty sexual banter with your lover adds to the atmosphere of sensuous relaxation. However, once you really get going, your strong sex drive takes over and the verbal chatter soon gives way to physical passion.

Tips for Your Ideal Lover

When you're out on the town, a mischievous look or provocative remark from your spouse serves as a turn-on for a later assignation. You shine in unhurried moments alone with your lover, where you enter into the erotic rhythms of passionate lovemaking. The glow of candles adds atmosphere and comfort to your romantic encounters.

July 22, *Cancer 4*

What Makes You Tick

Under most circumstances, you exude self-confidence, but where love is concerned, you can be reticent. You are afraid of rejection, and your feelings are so sensitive and deep that you don't want to go too far out on a limb and risk getting hurt. However, you thrive with a partner who shows you the devotion and affection you crave. In return, you provide your mate with unconditional support.

Between the Sheets

Despite your strong sensual nature, sex without love probably doesn't appeal to you. You enjoy being the center of your mate's attention, and romantic gestures such as candlelit dinners and thoughtful gifts make you feel cherished and appreciated. In bed and elsewhere, you get off on the pleasures of a luxurious setting. Your ideal lover matches you in playful abandon beneath the covers, while being extremely careful not to trample on your vulnerable emotions. In the privacy of the bedroom, sexy attire and toys are fun props that spark your lusty libido. Gifted at soothing the daily stresses of your significant other with tender caresses, you expect the same type of loving consideration.

Tips for Your Ideal Lover

Romantic evenings of subtle seduction stir your passions. Good food and great sex turn you on, and a romantic dinner followed by major cuddling with your lover satisfies several of your most basic desires. In bed, sensory pleasures like sharing succulent edibles such as exotic fruits and sweetmeats can turn into an erotic free-for-all.

July 23, *Leo 5*

What Makes You Tick

The fire of desire begins in your mind, and you need a relationship where love and friendship can coexist. Drawn to original thinkers, you will soon lose interest in a partner with whom you have no intellectual connection. Although romance may not be first on your list of priorities, you value intimacy. Emotionally you can be detached, but there is nothing cool about your smoldering sexuality.

Between the Sheets

A dramatic and demonstrative lover, your aim is to soar to heights of joy with your partner. The intuitive lover who encourages you to abandon yourself to pleasure is the ideal match. Although you usually prefer making the first moves in a new romance, you can be swept away by an obliging suitor who makes you feel utterly irresistible. In the bedroom and elsewhere, you are the star of your own drama, and you get off on your significant other's admiration and adulation. Naturally giving and considerate, you make a real effort to please your bedmate in return. Blessed with thoughtfulness and imagination, you are able to adapt to whatever pace or rhythm your partner requires.

Tips for Your Ideal Lover

For you, lovemaking should be full of adventure, drama, and excitement, and an attentive lover with original ideas keeps you intrigued. Your delight in erotic pleasure can evolve into ecstasy during fantasy and role-playing games. More than anything, you need an energetic bed partner with the physical stamina to keep up with you.

July 24, *Leo 6*

What Makes You Tick

A genuine romantic, you probably don't feel complete without a loving companion in your life. With romance as a priority, you invest a lot of energy in making yourself appealing to potential suitors. Consequently, you rarely have to look for love, because it finds you. Your desire for intellectual companionship is as strong as your need for affection, and you prefer the company of mentally stimulating individuals who share your many interests.

Between the Sheets

You expect so much from an intimate union that reality rarely lives up to your mental image. Yet without a warm, loving relationship, you may feel only half alive. When you do find your true love, you make a most generous, caring, and enthusiastic life partner but also an extremely demanding one. Your lover's eyes are the mirrors in which you see yourself, and his or her good opinion is truly important to you. In bed or out of it, you thrive in the company of a partner who showers you with attention and approval. Despite your strong sexual appetite, your ultimate aim is to take lovemaking to a higher level than mere physical gratification.

Tips for Your Ideal Lover

You delight in all the trappings of romantic courtship, and you particularly enjoy excursions to exotic locations that provide a luxurious backdrop for loving. Making love in lavish comfort appeals to you, and while you may enjoy an occasional quickie, you're not likely to grab it in the back of a cramped automobile.

July 25, *Leo 7*

What Makes You Tick

You pour yourself into an intimate relationship, and when things go well, you are on top of the world. However, if the union should turn sour, you feel totally devastated. Dull people weigh you down, and you much prefer spending your time with upbeat individuals. Your sexual expression evolves naturally, and if you sometimes seem nonchalant about the physical side of lovemaking, it's because you have other things on your mind.

Between the Sheets

Your exuberant surface personality conceals a rather un-Leo-like inner nature that can be secretive and mysterious. Although your inner lion craves the spotlight, another part of you prefers operating from behind the scenes. In love and romance, you are intensely passionate, extremely complex, and determined to have things your own way. Although fervently loyal to your beloved, you can also be fervently jealous and possessive. Your physical passions and sexual prowess may be equal to that of the most ardent Aries or Scorpio, but your leonine ego is surprisingly fragile and requires frequent encouragement and reassurance. Since flattery is Leo's ultimate aphrodisiac, nothing turns you on faster than attention and approval from a loving bedmate.

Tips for Your Ideal Lover

Sensuality is your weakness, and you enjoy being stroked, fondled, and fussed over. You particularly like it when your bed partner makes a special effort to seduce you with erotic toys, sexy apparel, or provocative language. Good communication is important to you, and talking things over in bed helps you avoid misunderstandings.

July 26, *Leo 8*

What Makes You Tick

The typical lion is an extrovert who expects to be noticed and admired, and even the shyest of the great cats craves the approbation and applause of an audience. In matters of the heart, you're caring and loyal, but you have high standards and you expect your significant other to live up to your expectations. Moreover, your proud nature and rather fragile ego require constant reassurance from your mate.

Between the Sheets

Despite your lusty libido, you bring caution to the mating dance. Casual affairs hold little appeal for you, and you control your desires until you're sure the person you are with is the right one for you. However, once your mind is made up, you are anything but shy. Behind closed doors, you're a fiery, dramatic bedmate with an exceedingly physical approach to lovemaking. Endurance is your forte, and your stamina in the bedroom virtually guarantees your lover's continued satisfaction. You have great respect for traditional ideas, and you want permanence in a loving union. Although you can be rather demanding, you're caring, protective, generous, and loyal when you feel safe and secure in an intimate union.

Tips for Your Ideal Lover

Your ideal lover is sensual and passionate and shows affection through deeds as well as words. You possess a vivid imagination and acting out erotic fantasies appeals to your sense of the theatrical. Sexy attire turns you on, and with a partner you trust, you enjoy simulating fanciful scenes of torrid seduction.

July 27, *Leo 9*

What Makes You Tick

Although your inner lion craves the spotlight, the number 9 vibration prefers operating from behind the scenes. A dreamer as well as an idealist, you pour your heart and soul into an intimate union. In love, you're a total romantic, and when you fall for someone, you expect it to last forever. However, if the relationship doesn't go well, you don't let disappointment prevent you from seeking another love.

Between the Sheets

You are quite capable of enchanting your lover with subtle seductive moves one night, then dazzling him or her with sizzling intensity and wild abandon the next. You dream big dreams, and you enjoy acting them out in the bedroom with your beloved. Sex and sensuality are part of the entire package that makes up any romantic alliance. However, you crave emotional fulfillment along with physical gratification. Setting the stage with luxurious things provides the proper backdrop for your highly sensuous, romantic lovemaking. You are so psychic that you pick up your partner's thoughts all the time, and your ability to intuit your mate's desires makes it easy for you to gratify them.

Tips for Your Ideal Lover

In a subtle way, you like to control and direct the bedroom activity. A mood-setting romantic atmosphere relaxes you as it stimulates you and turns you on. Once trust is established, you are capable of letting go completely and losing yourself in the wild expanse of desire generated by your intrinsic love and passion.

July 28, *Leo 1*

What Makes You Tick

Colorful people who are exciting and slightly outrageous appeal to your dramatic, theatrical nature. You'll probably experience a few hard tumbles in your love life, before deciding to settle down. Although your pride is likely to be wounded if things go awry, you rebound from love's trials with remarkable ease. You like being the center of your mate's attention, and you're a generous, affectionate, considerate partner in return.

Between the Sheets

Early in a relationship, you do everything possible to fascinate a potential partner, and get him or her to want to know you better. You adore the spotlight and tend to view your activities, both in and out of the bedroom, as command performances. Since you can't resist the temptation to play to an audience, you get off on turning your lovemaking into a major production. You're rarely shy about asking for what you want. It doesn't take much to rouse your lusty sexual appetite, yet true love is still your best aphrodisiac. It is because your romantic idealism is so intense that you view a love relationship as sacred and somewhat larger than life.

Tips for Your Ideal Lover

Your energetic style of lovemaking is not for the faint of heart, and you're clear about what you like in bed. However, it takes more than just sex to hold your interest. You crave more than mere physical satisfaction and your real aim when making love is to turn sexual union into a transcendent experience.

July 29, *Leo 2*

What Makes You Tick

You know how to live and love. In an intimate union, you are openhearted and generous, but also exacting and demanding. Although more than willing to pamper and indulge your partner, you expect to be appreciated, admired, and catered to in return. If a relationship turns sour, you may feel devastated but you won't remain alone for very long.

Between the Sheets

Sensual and strongly sexed, your deep-seated need for love and affection makes you an ardent and passionate lover. When you care for someone, you are quite lavish in expressing your feelings. Your intimate encounters virtually explode with passion, and demonstrations of love invigorate you and make you feel totally alive. In the bedroom, you enjoy luxuriating in long, lazy sessions of erotic lovemaking. When you are in the mood for love, which is quite often, you pursue the object of your affection with leonine intensity. You view lovemaking as a carnival of the senses and your bed as an intimate stage for erotic enjoyment. Moreover, few bed partners have your stamina between the sheets.

Tips for Your Ideal Lover

Your ideal mate values your sensuality and willingly overlooks your bouts of stubbornness. Your passion and sexual prowess may be equal to that of any sign in the zodiac, but your ego is surprisingly fragile and requires frequent reassurance. Since flattery is Leo's ultimate aphrodisiac, nothing turns you on faster than the approval of a loving bedmate.

July 30, *Leo* 3

What Makes You Tick

Yours is a gregarious, outgoing nature. In a social setting, you're a riveting storyteller and unabashed flirt, with a decided knack for keeping either an audience or a single listener totally enthralled. Your ideal life partner is someone who has many interesting aspects to his or her character and who doesn't mind sharing you with your many friends and various creative pursuits.

Between the Sheets

Less dramatic than other members of your Sun sign, you have a relaxed, laid-back approach to love and sexuality. Your fun-and-games tactics in the bedroom practically guarantee a good time between the sheets. Your ideal relationship provides both mental and physical stimulation. Essentially more cerebral than emotional, you have a way with words that rarely fails to interest and arouse your bed partner. The ability to please as well as be pleased is important to you, and you pride yourself on remembering the little details that make your significant other feel truly loved. While you're not in a hurry to make a long-term commitment, you do make a generous, devoted life partner.

Tips for Your Ideal Lover

Your attitude toward sex is playful and uncomplicated. You're turned on by an inventive lover who enjoys surprising you with innovative ways to increase your mutual pleasure. Since your approach to lovemaking is as much cerebral as physical, fresh ideas spark your libido and keep you coming back for more.

July 31, *Leo 4*

What Makes You Tick

Although exuberant and outgoing in social situations, you prefer keeping your true emotions hidden until you are sure that your prospective partner shares them. However, once you are committed, you're a generous and strongly protective lover. You like to make a theatrical production out of everything, and you particularly enjoy the rituals of courtship, especially those that engender grand and glorious moments of love and romance.

Between the Sheets

Inherently sexy and passionate, you're driven by a lusty libido and a strong sense of the dramatic. Your exceptional intuition helps you pick up on your partner's feelings and anticipate his or her needs and desires. This ability to provide what the other person wants makes you virtually irresistible as a lover. A genuine romantic, you tend to dramatize and mythologize every aspect of your life. In matters of the heart, you are warm, passionate, and exceedingly generous, but you can also be rather possessive and demanding. Since you require a good deal of emotional pampering, you are at your best in a love union where you get the devotion you crave.

Tips for Your Ideal Lover

Play and spontaneity bring a festive atmosphere to the bedroom, and you respond well to a bed partner who carefully sets the stage for sensual pleasure with candles, well-spaced mirrors, and erotic novelties. Sexy, intimate apparel and silky fabrics turn you on, while a feather trailed along your skin really tickles your fancy.

August 1, *Leo 1*

What Makes You Tick

Sociable and gregarious, relationships are at the heart and soul of your existence. You like most people, and thanks to your sunny, outgoing, fun-loving nature, they want to get to know you better. In an intimate union, you are caring and generous. However, you can also be rather demanding. You expect your lover to flatter and pamper you and to stroke your ego. In return, you offer love, romance, and infinite generosity.

Between the Sheets

You're a star in the bedroom, and you know it. Highly sexed and dramatic, you get off on turning lovemaking into a staged production. With your lover as the muse for your creativity, you enjoy acting out your fantasies of fiery passion and sensuous seduction. A sumptuous setting adds to the feeling of regal grandeur. Spontaneity and imagination make for endless thrills. It doesn't take much to arouse your sexual appetite, because love is your best aphrodisiac. You are a playful, passionate bedmate, with strong desires and an insatiable curiosity about various sexual techniques. Since you view sexuality as an art form, you become impatient with dull routine and constant repetition in the boudoir.

Tips for Your Ideal Lover

It may not take much to spark your passions, but you crave more from a physical union than mere sexual satisfaction. Lovemaking for you must be both a dramatic production and a transcendent experience for you and your bedmate. Showy gestures of love, such as unexpected gifts, add fuel to your erotic fire.

August 2, *Leo 2*

What Makes You Tick

In love, you are exceedingly magnanimous in expressing your feelings. You willingly give your all to your beloved, and you require the same type of devotion in return. However, at times you get so caught up in the glamour of romance that you ignore the everyday realities of the relationship. Although you expect constancy from your partner, your own need for adoration can make you into something of a flirt.

Between the Sheets

A decidedly theatrical flair emerges in the privacy of your bedroom. Your sexual approach is a wonderful combination of fiery passion and languid sensuality. Since your pleasure-seeking instincts are so strong, you're eager to experience all the joys of lovemaking. However, there is a touch of conservatism in your hedonism that prevents you from straying too far outside traditional boundaries. Even so, you possess an exciting, extensive sexual repertoire that you engage in with evident enthusiasm. You get off on wooing and being wooed luxuriously, as befits your regal leonine status. You are proud of your sexual prowess and ability to please your bedmate, and the more enthusiasm your partner shows, the happier you are.

Tips for Your Ideal Lover

The lover who prepares an exotic feast to indulge in before or during lovemaking has an edge. Long sensuous foreplay taps into your deepest need to be courted and pampered. A slow erotic massage with specially chosen aromatic oils and lotions imbues your entire torso with pure physical pleasure.

August 3, *Leo 3*

What Makes You Tick

More flexible than the average lion, you're less inclined to stay with any one thing forever. New people provide stimulation, and a craving for variety and change impels you to seek out fresh challenges. Eminently sociable, you enjoy people and you're not averse to using your charm to entertain and impress them. You live for attention and approval, and you need a partner who provides positive feedback.

Between the Sheets

You need understanding and respect from your significant other. In exchange, you are prepared to be supportive, generous, loyal, and loving. Despite a streak of independence, your affections tend to remain constant with the right mate. Your attitude toward sex is playful and far less serious than that of other Leo natives. An inventive lover, you try to infuse a spirit of discovery and a sense of fun and games into your bedroom antics. In intimate situations, you enjoy pillow talk and an exchange of spicy verbal banter with your partner. A riveting storyteller, you glory in recounting your own fantasies or spinning torrid little tales to amuse and arouse your bedmate.

Tips for Your Ideal Lover

Your approach to love is mainly mental, and just the thought of making love can serve as a turn-on. Inside your head, you envision the ensuing coupling as a big event, full of drama and excitement. The air around you is charged with erotic anticipation, and your ideal lover kindles the spark and turns it into a raging fire.

August 4, *Leo 4*

What Makes You Tick

You're warm, passionate, and generous, but you can also be somewhat demanding and possessive. Since you require a good deal of emotional pampering, you are at your best when you get all the devotion and attention you crave. You're so hardworking, dedicated, and ambitious on the job that you need a mate who truly loves you and is firmly ensconced in your cheering section.

Between the Sheets

A genuine overachiever, you excel at just about everything you do, and your sex life is no exception. A sense of drama permeates all areas of your life. In the bedroom and elsewhere, you gravitate toward the center of the stage. Although you're never small-minded or petty, you're quite capable of pitching a fit if your pride is hurt. An attentive lover, you demonstrate your abiding affection through deeds as well as words. Thanks to your love of luxury and beauty, you are a master when it comes to establishing a sumptuous, serene place for lovemaking. Once you forget about work and responsibility, your passion heats up and you become much more responsive.

Tips for Your Ideal Lover

The bed partner who knows how to create an atmosphere of sensuality is the one who turns you on. Being in or near water relaxes you, and lounging with your lover in a bubble bath or hot tub gets you in the mood for the erotic lovemaking to follow.

August 5, *Leo 5*

What Makes You Tick

There is a decidedly paradoxical side to your nature. You're warm-hearted and impulsive, yet rational and detached. Friendship is so important to you that you sometimes confuse it with love. You make a loyal mate as long as you're allowed the freedom to be yourself. Otherwise, you jump in and out of romantic relationships until you find Mr. or Ms. Right.

Between the Sheets

Your bubbling personality, charm, and generosity, both in and out of bed, make you a very desirable lover. While you're capable of intense physical passion, more often than not your intellectual side calls the shots. Despite your strong sex drive, you really get off on the intimacy of a close and lasting friendship. Inherently carefree and uninhibited, you want sex to be fun. Your open-minded, endless sexual curiosity makes you want to explore a variety of erotic pleasures. Consequently, you like experimenting with various positions and trying out new forms of sensual enhancement. Open to suggestion, you're prepared to try anything that enhances your shared sexual pleasure, and creating new moves keeps your lovemaking spontaneous and exciting.

Tips for Your Ideal Lover

Desire comes as much from the mind as from the body. The lover who makes you laugh also turns you on. Your ideal bedmate is adventurous, in sync with your unconventional ideas, and willing to join you in pulling out all the stops.

August 6, *Leo 6*

What Makes You Tick

You need someone to share your life, but you expect a great deal from an intimate union. Unfortunately, the realities of a close alliance may not live up to your romantic ideal of love. You long to be loved and cherished, however, your need for attention and appreciation can be rather hard on your partner. Nevertheless, with the right person at your side, you make a generous, ardent, and loyal mate.

Between the Sheets

Despite your strong sexual appetite, your real purpose between the sheets is to take lovemaking to a higher level than mere physical gratification. The idealism that touches every area of your life tends to manifest in the bedroom as a deep-seated emotional connection. A fiery lover, you possess a steadfast heart and delicate sensibilities. As the star of your own romantic drama, you graciously share the magnificence of your refined sexual artistry with your adoring costar. Lions equate flattery with love and affection, and even the most obvious attempts to gain your favor meet with success. A few heartfelt compliments are usually all it takes to draw you out of your lonely lion's den into the arms of your lover.

Tips for Your Ideal Lover

A charismatic lover who showers you with praise and genuine affection holds your attention. A warm sensual bath for two strewn with flower petals and surrounded by scented candles gets your juices flowing. An erotic massage with aromatic oils raises your temperature to a fever pitch.

August 7, *Leo 7*

What Makes You Tick

Your extroverted personality conceals the un-Leo-like secrecy of your somewhat solitary inner nature, and you need a mate who understands your shifting moods. Although fervently loyal, you can also be jealous and possessive. You fall in love fairly easily, but if the relationship becomes too confining, you begin to get antsy. While you treasure your independence, you have some difficulty granting the same freedom to your significant other.

Between the Sheets

In love and romance, you are passionate, complex, and determined to have things your way. A master of nonverbal communication, you express your innermost feelings through sensual contact with your beloved. The idealist in you views the sex act as an intimate dance that creates a harmonious exchange between partners. You equate your union with the mythos of a fairy tale, in which physical lovemaking symbolizes the unity of two souls. Ever attentive to your partner's needs and desires, you expect your consideration for him or her to be reciprocated in kind. In a loving relationship, having a good time together, in the bedroom and elsewhere, is a top priority.

Tips for Your Ideal Lover

The spirited, romantic playmate who showers you with warmth and affection, and also surprises you with sexy, slightly naughty little gifts, will spark your leonine passion. Acting out your fantasies together turns you on and engages your entire being in the game of erotic seduction.

August 8, *Leo 8*

What Makes You Tick

You're so self-assured that your majestic presence and logical mind make people think you know what you're talking about, even when you don't. You have very definite ideas about who should be in charge in any given situation, and anyone who wants to score points with you will make it seem as if you are running the show, even when you're not. Although demanding in relationships, you're also generous, protective, caring, and loyal.

Between the Sheets

Casual bedroom dalliances don't really appeal to you; you prefer saving your passion for a grand affair of the heart. Fearful of rejection, you restrain yourself until you're sure that you and the object of your affection are on the same page. Even when your ardor burns red-hot, you manage to maintain an air of reserve in public. Behind closed doors, however, you're a fiery, dramatic bedmate with an exceedingly physical approach to lovemaking. A powerhouse of sexual energy, you like being the one in control of your encounters. In the right situation, with the right person, you dazzle your mate with a lusty combination of aggressive moves and lingering sensual caresses.

Tips for Your Ideal Lover

Erotic massage turns you on, as it relaxes you into a state of mellow sensuality, and sharing an aromatic bubble bath with your partner puts you in a playful mood. Drama is in your blood, and you enjoy making a production of your lovemaking with sexy attire, sumptuous bedding, candles, and music.

August 9, *Leo 9*

What Makes You Tick

You regard love as vital to personal happiness, and you project a magical allure that inevitably draws love and romance into your life. Fiercely loyal and caring, when you find Mr. or Ms. Right, you pour your whole heart into the relationship. Your idealistic attitude leads you to expect lots of give-and-take, and in a loving relationship, you are as sensitive to your mate's needs as to your own.

Between the Sheets

A nurturing, attentive, and compassionate partner brings out the best in you. However, if the alliance should end badly, your joy can quickly turn into despair. Your strong sex drive demands expression, and you like a lot of drama and excitement in the bedroom. However, the physical side of love by itself just doesn't do it for you. Without a feeling of emotional intensity in your lovemaking, you may not be totally satisfied. You are a very complex mixture of confidence and uncertainty, and when you feel appreciated and admired, you make an innovative and creative bedmate. The lover who continually reassures you of your desirability reaps the rewards of your generosity, consideration, and legendary sexual prowess.

Tips for Your Ideal Lover

You appreciate sophistication and elegance in a suitor, and you enjoy dressing up and being wined and dined in opulent surroundings. However, when it comes to sex, you just want to forget about propriety, and be swept away on an erotic wave of passion.

August 10, *Leo 1*

What Makes You Tick

Naturally romantic and idealistic, you have a penchant for dramatizing and mythologizing your life; mediocrity has no place in your scheme of things. Since you equate admiration with love, you thrive on the approval of your significant other. In an intimate union, you're passionate and generous but also quite demanding. It's difficult for you to accept second place, and you become jealous at the mere hint of a rival.

Between the Sheets

A genuine bombshell in bed, you make a fiery, ardent lover. When creating a romantic setting for lovemaking, you prepare the stage with flowers, candles, soft music, and whatever else seems appropriate to the upcoming performance. As a natural actor, you adore the spotlight and tend to view your activities inside and outside the bedroom as performances. Even in life's most intimate moments, you usually can't resist the temptation to play to your audience of one. Since your torrid sexuality thrives on novelty and excitement, you're willing to try anything at least once. Your ideal partner is as high-spirited, playful, and enthusiastic under the covers as you are. An open-minded, affectionate, and adventurous bedmate turns you on.

Tips for Your Ideal Lover

Provocative language and erotic attire in a sumptuous setting get your juices flowing. You are not shy or hesitant about sex and a sizzling frolic in a well-lighted or strategically mirrored room may be just the ticket to chase away the blahs of a dull or routine love life.

August 11, *Leo 2*

What Makes You Tick

A model mate, you're more than willing to cater to and pamper your partner. However, you need to be petted and admired in return. You dislike disagreements, and you're usually the first to make up after an argument. Even so, you refuse to put up with disloyalty, and you are not shy about calling your mate to task for failing to live up to your expectations.

Between the Sheets

You are strongly sexed and highly attuned to your physical needs and those of your bed partner. You employ your flair for theatrical presentation to create a lavish setting for your sensory pleasures. The sanctuary of your bedroom becomes an intimate stage for erotic enjoyment. Making love in lavish comfort, on luscious fabrics, gratifies your taste for glamour and opulence. For you, a well-orchestrated seduction can be totally intoxicating. Your lover may entice you with teasing sexual play, using sensual aromatic oils to stimulate your desires. Sultry verbal suggestions turn you on by engaging your imagination. Exchanging spicy stories and sharing exotic fantasies act as tantalizing foreplay before a night of steamy sex.

Tips for Your Ideal Lover

Despite a taste for the extreme, the conservative side of your nature shows itself in your need to always be in control of the bedroom activity. Your ideal lover encourages you to throw caution to the wind and follow your basic pleasure-seeking instincts. Once drawn out, your lusty libido assumes a passionate life of its own.

August 12, *Leo* 3

What Makes You Tick

You need to be able to respect and admire your lover, and you require his or her good opinion in return. Your lively, inquisitive mind never stops for very long, and your ideal mate shares at least some of your numerous interests. Outgoing, friendly, and charming, your magnanimous nature makes you popular and well liked. Although you're in no hurry to make a commitment, you are loyal and devoted when you finally do.

Between the Sheets

Despite your gregarious nature, you enjoy spending time alone with your beloved. Glamorous surroundings bring out your romantic side, and you like to create an atmosphere of luxury for your lovemaking. Grand gestures of love and devotion make you forget mundane concerns. Innately inventive and original, you're full of surprises, both inside and outside the bedroom. Communication is the essential ingredient in creating a natural flow of erotic energies. Readily open to suggestion, you're prepared to try anything that enhances your shared sensual pleasure. You are turned on by spontaneous attempts to inflame your sexual appetite and your desire for pleasure grows as you engage in sensuous foreplay.

Tips for Your Ideal Lover

The lover who wants to score points with you flatters you and makes you feel special. Your perfect bedmate knows how to continually rekindle the initial spark of desire and maintain that brand-new feeling of attraction. Sexy conversation is a major turn-on, and playful bedroom banter inflames your lusty leonine libido.

August 13, *Leo 4*

What Makes You Tick

In matters of the heart, you're ardent, caring, and loyal, and you exude a type of smoldering sexuality that potential suitors find exceedingly appealing. However, you require lots of pampering and attention. In your most intimate relationships, you're passionate and affectionate with a theatrical approach to love and sex. Even so, romance actually matters less to you than intellectual rapport and common interests.

Between the Sheets

Your high ideals hold sway even in the bedroom, and a casual love affair has little temptation. You prefer the lasting devotion of true love to the reckless excitement of a one-night stand. Since you enjoy playing benefactor, you are inclined to put your bedmate's pleasure on an equal par with your own. Moreover, there is a delicate sensibility to your love nature that abhors crude and boorish behavior. Your ideal lover is thrilling and entertaining, without overstepping the bounds of good taste. Your deeper layers of sexual desire need to be drawn out slowly, over time. A patient bedmate melts your reserve and stirs your passions with seductive moves and erotic foreplay.

Tips for Your Ideal Lover

Mr. or Ms. Right intuits your moods and knows instinctively when it is time to take the initiative and when to take a step back and let you shine in the spotlight. A sumptuous setting for lovemaking with erotic attire and a sultry striptease is virtually guaranteed to entice you and get all your juices flowing.

August 14, *Leo* 5

What Makes You Tick

Even though romance is not always the first thing on your list of priorities, you put a high value on partnership and companionship. Because you're drawn to social causes and crusades, a loving mate helps balance your perspective by reminding you of the joyful side of life. Although you prefer being the aggressor in romantic situations, you can be swept away by an admiring suitor who flatters your leonine ego.

Between the Sheets

You throw yourself headlong into everything you do in life, and sex is no exception. In an intimate relationship, you like to keep things fresh and exciting. Nevertheless, for you to feel completely satisfied, in addition to physical attraction there needs to be a mental component to your lovemaking. An intelligent, intuitive lover who encourages you to forget the world's troubles and abandon yourself to sensual pleasure is an ideal mate. Adulation is your biggest turn-on, and you love it when your bed partner makes you feel irresistible. You respond to luxury and glamour between the sheets, and you give your best performances on a stage that is appropriately set for lovemaking.

Tips for Your Ideal Lover

An attentive lover with an imaginative approach to romance keeps you intrigued. The witty partner who charms and entertains with innovative ideas and funny stories diverts your attention from outside concerns. Once your mounting desire turns into smoldering urgency, your delight in the pleasures of Eros can evolve into a passionate fantasy for two.

August 15, *Leo 6*

What Makes You Tick

As a super-romantic, you naturally expect a great deal from an intimate relationship. You need someone to share all aspects of your life, and you probably don't feel complete without a partner. Unfortunately, the reality of an intimate association may not live up to your romantic ideal. Although you long to be loved and cherished, your need for constant attention and appreciation can be rather hard on your partner.

Between the Sheets

You are so warm-hearted and friendly that it is difficult to find anyone who can resist your charm. Your sexual appetite is strong, but it is infused with a desire to take lovemaking to a higher level than mere physical gratification. The idealism that touches every area of your life tends to manifest in the bedroom as a deep-seated emotional and spiritual connection. Since lions equate flattery with love and affection, a few heartfelt compliments are usually all that is needed to draw you out of your den and into the arms of your lover.

Tips for Your Ideal Lover

Sensual pleasure finds its fullest expression in dramatic scenes of mythic proportions. Making love in a lush atmosphere and surrounded by beautiful things appeals to your artistic nature and refined tastes. The ecstasy is further heightened for you in a carefully staged ambiance with fresh flowers, flickering candlelight, and soft background music.

August 16, *Leo 7*

What Makes You Tick

You are a genuine romantic, yet relating is more than just romance for you. You want your sweetheart to be a friend, companion, and intellectual equal as well as a lover. Although you crave commitment, you need to be in a relationship that doesn't stifle your creativity. An attentive mate, you demonstrate through word and deed that your partner is the most important person in your world.

Between the Sheets

Inherently sexy and passionate, you're driven by a lusty libido and a strong sense of the dramatic. In the bedroom, you're warm, ardent, and exceedingly generous, but you can also be moody and demanding. You require a good deal of emotional pampering, and you're at your best in a love union where you get the attention and devotion you crave. For you, the ability to share your most intense feelings with your mate or partner is what makes an intimate relationship truly special. You are so psychic that you often read your partner's mind, and your ability to discern his or her needs and desires makes it relatively easy for you to gratify them.

Tips for Your Ideal Lover

An attentive lover with an imaginative approach keeps you intrigued, and innovative lovemaking makes you feel vitally alive. The bedmate who sets the stage with beautiful things provides the most appealing backdrop for your passionate sensuality. Erotic pleasures spark your desire. In fact, few things delight you more than a full-body massage with warm scented oils.

August 17, *Leo 8*

What Makes You Tick

Since you have a tremendous respect for traditional ideas, you need permanence in an intimate relationship. You can be bossy and demanding, yet you make a considerate and dependable partner when you're emotionally secure. It is more difficult for you, than for others of your Sun sign, to express deep feelings and emotions. As a result, there are times when you may come off as rather cool and distant.

Between the Sheets

Inherently romantic, sincere, and devoted, you are a caring, ardent, and generous lover. Although your physical passions are red-hot, you may feel the need to control them. You restrain yourself until you're sure that you and your partner are on the same page. You don't deal well with rejection, and your proud nature and fragile ego require constant reassurance in the form of compliments and encouragement. Daily doses of affection and approval warm your heart—and ignite your smoldering desires. Although you never quite throw caution to the wind, when your ardor is ignited and your mate willing, you are one of the sexiest lovers in the zodiac.

Tips for Your Ideal Lover

Your affectionate nature seeks a private stage where you can show off your most dramatic bedroom moves. You appreciate an exciting, adventurous partner who lets you know how much you are adored and admired. Once you feel secure, your spouse's caresses quickly melt your reserve, and your fiery sensuality emerges in a burst of passion.

August 18, *Leo 9*

What Makes You Tick

You tend to be more restless and unpredictable than the typical Leo Sun native. You regard love as vital to personal happiness, and luckily you project a magnetic allure that draws it into your life. Romantic and compassionate, you are as likely to fall in love with an ideal as with a person. When reality doesn't live up to your dreams, you can be severely disappointed.

Between the Sheets

Your changeable personality provides endless fascination in the bedroom. You can enchant your lover with subtle seductive moves one night and then dazzle him or her with sizzling intensity and wild abandon the next. By creating an otherworldly atmosphere, you intensify your feelings of intimacy with your soul mate. You respond passionately to visual entertainment and dramatic lovemaking, and engaging in ecstatic sex makes you feel vitally alive. Taking time for slow, deliberate foreplay opens up all your senses and sparks your libido. When you find your special someone, you're loyal and devoted to his or her happiness, and your innate ability to intuit your partner's needs and desires makes it easy for you to gratify them.

Tips for Your Ideal Lover

Although you may think you want a tranquil existence, your fiery leonine nature craves action and excitement. A sultry, exotic striptease is a guaranteed turn-on for you. Your ideal lover is open to suggestions for spontaneous play and eager to join you in acting out your amorous daydreams.

August 19, *Leo 1*

What Makes You Tick

You like doing things on your own and carrying out your plans without asking anyone for advice or opinions. Even so, being half of a couple appeals to you. A true romantic, you love the idea of being in love. However, relating is more than sex and romance for you. You want a mate who can match your drive and enthusiasm and enjoys participating in your exciting, adventurous life.

Between the Sheets

Your sense of drama spills over into every life area, and the bedroom is no exception. Since you think more with your heart than your head, you want a love relationship that intoxicates you with its many joys and delights. Sexually, you're a delightful mixture of tradition and innovation. Not one to allow your intimate times to go stale, you're constantly seeking new twists on old activities. As a lover, you're generous and very responsive. You prefer taking the lead in the bedroom to make sure that your desires and those of your bedmate are met. Nothing makes you happier than giving joy to a bed partner who willingly returns the favor.

Tips for Your Ideal Lover

Big, showy gestures of love, such as unexpected gifts, fuel your sexual ardor. You libido is aroused by provocative attire in the bedroom, and you get off on acting out your secret fantasies. Since you enjoy being a star, the more adoration and appreciation your partner shows you, the more turned on you become.

August 20, *Leo 2*

What Makes You Tick

As someone who wants everything that life has to offer, you enjoy living in a pleasant atmosphere of comfort and luxury. Although generous and caring, you're also jealous and controlling. In an intimate union, you can be both giving and demanding. Your tendency is to think in pairs, and you willingly share all that you have with your beloved. In return, you expect an equal measure of loving consideration.

Between the Sheets

Your sensuality is spiced with a flair for the dramatic, and a loving union brings out the sexiest aspects of your leonine character. Your moments of deepest intimacy crackle with fiery intensity. Under the right circumstances and with the right person, you are always prepared to pounce and play. Behind closed doors, you enjoy indulging your theatrical flair and proclivity for provocative exhibitionism. You love showing off in the privacy of the bedroom, and your ideal partner is the lover who encourages your spontaneity and sexual creativity, and applauds the results. However, the person who holds the key to your heart must stimulate your mind along with your body.

Tips for Your Ideal Lover

Sex is as fundamental as eating, and just as necessary. With a lover who also adores performing, you are a rapturous audience for exotic bedroom antics such as a tantalizing striptease. Props like sex toys and fun novelties get your sexual juices flowing, and add spice to your playful, erotic frolicking.

August 21, *Leo* 3

What Makes You Tick

You are more relaxed and less dramatic than other lions. You like to flirt, and you're in no hurry to make a firm commitment. Intellectually, you need to be able to admire and respect your significant other. Since you're bright and outgoing, your best possible mate is someone who is also friendly and easygoing and doesn't mind sharing you with your many acquaintances.

Between the Sheets

You're gregarious and enjoy being the center of attention, in and out of the bedroom. A brilliant conversationalist, you have a way with words and you're never dull or boring. The ongoing exchange of witty sexual banter with your lover adds to the atmosphere of lighthearted amusement. Sexy comments inflame your lusty libido, and your frolicsome nature virtually guarantees you and your partner a fun time between the sheets. However, once you really get going, your strong sex drive takes over and spicy chatter swiftly gives way to ardent physical passion. You enjoy stolen kisses in public places, because they remind you of your lover's desire for you. Flattery always gets your attention, and the bedmate who wants to please should shower you with compliments.

Tips for Your Ideal Lover

The spontaneous part of you is rejuvenated by unplanned erotic moments that you and your partner manage to steal when no one else is around. A bit of impromptu devil-may-care lovemaking can serve as a real turn-on and keep your love life fresh and alive.

August 22, *Leo 4*

What Makes You Tick

When you love, you do it with your whole heart. Consideration and good manners are important to you in a relationship, and people who are courteous and thoughtful have an edge. You believe that two people working together can build a better, more secure life than either one alone. Consequently, you want a committed union where each partner is willing to stand firmly by the other's side.

Between the Sheets

Once you feel confident about your partner's feelings toward you, you plunge into intimacy with total abandon. The physical side of love is important to you, and you like to keep things exciting between the sheets. A strongly physical lover, you make love with ardor and great staying power. Your ideal union retains a lifelong feeling of romance, and you continue to go out of your way to keep the relationship fresh and vital. Although you ooze charm and can be very generous and considerate, you often resent having to share your beloved with others, and at times you can be quite possessive and demanding. Flattery is your weakness, and you're an absolute sucker for an adoring mate who showers you with compliments.

Tips for Your Ideal Lover

Good sex puts you at ease, and you enjoy sensuous foreplay that includes the soothing erotic pleasures of soaking in a hot tub together or massaging each other with scented oils. A romantic ambiance that includes candlelight and soft music inspires you and turns you on.

August 23, *Virgo 5*

What Makes You Tick

You project an air of aloof detachment, yet you're more in need of affection and companionship you're willing to let on. While basically self-sufficient, you also like the comfort and security of a committed relationship. Your first connection with a potential suitor is invariably a mental one, and the person with innovative ideas and far-out plans can catch and hold your interest.

Between the Sheets

Because you believe that the head should rule the heart, strong emotions make you uncomfortable. The problem is that you are more comfortable analyzing and categorizing your feelings than experiencing them. Although you dislike having people telling you what to do, you can be quite critical of the way others live their lives. Nevertheless, you have a freer, more uninhibited approach to lovemaking than most other Virgo natives. Emotionally, you may fear too much intimacy, but physically you're open to just about anything that brings pleasure to both parties. Behind closed doors, you're warm, witty, and extremely sexy. However, you require an intellectual connection along with the physical one; when your mind is engaged, your body naturally follows.

Tips for Your Ideal Lover

Relaxation draws out your elusive passions, and seductive play and teasing heighten the sexual tension. Your earthy libido responds well to slow, sensuous foreplay leading to ardent lovemaking. You are particularly responsive to a witty lover who uses charm and humor to divert your mind from the petty concerns of daily life.

August 24, *Virgo 6*

What Makes You Tick

Because you dislike being alone, partnership holds a high priority for you. Even though love is important to you, you rarely lead with your heart, and you think things through very carefully before making a serious romantic commitment. Your sensitive nature and refined sensibilities are easily upset by too much drama and intensity. Ultimately, you prefer a love relationship that can be kept on an even keel.

Between the Sheets

Inherently cautious, you're not one to leap into a romantic union with reckless abandon. You need to get to know a potential lover first, preferably through sharing common interests both inside and outside the boudoir. However, once you commit to a close relationship, you expect to stick with it in good times and bad. At times, you may appear less interested in love and sex than you actually are. However, once you stop overanalyzing every move you make and start heeding the promptings of your body and emotions, you make an exceptionally passionate, considerate lover. You have plenty of sexual curiosity, and you are always seeking new ways to excite and please your mate.

Tips for Your Ideal Lover

Your passions emerge full-blown in an elegant ambiance, and you enjoy little touches of romance in the bedroom such as scented candles and luxurious bed linens. The wise lover creates a setting for lovemaking that engages all the senses. You respond especially well to symbolic gestures of courtship that include flowers and candy.

August 25, *Virgo* 7

What Makes You Tick

Although sensitive and kindhearted, you're also somewhat dispassionate and you prefer thinking about your emotions rather than actually feeling them. As a result, you have a tendency to blow hot and cold in intimate relationships. In love and in life, you play your cards close to the chest. You don't grant many people access to your inner sanctum, but when you're absolutely certain about someone, you make a thoughtful, devoted, and romantic partner.

Between the Sheets

You are loving but critical of anyone who doesn't measure up to your high standards. Innately cautious, you're not one to leap into a close alliance with reckless abandon. You need to get to know a potential lover first, preferably through sharing common interests outside the bedroom. As a confirmed workaholic, you may appear less interested in sex and romance than you actually are. However, behind closed doors, the sensual side of your nature comes to the fore. You have plenty of sexual curiosity, and you are always seeking new ways to excite and please your mate; sharing your ideas and insights makes you feel closer to your bed partner.

Tips for Your Ideal Lover

Your ideal lover understands your need to be pampered. Erotic foreplay turns you on and sets the stage for deeper, more meaningful lovemaking. A slow artful seduction appeals to your refined sensibilities. Although you ease into intimacy slowly, once you get going, the many layers of your earthy sensuality unfold.

August 26, *Virgo 8*

What Makes You Tick

Although slow to warm up in public, you are affectionate and caring in private. Your natural sex drive is strong, and when you let yourself go completely, you're quite the sensuous lover. Still, even in your own boudoir, it may take time for your cool exterior to melt. Your ideal lover knows how to draw out your hidden passion with a careful, measured approach.

Between the Sheets

While you may appear composed on the surface, you often feel insecure and emotionally vulnerable. Your feelings run deep, and at times you have difficulty expressing them. Moreover, your true emotions are not likely to be revealed until you get to know your prospective partner well. Naturally hardworking and ambitious, you lead a busy life that allows little time for dreamy romantic interludes. You want nothing less than a secure romantic union, and casual suitors with empty promises are swiftly dismissed. However, behind closed doors, you are able to drop your reserved demeanor and reveal your inherently passionate nature, and the bedmate who patiently draws out your hidden desires is sure to be well rewarded.

Tips for Your Ideal Lover

Erotic massage with scented oils energizes you and helps connect you to your lusty physicality. Verbal rapport and sexy talk bridges the distance between inner desire and action. Talking with your beloved about what you are planning to do to each other creates intimate moments of tenderness and passion.

August 27, *Virgo 9*

What Makes You Tick

Your emotional side, as indicated by the number 9 vibration, places a high priority on close, loving relationships. However, your cerebral Virgo Sun sign also craves companionship of the thoughtful, intellectual variety. Moreover, you are a genuine romantic and as likely to fall in love with a romantic dream as with a real person. If everyday reality doesn't live up to your expectations, you can be deeply disappointed.

Between the Sheets

While the dreamy part of you casts an invisible web of seduction around potential suitors, your own two feet are planted firmly on the ground. Although your ultimate desire may be to merge sexual pleasure with spiritual union, you need to know that there will be an earthy, practical side to your life together as well. Sensual, sensitive, and concerned, you're an easy person to love. Making your partner feel cherished and appreciated is your special talent, in bed and out of it. For you, physical love is a tender expression of deeper feelings, a complete mingling of body, mind, and soul. When you find the true love you're seeking, you willingly sacrifice everything for your partner.

Tips for Your Ideal Lover

Your ideal lover is subtly seductive and able to melt your reserve with a smile or a gentle touch. Sharing a bath or an invigorating shower with your lover can serve as playful foreplay for a night of vigorous lovemaking. Spicy pillow talk calms your restless mind as it arouses your slumbering sexual passion.

August 28, *Virgo 1*

What Makes You Tick

You may often feel as if you're being torn apart by opposing influences. On the one hand, you're dedicated to your partner's interests; on the other, you yearn for freedom and independence. Physically, you're ardent, but emotionally, you vacillate. Your ideal mate is capable of seeing past your emotional barriers to the passionate you beneath.

Between the Sheets

Considerably more romantic then you care to admit, your cool Virgo façade and desire for perfection melt under your sizzling sexual intensity. A totally different person in private than in public, you drop your reserve behind closed doors and give full rein to your sensuality. Moreover, once you develop a sense of trust, you're able to let go and become the amorous lover you were meant to be. Although naturally critical, you are kind and generous in the bedroom and willing to consider your bedmate's preferences along with your own. Although romance truly matters to you, so does intellectual rapport. Casual affairs hold little temptation, because you crave the lasting devotion of true love.

Tips for Your Ideal Lover

Your erotic side smolders like a dormant volcano until released with the help of a seductive partner. With the right person, your shyness and inhibition are swiftly overcome in a loving and passionate embrace. Bathing or showering together beforehand relaxes you, as does a sensuous full-body massage with scented oils.

August 29, *Virgo 2*

What Makes You Tick

Initially cautious in love, you prefer building a long-lasting relationship on a strong, solid foundation. Since you refuse to ignore responsibility in favor of fun and games, one-night stands have no place in your love life. Once you find a compatible mate, you're loyal and dependable but also sexy and extremely sensual. Tactile by nature, you communicate with your lover as much through touch as with words.

Between the Sheets

While it doesn't take a lot of fancy moves to entice you, you do appreciate the beauty of elegant surroundings. When preparing for lovemaking, you like to pay attention to detail. A beautifully appointed room, with fresh flowers and candlelight puts you in the mood for love. While some romantic partners may be more exciting than you, few are as dependable or trustworthy. In an intimate union, you are tender, loving, and affectionate. Although practical and down-to-earth in the rest of the house, your old-fashioned romanticism and consideration for your partner make you a dream lover in the bedroom. You enjoy touching and being touched, and your heightened sensory perception enhances the pleasure you share with your mate.

Tips for Your Ideal Lover

In the bedroom and elsewhere, you don't like being rushed, and slow, seductive foreplay that engages all your senses evokes your slumbering passions. Sensuality begins with touching and stroking. You communicate freely through nonverbal language, and you like it best when you and your lover slowly explore each other's bodies.

August 30, *Virgo 3*

What Makes You Tick

Inherently friendly and sociable, you like people and enjoy communicating and exchanging thoughts and ideas with everyone you meet. Although you adore partying and flirting, you actually require the stability of a long-term love union in your life. Because you value friendship and companionship as much as love, you need to find a significant other who is your intellectual equal and able to keep up with you mentally.

Between the Sheets

Variety truly is the spice of your life . While your approach to love and sex may come off as rather lighthearted, you have a serious appreciation for the physical joys of lovemaking. A skilled lover, you are fascinated with the mechanics and techniques of sexuality. Nevertheless, your approach to sensual pleasures is earthy, direct, and essentially unpretentious. You will go to a lot of trouble to please your bed partner, as long as things don't get too emotionally intense or demanding. Since you're motivated as much by curiosity as by desire, change and diversity keep your love life fresh and also keep you interested in and out of bed.

Tips for Your Ideal Lover

You channel a lot of energy into intimate dialogue with your lover, and one of your favorite topics of conversation is your sex life. You respond amorously to spicy verbal banter and playful sex games, and while erotic toys and literature may shock you at first, they can also serve as a major turn-on.

August 31, *Virgo 4*

What Makes You Tick

As a lover or friend, you are loyal and dependable, but you're also anxious and inclined to be overprotective. Inherently cautious, you're not one to leap into a romantic union with reckless abandon. You need to get to know a potential lover first, preferably through sharing common interests outside the boudoir. However, once you commit to a close relationship, you expect to stick with it in good times and bad.

Between the Sheets

Although sensitive and kindhearted, you're rather cool and dispassionate and tend to think about your emotions instead of feeling them. However, once you stop overanalyzing every move you make, and start heeding the promptings of your feelings and emotions, you make an exceptionally passionate, considerate partner. Little is left to chance in your love life, as you like to plan all the details of a romantic encounter in advance. Naturally sentimental, yet apprehensive about expressing your true feelings, you prefer demonstrating affection through thoughtfulness and consideration for your partner rather than with words of love. While your hidden passions can be stirred by a persistent suitor, it generally takes time for you to reveal your deepest desires.

Tips for Your Ideal Lover

In the privacy of the bedroom, the sensual side of your nature comes to the fore. You have plenty of sexual curiosity, and the lover who distracts you from daily cares is rewarded with an explosion of earthy passion. Your ideal bed partner continually seeks new ways to arouse and excite you.

September 1, *Virgo 1*

What Makes You Tick

Beneath your calm façade, you're a restless bundle of nervous energy. At times, you feel torn between your love of freedom and independence, and a genuine desire to help others. You take your obligations very seriously, but you can be overly critical and judgmental. Problems may arise in an intimate union if you feel compelled to help your beloved by remaking him or her into your idea of perfection.

Between the Sheets

You tend to be more sexually aggressive than other Virgo lovers. You're not afraid to take the lead and voice suggestions for making your sex life more spontaneous and exciting. Your initial approach tends to be rather refined, yet with a little encouragement from your lover, your hidden desires morph into tempestuous passion. Although the idea of using erotic toys in your lovemaking may shock you at first, they can add a playful, slightly naughty aspect to your lovemaking under the right circumstances. Your mind is your major erotic zone, and you find words as seductive as deeds. Talking or fantasizing about torrid sexual pleasures inflames your imagination and gets all your juices flowing.

Tips for Your Ideal Lover

You are sexually inquisitive, and pillow talk that includes tidbits of salacious gossip about other peoples' sexual behavior can serve as a major turn-on. Your physical vitality thrives on high-energy lovemaking. Your erotic side smolders just beneath the surface, and any inhibitions you may feel are swiftly overcome in moments of passion.

September 2, *Virgo 2*

What Makes You Tick

You take commitment seriously and show how much you care by being generous and dependable. Once involved, you do everything possible to accommodate yourself to your significant other. Typically more concerned with pleasing than with being pleased, you are an exceedingly thoughtful and affectionate romantic partner. The dark side of your love nature is a tendency to be hypercritical and judgmental, especially of people close to you.

Between the Sheets

Satisfying the one you adore, in and out of the bedroom, is really what it's all about. You want an intimate union that truly touches your heart. Since you also crave beauty and order in your life, you enjoy creating a pleasant atmosphere where you can love and be loved. You particularly appreciate the refined elegance of tasteful surroundings, with fresh flowers, soft lighting, and music playing in the background. The temptation of a casual liaison holds little appeal for you. You want to be with a lover you trust, who cherishes and understands you and shares your high ideals. Just the thought of sharing your most precious moments with your true love fuels your romantic fantasies.

Tips for Your Ideal Lover

Your ideal lover builds sexual bonds on a strong, solid foundation. Since you like to ease into intimacy slowly, you appreciate a bed partner who sets the stage for lovemaking with protracted foreplay. Although you enjoy being seduced with romantic words, you respond ardently to nonverbal language as well.

September 3, *Virgo 3*

What Makes You Tick

In an intimate relationship, you are romantic and idealistic, but too much emotional intensity makes you feel anxious and uncomfortable. Since you value companionship and friendship almost as much as love, you need a significant other who challenges you intellectually. Although you like to party and flirt, you need the security of a stable love union. When you find the right person, you'll probably stay together for a lifetime.

Between the Sheets

A highly skilled bedmate, you're fascinated with the mechanics and techniques of sexuality. Although your style of lovemaking tends to be freewheeling and lighthearted, you have a serious appreciation for the physical joys of lovemaking. Your approach to the lusty pleasures of the body is direct, earthy, and unpretentious. Mental affinity with your lover is as important to you as physical rapport. Since you're mainly motivated by curiosity, variety spices up your love life and holds your interest between the sheets. The intimate banter of sex games and other verbal enticements have a major impact on you. Whispering sweet nothings turns you on, and you absolutely love it when spicy conversation morphs into sexy reality.

Tips for Your Ideal Lover

Talking about your secret sexual desires inflames them and clues your lover in to what you like doing and having done to you in bed. You respond eagerly to sexy chatter, and a gentle massage with aromatic oils relaxes you and prepares your body for the erotic celebration to follow by calming your racing mind.

September 4, *Virgo 4*

What Makes You Tick

Exceedingly sensitive to your surroundings, you require an ordered environment in which to live and work. You are kindhearted and affectionate, and you bring sincerity to all your relationships. In affairs of the heart, you are happiest when involved in a permanent union. Thoughtful and attentive to small details, you pick up on little things that most others seem to miss. As a result, you know most of your partner's likes and dislikes and act accordingly.

Between the Sheets

There is nothing superficial about you; you think and feel very deeply. Even so, you want a relationship with your spouse that provides escape from the mundane. In your lover's arms, you forget about the responsibilities and stresses of the world outside your bedroom. Your ideal mate is sweet-natured and loving, yet bright enough to engage in intelligent conversation. In your romantic dreams, love and sex are always intertwined. The partner who showers you with TLC knows the way to your heart. You enjoy all the accouterments of courtship, including flowers, champagne, and sweetmeats. A romantic ambiance, with scented candles and soft music puts you in the mood for lovemaking.

Tips for Your Ideal Lover

Since little is left to chance in your life, you like to schedule your sex dates in advance, thereby giving you something to look forward to at the end of a day's work. The promise of the lovemaking to come fuels your fantasies and readies you for moments of breathtaking intimacy.

September 5, *Virgo 5*

What Makes You Tick

Basically self-contained, you may give the impression that you're not interested in commitment, but you actually prefer coming home to the security of a permanent love union. Moreover, once involved, you make a loyal and devoted mate. You do need your personal space, and if your partner tries to tell you what to do or whom to see, your inclination is to withdraw and shut down emotionally.

Between the Sheets

Sexual arousal usually begins in the mind. While Virgo 5s may shy away from public displays of affection, they are as sexy and sensuous in private as any zodiacal combination. Your ideal bedmate knows how to draw out your elusive passions by appealing to your intellect along with your body. The clever, innovative lover loosens you up with provocative language and witty sexual banter. In the bedroom and elsewhere, anything new and unusual intrigues you and diverts your attention away from your everyday concerns. Relaxation draws out your elusive passions, and an amorous, enticing seduction inflames your lusty libido and helps you forget about everything except the luscious sensuality of the moment.

Tips for Your Ideal Lover

An earthy, aromatic massage leading to erotic play and teasing builds a delicious sexual tension that heightens your physical desire. A surprise gift of sex toys may shock you at first, yet it ultimately thrills you beyond your wildest dreams. Reading sophisticated erotica with your lover merges your inquiring mind with your primal urges.

September 6, *Virgo* 6

What Makes You Tick

You may appear self-sufficient, but you actually need other people. High expectations can make it difficult for you to reach a decision regarding the future of a romantic relationship; you prefer taking your time before making a commitment. However once you decide, you expect to stay involved for a lifetime and you invest a lot of energy in crafting an intimate union that is totally satisfying.

Between the Sheets

Naturally amenable, you do whatever you can to avoid disagreement and discord inside or outside the bedroom. You have discriminating tastes and your main objective when making love is to create a memorable experience. Since you view love as a two-way street, you expect the same type of consideration in return. In your image of a perfect union, your connection with your lover goes well beyond the physical. You want an intimate union that includes intellectual and emotional bonding. Easily overwhelmed by aggressive ardor, you prefer a slow, artful seduction in a serenely romantic setting. Your hidden passions emerge in surroundings that are replete with all the accouterments of love and romance.

Tips for Your Ideal Lover

Traditional courtship rituals turn you on, and you adore the playful games and flirtatious banter that lead to sexual arousal. Your passions emerge full-blown when surrounded by beauty and comfort, and your ideal bedmate knows how to fashion a harmonious setting for love and romance that engages all the senses.

September 7, *Virgo 7*

What Makes You Tick

Virgo's perfectionism can make you appear overly critical. Yet if your emotional demands are met, you willingly give your all for love. More concerned with pleasing than with being pleased, you make a caring and thoughtful romantic partner. However, your feelings are easily hurt, especially if you think your love and devotion are unappreciated. Knowing that your partner is truly committed to the relationship makes you feel safe and secure.

Between the Sheets

When you are attracted to someone, you stop to analyze your feelings instead of acting on them. Typically, you will not proceed to the next step until you convince yourself the relationship isn't a mistake. Communication is essential to you, and your ability to analyze any situation makes you a methodical, yet creative and innovative lover. Sharing your ideas and insights in and out of bed makes you feel closer to your mate. Your ideal partner first engages your mind, then your heart, and last but not least, your body. Because you shoulder so many responsibilities, you need a partner who can entice you away from your worries; a loving and considerate bedmate sustains your affection.

Tips for Your Ideal Lover

Witty and provocative erotic suggestions stimulate you physically by arousing you mentally. An exciting romantic evening on the town starts melting your resistance and inciting your passions before you even return home; the seductive game that began with spicy sexy banter grows deeper and more satisfying with physical intimacy.

September 8, *Virgo 8*

What Makes You Tick

You may appear cool and aloof on the outside, but you're loving and emotionally vulnerable on the inside. Your true depths of feeling are revealed when you get to know your prospective partner well. Even in an intimate relationship, you're difficult to understand and may remain something of an enigma to your significant other. Nevertheless, when you overcome your doubts and misgivings, you're capable of a prodigious amount of caring.

Between the Sheets

Although modest and controlled in public, your innate passion and earthy sensuality come to the surface in private. A skillful bedmate, you like to begin the foreplay with slow, languid caresses. During lovemaking you take the time to build to a heightened state of ecstasy. You may further enhance the feelings of intimacy by employing a combination of tender touch and provocative suggestions. Since spontaneity is not your thing, little is left to chance in your love life. You like to preplan lovemaking, in order to savor every moment and make each sexual encounter as perfect as possible. You respond amorously to an erotic massage that relaxes your body and eases your harried mind.

Tips for Your Ideal Lover

Though generally private about your deepest feelings, you can be wildly passionate in the security and comfort of hearth and home where your pent-up passions erupt with playful abandon. Since endurance is your forte, you hate to rush things and the patient lover who cultivates an unhurried atmosphere of seduction turns you on.

September 9, *Virgo 9*

What Makes You Tick

Although the emotional side of your nature wants love, your cerebral side craves companionship of a more intellectual variety. When you find your soul mate, you willingly sacrifice everything for your beloved. A genuine romantic, you're as likely to fall in love with a dream as with a real person. If reality doesn't live up to expectations you're deeply disappointed yet predisposed to move on to another "ideal" lover.

Between the Sheets

Making your partner feel cherished is your special talent, and you have no qualms about catering to your lover's whims, either in bed or elsewhere. Physical love is an expression of deeper feelings, an emotional mingling of mind and body. Sensitive and concerned, you're an exceptionally easy person to love. You concentrate on the needs and desires of your beloved, and hope for similar consideration in return. Relaxation draws out your passion. A pampering bath laced with aromatic oils, followed by an invigorating massage soothes your nerves and awakens your lusty sensuality. Pillow talk makes you feel closer to your lover, and you get off on sharing your most intimate secrets with your bed partner.

Tips for Your Ideal Lover

Your goal is to merge sexual pleasure with spiritual union, and the lover who joins you in celebrating the sacredness of the body has an edge with you. A sensuous massage with warm scented oil awakens your lusty physicality, and the bedmate who employs subtly seductive caresses easily melts your sexual reserve.

September 10, *Virgo 1*

What Makes You Tick

A true meeting of the minds is considerably more important to you than moonlight and roses. While a cautious inner voice usually reminds you to think twice, there is an impulsive side to your character that prompts you to rush headlong into new relationships. Physically, you're passionate, but emotionally, you blow hot and cold. Even so, when you find security and contentment in a love union, you make a caring partner.

Between the Sheets

As a lover, you're more athletic, eager, and aggressive than other members of your Sun sign. In an intimate union, mental rapport may be your first requirement, but fiery sexual ardor runs a close second, and your dynamic physical vitality thrives on high-energy lovemaking. When you're away from your beloved, your passionate desire smolders like an awakening volcano. Although your approach to sensual pleasure may be rather refined, in your most intense intimate moments your Virgo reserve tends to melt away like snow on a hot stove. Your innate generosity makes you want to please your significant other in bed and elsewhere, but in return you expect nothing less than his or her undying appreciation.

Tips for Your Ideal Lover

Your brain is your most sensitive erogenous zone, and expressing your sexual desires verbally can be a real turn-on. When your partner is out-of-town, you enjoy engaging in hot phone sex and swapping torrid text messages. When you're together, getting physical with your lover is like a minivacation from the world's problems.

September 11, *Virgo 2*

What Makes You Tick

It is hard for you to talk about your emotions, preferring to show your beloved how much you care by being helpful and dependable. In an intimate union, you are loving, tender, and affectionate. You take your commitments seriously, and devotion and loyalty are key elements in all of your relationships. You are a perfectionist and can be quite critical when your partner is unable to live up to your high standards.

Between the Sheets

Your sensuality and lusty appetite for life's delight set you apart from other Virgo natives. A down-to-earth lover, you view sexuality as a natural, wholesome form of expressing deep feelings of love and affection. You prove your love by striving to please your mate, inside and outside the bedroom. Your style of lovemaking is innovative and inventive, and you continually come up with new and exciting ways of sharing your erotic imaginings. Every combination of sensual pleasure, from A to Z, seems to have a place in your romantic repertoire and you won't hesitate to try them all. Your methods of seduction are nonverbal; and chemistry, not words, directs your libido.

Tips for Your Ideal Lover

Inherently tactile, you get off on touching and being touched. Your ideal lover attends to all the little details that will make your time together truly memorable. When the scene is set for lovemaking with perfumed sheets, candlelight, and beautiful music playing in the background, how can you possibly resist?

September 12, *Virgo 3*

What Makes You Tick

Naturally sociable and friendly, you enjoy being around people, cheerfully exchanging ideas and swapping stories with everyone you meet. In your private life, you need a loving partner who is your intellectual equal and challenges you mentally. In an intimate relationship, you value friendship and companionship as much as love and romance. When you let yourself go emotionally and express your true feelings, you make a loving, caring, helpful romantic partner.

Between the Sheets

Gratifying your partner's sexual desires is important to you. A great talker and a good listener, you make it your business to find out what he or she likes to do beneath the covers. You thrive with a lover who is intelligent and knowledgeable enough to hold your interest. Although you prize your independence, you want stability and commitment in a romantic alliance. As far as you are concerned, sharing ideas and activities keeps your relationship fresh and exciting. You crave variety in your love life and enjoy experimenting with different positions and techniques. Sexy role-playing fantasies are a major turn-on, and you enter into the world of your erotic imagination easily and eagerly.

Tips for Your Ideal Lover

Intense drama really doesn't appeal to you, and while you thoroughly enjoy sex games, you prefer the ones that are light, playful, and fun. Perusing erotic literature in bed with your lover merges your sharp, literate mind with your primal sexual desires.

September 13, *Virgo 4*

What Makes You Tick

You need a mate who makes you feel cherished and appreciated. Despite your critical nature, you're sensitive to criticism and your feelings are easily hurt. Discord really bothers you, and when you feel insecure, you become anxious and overprotective. In an attempt to keep your emotions on an even keel, you may try to bury your negative feelings. However, eventually, unexpressed anger can turn into long-term resentment.

Between the Sheets

When you find the security you seek in an intimate relationship, you are affectionate, considerate, generous, and caring. Initially you may appear somewhat cautious and reserved, but once you feel comfortable with your partner, you make an amazingly skilled, thoughtful lover. Pleasing your significant other is always uppermost in your mind. You're able to sense how well he or she responds to your lovemaking, and then you store the knowledge in your memory banks for future use. A methodical, yet inventive bed partner, you pride yourself on your ability to keep the activities new and interesting. You respond especially well to small touches that help create a serene bedroom environment free of disturbances and distractions.

Tips for Your Ideal Lover

Behind closed doors, you're able to shed your controlled, ultraresponsible image and unwind. You are turned on by simple pleasures, and getting physical with your lover relaxes you and takes your mind off your day-to-day worries. The glow of candlelight and the scent of fresh flowers help create a pleasant atmosphere for making love.

September 14, *Virgo 5*

What Makes You Tick

Since you are self-contained and could enjoy a single life quite comfortably, you may be rather cautious when it comes to committing to a life-long partnership. However, once you agree to a commitment, you expect to stick around for the long haul. You want a relationship that combines love with companionship, and your ideal union is one in which you and your partner share similar interests and ideas.

Between the Sheets

Your innate sensuality finds its fullest expression in a secure romantic union. Although reticent and not overly demonstrative in public, there is nothing you won't try in private if it makes you and your bedmate happy. When making love, you pride yourself on your dexterity and ability to please your partner. Because you're sensitive to your significant other's needs and desires, you're usually able to anticipate them. However, you expect your spouse to anticipate your wants as well, and you appreciate a partner who takes the trouble to find out what you like. You enjoy trying new things, and playing out your fantasies may be one of your favorite forms of sexual recreation.

Tips for Your Ideal Lover

Relaxation calms you and draws out your elusive passions, and a sensuous massage with aromatherapy oils awakens your deep sensuality. Physical arousal begins with words, and talking about what you're about to do turns you on. Erotic play and teasing puts you in the mood by building sexual tension that heightens the ensuing lovemaking.

September 15, *Virgo 6*

What Makes You Tick

While outwardly cool and detached, you actually crave love and affection and may not be content without a life partner. Despite the practicality of your Virgo Sun sign, the number 6 vibration makes you profoundly idealistic and romantic. You are looking for the perfect mate, and you refuse to settle for anything less. Moreover, you fear rejection and you are likely to think twice before risking your heart on a whim.

Between the Sheets

A sensual, patient lover, you are willing to wait for the most agreeable situation before you make a move. A slow artful seduction is more your style than fast, furious, or aggressive lovemaking. You enjoy flirting, romantic games, and other traditional rituals of courtship almost as much as the act itself. Giving, sharing, and making your partner happy is what it is all about for you. You see honest communication as an essential ingredient of sexual interaction because it keeps the bedroom activity lively and mutually gratifying. Comfort and congeniality contribute to your sexual enjoyment, and you prefer simple, harmonious surroundings to showy opulence.

Tips for Your Ideal Lover

Inherently civilized and cultured, you have delicate sensibilities and a great appreciation for all things beautiful and artistic. You enjoy small touches such as a romantic ambiance with candlelight, fresh flowers, soft music, affectionate gestures, and words of love that turn you on and put you in the mood for lovemaking.

September 16, *Virgo 7*

What Makes You Tick

One part of you craves excitement, variety, and independence, while the other part prefers the emotional security of a permanent union. In love as in life, you play your cards close to the chest. Critical of those who do not live up to your high standards, you don't grant many people access to your inner sanctum. However, once you are absolutely certain about a potential suitor you make a caring, romantic life partner.

Between the Sheets

Communication is essential for you in all aspects of your life. Sharing your ideas and insights makes you feel closer to your mate or partner. Sexually, you're tender and ardent, and you like to spoil your lover. You will do everything possible to satisfy your mate, but you expect the same in return. Your ideal bed partner understands your need to be catered to, pampered, and appreciated. Erotic foreplay turns you on and sets the stage for deeper, more meaningful lovemaking. A slow, artful seduction appeals to your refined sensibilities. Although you ease into intimacy slowly, your earthy sensuality begins to unfold as passions rise.

Tips for Your Ideal Lover

Your sensual nature simmers just below the surface, and provocative talk and spicy banter help liberate it along with your quick sense of humor. An invigorating shower can serve as playful foreplay. Once ignited, your libido overcomes your inhibitions, revealing an earthy sexuality and deep enjoyment of physical pleasure.

September 17, *Virgo 8*

What Makes You Tick

Inwardly, you're rather shy and less confident than you appear. However, you're so good at hiding self-doubt that most people are not even aware of your tendency to worry about every little thing. In matters of the heart, your calm appearance may cause others to see you as cool and unemotional. However, you're actually warm and caring.

Between the Sheets

Your emotions run deep, but you have difficulty expressing them. Yet once you learn to trust and open up to your partner, you make a steadfast, loyal, and giving mate. You are hardworking and ambitious, and the busy life you lead leaves little time for dreamy romantic interludes. Even so, your physical drives are quite strong, and when you take time for loving, you're a very sexy, sensual lover. Sometimes you're so suffused with desire that you give off heat like a smoldering volcano. Behind closed doors, you drop your reserved demeanor to reveal your passionate self, and the patient, thoughtful bedmate who knows how to draw out your controlled desires is well rewarded.

Tips for Your Ideal Lover

Your cool exterior takes time to melt and you may need a little coaxing after a long, grueling workday; however, dormant passions quickly ignite as you relax and unwind. An erotic massage, or a soak in a warm tub with aromatic oils, soothes you and sparks your lusty appetite for sensual pleasure.

September 18, *Virgo 9*

What Makes You Tick

Your kind, sympathetic nature makes you eager to help others, and you have a romantic, sentimental side that places a high priority on being half of a loving couple. There is also a more cerebral side to your character that craves love and companionship, of the more thoughtful, intellectual variety. Either way, you want an intimate relationship based on mutual respect, love, and affection.

Between the Sheets

Highly attuned to your partner's wants, needs, and desires, you make a thoughtful, considerate lover. Moreover, your earthy Virgo sensuality becomes ever richer with age and experience. When you find a new way to please your mate, you will hone the technique until it approaches perfection. However, you crave intimacy that goes much deeper than mere sexual satisfaction. You long to connect with your beloved mentally and spiritually, as well as physically. You get off on talking about sex and may spend a lot of time daydreaming and fantasizing about love and romance. Your imagination is so vivid that it may take only a few provocative suggestions to put you in the mood for making love.

Tips for Your Ideal Lover

Even though it makes you blush, foreplay that includes a detailed conversation about what you and your lover plan to do is a major turn-on. Your ideal bed partner is creatively seductive, dazzling you with romantic touches such as rose petals on the coverlet and chocolates and champagne on the bedside table.

September 19, *Virgo 1*

What Makes You Tick

More of an individualist than other Virgo natives, you want to be free to do as you please and dislike having anyone interfere in your plans or tell you what to do. Even so, you're more passionate and romantic than you let on, and you want a partner to share your life. Moreover, you're seeking a mate who can see past the emotional barriers you impose to the real you underneath.

Between the Sheets

You often feel torn between your independent nature and your sense of duty and obligation, but when you find your soul mate, you'll do whatever you can to make the relationship work. A totally different person in public, you drop your reserve and give full reign to your sexuality behind closed doors. An ardent, determined bedmate, you pride yourself on your sexual prowess. Your approach to lovemaking is a blend of earthy sensuality and torrid passion. Gratifying your lover's desires along with your own is important to you and you're good in bed. Your powers of seduction peak when inspired by a mate who offers trust and encouragement.

Tips for Your Ideal Lover

Your appetite for sexual pleasures increase and your physical desires erupt with passionate abandon during a romantic getaway with your lover. Going off for a change of scene, and leaving behind the routines of everyday life, revitalizes your love life. Even an impromptu overnight stay can relieve stress and make you feel sexually reborn.

September 20, *Virgo 2*

What Makes You Tick

You want to love and be loved, and in an intimate union, you are caring and affectionate. You crave beauty and order in your life and enjoy creating a pleasant atmosphere for lovemaking. Although you consider intellectual rapport as important as passion and romance, the urge to merge with your true love is one of your main motivators. You're faithful and devoted where love is concerned, and you expect no less in return.

Between the Sheets

Innately thoughtful and sentimental, you notice the things that make your partner happy, and you try to provide them. Communication is your forte, in and out of bed, and sharing thoughts and feelings brings you closer to your lover. When problems arise, you try nipping them in the bud by talking things through. However, physical pleasure matters to you as well, and if words don't do the trick, you will rely on your earthy sexuality to help calm troubled waters. Aggressiveness, however, doesn't work with you. You view the pleasures of lovemaking as an erotic feast for the senses, and you prefer slow, languid seduction that leads to a deeper, more meaningful sensual exploration.

Tips for Your Ideal Lover

You don't like to be rushed, preferring to ease into intimacy slowly. You particularly like taking your time when making love, and your ideal lover knows exactly what to do to awaken your hidden desires. Massaging each other with flavored oils or sharing exotic edible delicacies can enhance your mutual satisfaction.

September 21, *Virgo 3*

What Makes You Tick

In an intimate union, you're affectionate and romantic. Even so, you value friendship and companionship as much as love and need a partner who challenges you intellectually. Close relationships can be problematic, because your mistrust of emotion makes it hard for you to open up. However, once you feel comfortable with your partner, you make a caring, helpful mate, and if you find the right person, you will probably stay together for a lifetime.

Between the Sheets

Your approach to the erotic pleasures of the body is direct, earthy, and unpretentious. Although your style of lovemaking is emotionally cool and light-hearted, you appreciate its many physical joys. Mental affinity with your significant other is as important to you as physical rapport. Since you're motivated as much by curiosity as by desire, variety can spice up your love life and keep you interested between the sheets. The intimate banter of pillow talk and other verbal enticements have a major impact on you. Expressing your secret desires verbally inflames them further and also clues your lover in to what you like doing and having done to you in bed.

Tips for Your Ideal Lover

A highly skilled bedroom participant, you are fascinated with the mechanics and techniques of sexuality. Spicy conversation awakens your libido, and the lover who makes you laugh draws out your naughty side. Whispering sweet nothings turns you on, and you particularly like it when the lusty words morph into a sexy reality.

September 22, *Virgo 4*

What Makes You Tick

Very much your own person, you sometimes exude an air of cool detachment, yet even when your outer demeanor is reserved, you are warm and caring beneath the surface. In an intimate union, you need a partner who makes you feel cherished, because when you feel insecure you become overly critical of your beloved. Even so, once you enter into a close relationship, you stick with it through good times and bad.

Between the Sheets

Inherently cautious, you are not one to leap into love or romance with reckless abandon. You prefer getting to know a potential lover first by sharing common interests outside the bedroom. In public, you keep your emotions under control. However, in your private moments, you are as loving and sensual as any other member of the zodiac. Your true feelings are only revealed in the intimacy of an enduring bond. With trust established and the vagaries of courtship out of the way, the complex layers of your earthy sensuality begin to unfold. You actually have very few sexual hang-ups, and you will do most anything that feels good and that both you and your partner find pleasurable.

Tips for Your Ideal Lover

When you perform a seductive striptease for your lover, you reveal the true eroticism behind your apparent reserve. Playful flirtation and provocative verbal suggestions intrigue you and add to your decadent mood. Your ideal mate builds delicious sexual tension with sultry teasing movements that heighten physical desires for both of you.

September 23, *Libra* 5

What Makes You Tick

You genuinely like people, yet you find it difficult to communicate with others on an emotional level. The truth is that feelings strike you as rather messy and embarrassing. Instead you reach out intellectually to those around you and respond most readily to signs of mental rapport. Where long-term commitments are concerned, your desire for freedom and independence is constantly at odds with your belief that life is incomplete without a partner.

Between the Sheets

Your Libra Sun sign makes you yearn to belong to another person, while the number 5 vibration prefers an independent lifestyle. The best alliance for you may be the one that begins as a close friendship and slowly evolves into a more intimate bond. Ultimately, you favor the charming rituals of love and courtship to the unbridled passion of steamy sexual encounters. Even so, you're a generous lover and you won't hesitate to put your needs on hold to accommodate those of your partner. In bed, you're innovative and inventive without ever being crude or vulgar. Verbal communication is your forte and discussing your impending lovemaking with your bedmate can act as a major turn-on.

Tips for Your Ideal Lover

Although you thrive in the world of high ideas, physical pleasure brings you down to earth. Talking during sex engages your imagination and verbal teasing can be a thrilling prelude to ecstatic lovemaking. You respond with enthusiasm to the lover who creates a sensuous romantic atmosphere with candles and flowers.

September 24, *Libra* 6

What Makes You Tick

Your amiable nature and willingness to compromise make you particularly easy to get along with. Where love and sex are concerned, you enjoy being an object of desire, and your charismatic allure makes the very air around you crackle with erotic excitement. However, once you enter into a loving union, you give it your all. Romance is in your blood; you consider life without love as barely worth living.

Between the Sheets

You thrive on the affection and attentions of your mate, and you are easily influenced by his or her opinions and ideas. Your sensitive nature and romantic idealism make you extremely vulnerable in an intimate alliance. Disloyalty or disaffection upsets your emotional equilibrium. If you are disappointed by your lover, you become quite distressed. Your refined nature wants lovemaking to be serene and beautiful, and romance is as important to you as passion. Thoughtful and considerate by nature, you tend to put your bed partner's happiness and satisfaction ahead of your own. You do, however, expect the same consideration in return. If you don't get it, you may be severely disillusioned.

Tips for Your Ideal Lover

Your romantic, idealistic nature opens to the magic of romance, sometimes even making the sex act an afterthought. Your ideal mate creates a setting for lovemaking that engages all the senses. Although an occasional vigorous bedroom romp may be in your repertoire, you routinely reject crude or unrefined physical lovemaking.

September 25, *Libra 7*

What Makes You Tick

The romantic idealist in you expects so much from a relationship that reality rarely lives up to your dream. Even so, you probably won't feel fulfilled in life without someone special sharing it. Emotionally, you can be rather high maintenance, yet no one makes a more thoughtful companion. Attentive and caring, you do many little things to enhance your partner's quality of life.

Between the Sheets

Because you dislike being alone, partnership holds a high priority, and you are prepared to invest a great deal of energy in creating a satisfying love life. Even so, your idealism and exceedingly high expectations can make it difficult to sustain a harmonious romantic relationship. Your amorous nature thrives on the rituals of traditional courtship. You get off on sensuous accouterments such as sultry nightwear, silky sheets, and soft lighting. You may not expect to be swept away by wild passion, but you do appreciate a bedmate skilled in the ways of love. Dull or routine sex turns you off, and you prefer a creative lover who knows how to keep you guessing.

Tips for Your Ideal Lover

You don't like confrontation, and your ideal lover knows how to create and maintain an atmosphere of peace and harmony in the bedroom. Spontaneous romantic gestures add sparkle to your activities between the sheets. Whether you're the one watching or actually performing, a sultry, sensual striptease energizes your libido and gets all your sexual juices flowing.

September 26, *Libra 8*

What Makes You Tick

A study in contrasts, you're outgoing in intimate company, yet you can swiftly clam up among strangers. In romantic situations, you're warm and affectionate one moment, cool and mysterious the next. You like being in control in a relationship, which can lead to power struggles with your significant other. It takes more than love to catch and hold you because you want a life partner who shares your worldview.

Between the Sheets

Outwardly, you appear as easygoing as other Libras, yet a fierce determination to succeed at everything is lurking just beneath the surface. In a loving union, you're capable of total loyalty and devotion. Your sexual feelings may run hot and cold, but when they're hot, they sizzle. As a result, you're sentimental and affectionate some of the time, lusty and passionate at others. Between the sheets, endurance is your forte, and your appetite for sensual pleasures tends to increase with age. The longer you and your lover are together, the more uninhibited you become in his or her embrace. During your wilder moments, you pull out all the stops and give full reign to your carnal desires.

Tips for Your Ideal Lover

A sensual massage with aromatic oils opens up the steamier passions that well up from deep within you. Outwardly refined, you prefer sending out provocative hints of what you like in bed to making overt suggestions. Your ideal lover picks up on your subtle advances and acts on them without hesitation.

September 27, *Libra 9*

What Makes You Tick

You don't enjoy making waves. Your romantic idealism compels you to seek your other half, yet once you find your soul mate, it's easy for you to slip into emotional dependency. Since you like everything to be calm and congenial, you do what you deem necessary to maintain peace and harmony, including clinging to a bad relationship for too long rather than upsetting the status quo.

Between the Sheets

In the bedroom, you're an irresistible combination of passion and old-fashioned romance. Your amorous nature thrives on the rituals of traditional courtship, and you get off on romantic touches such as sultry nightwear, silky sheets, music, and soft lighting. The glamorous aura you project can be utterly captivating. Yet despite your romantic inclinations, you are quite discriminating when it comes to serious involvement. You are looking for true love and refuse to settle for less. When you find your Mr. or Ms. Right, you pledge your undying love and affection. However, if you ever feel betrayed, you won't accept defeat lightly, and the love that once burned like fire turns as cold as ice.

Tips for Your Ideal Lover

Although depth of emotion matters more to you than specific actions, the thoughtful lover who creates a luxurious setting for lovemaking has the edge. Sharing exotic fruits, chocolates, and wine in the boudoir with your bedmate appeals to your sensual nature and puts you in the mood for love.

September 28, *Libra 1*

What Makes You Tick

In love with the idea of love, you may regard romance as a game. Eventually, however, you'll need to choose between independence and the comfortable feeling of being half of a couple. When you find Mr. or Ms. Right, you will probably settle down to a pleasant long-term intimate union, and once involved you'll set about creating a charming atmosphere with graceful surroundings where love can thrive.

Between the Sheets

In bed, you are generous and enthusiastic. Aggressive one moment, and cool and laid-back the next, you move unexpectedly between overt passion and subtle seduction. A harmonious atmosphere with luxurious bedding makes you feel sensuous and sexy. While the ardent side of your nature longs to be swept away in an erotic free-for-all, the other part of you prefers being wooed and won in an old-fashioned romantic courtship. Since boredom is an anathema to you, the side of you that longs to break the rules responds readily to the innovative lover who tempts you with provocative suggestions. You particularly like being seduced with kissing and touching designed to inflame your desire.

Tips for Your Ideal Lover

Your delicate sensibilities are easily offended by boorish behavior, and since you view sex as an art, you prefer a certain amount of sophistication and good taste in a lover. Although willing to take the lead in the bedroom, you also enjoy being coaxed and enticed into sweet submission.

September 29, *Libra 2*

What Makes You Tick

The "urge to merge" is your main motivation. You cannot imagine being alone for very long; you flourish in the warmth and security of a long-term, loving partnership. The idealistic part of you craves a significant other you can put on a pedestal and worship. However, your earthier, more sensual side wants a real life mate to share your most intimate moments.

Between the Sheets

You are among the most sensuous and sexually active members of your Sun sign, and you possess a sixth sense regarding your bed partner's needs and desires. Even though the lovemaking of your romantic dreams may seem to be just beyond your reach, you keep trying. A genuine romantic, you are happiest when you're alone with your spouse in a paradise of your own making. Between the sheets, you respond most readily to a slow, elegant style of lovemaking that builds toward the peak of desire. Like most Libra Sun natives, you crave beauty and order in your life and a harmonious bedroom environment puts you in the mood for love.

Tips for Your Ideal Lover

Erotic delicacies heighten the ecstasy, and you revel in a carnival of the senses created by luxurious bed linens, sultry nightwear, fresh flowers, scented candles, and soft music playing in the background. Your desire for touching and stroking makes your skin tingle, and your ideal lover knows what to do to satisfy your tactile sensuality.

September 30, *Libra 3*

What Makes You Tick

More intellectual than either physical or emotional, you tend to rely on your mind more than your feelings. It's not unusual for you to find a spirited discussion as stimulating and exciting as any passionate sexual encounter. Even so, you're an incurable romantic and prone to falling in love with the idea of love. Easily bored, you may go through several romances before deciding to settle down.

Between the Sheets

A delightful mixture of fun-filled companion and romantic lover, you're capable of caring deeply without taking things too seriously. When you find someone you like, your mind starts scheming to win the object of your interest. Even though you are willing to do whatever it takes to make your partner happy, you refuse to surrender your soul in the process. Your quick wit and fluency with language make words your most powerful means of seduction, and a little affectionate pillow talk adds to the sweetness of the moment. The bright, charismatic lover with the intelligence to keep you guessing most likely will catch and hold you.

Tips for Your Ideal Lover

To your way of thinking, elegance and sensuality go together and you long to be swept off your feet in high style. You get off on the charming rituals of courtship, and beauty and comfort gratify your refined tastes in the bedroom and elsewhere. Behind closed doors, erotic touching and teasing trigger your impulsive sexuality.

October 1, *Libra 1*

What Makes You Tick

Libra is the sign of "the iron hand in the velvet glove," because a steely will lies beneath the scales' amiable disposition. While you may be agreeable, you're no pushover. You think carefully before acting and rarely do anything you don't want to do. Relationships are central to your life, and you probably don't lack for romantic partners. Once involved, you're a model mate who remembers birthdays and anniversaries.

Between the Sheets

Pleasing your partner is your main objective, and you won't hesitate to explore wild sex if you think that it is what your lover wants. Given your druthers, you're more romantic than ardent. Not only do you expect lovemaking to feel good, you also think it should be a beautiful experience for both participants. However, there's also a passionate, playful side to your sexuality. You enjoy laughing, talking, and swapping erotic stories in bed. You are a dichotomy of independence versus dependence, yet partnership invariably wins out, because you want to be loved more than you want to be free. Although loyal and caring, if the romantic spark dies you could begin looking elsewhere.

Tips for Your Ideal Lover

Your sexual responses tend to heat up as your relationship grows and deepens. A part of you wants to let go and break all the rules. However, with your sophisticated tastes and delicate sensibilities, you usually opt for a more refined approach to lovemaking. Your ideal mate entices you with subtle moves and provocative suggestions.

October 2, *Libra 2*

What Makes You Tick

Sensuous, caring, and sentimental, you can't imagine being without a mate. In point of fact, love is everything to you, and you flourish in a secure, caring union. Sociable by nature, you may enjoy a little flirting from time to time, but what you really want is an ongoing relationship with your true love. Once you find your soul mate, it's quite natural for you to remain loyal and committed.

Between the Sheets

An idealist with regard to intimacy, you throw yourself into a relationship with your whole heart. In return, you expect your mate to fill your life with love, affection, and romance. When it comes to your bedroom activities, you possess a sixth sense that clues you in to your partner's deepest desires. Behind closed doors, you give all of yourself to your lover, and you want all of his or her attention in return. Not satisfied with dull routine, you crave some excitement between the sheets. Although variety and creativity turn you on, you are not really interested in kinky bedroom antics. Instead you have a weakness for romantic touches such as candlelight and music.

Tips for Your Ideal Lover

Your idyllic vision of love finds its best expression in the reality of a lusty sexual union. An aromatic massage that brings out your richly layered sensuality can become central to your lovemaking. Touching and stroking turn you on, and you shiver with anticipation as your lover slowly explores your entire body.

October 3, *Libra 3*

What Makes You Tick

The contradictions in your nature tend to surface in romantic relationships. Although you yearn for companionship, you are more independent than other members of your Sun sign. You want a committed relationship, but you refuse to be bossed or smothered. Consequently, you may go through a number of romances before settling down. However, when you do enter into an intimate union, you make a loving, considerate, tender partner.

Between the Sheets

You are a delightful mixture of breezy, fun-loving companion and idealistic, romantic lover. Since you know how to love deeply without taking it all too seriously, you'll do almost anything to make sure that your partner is happy; you won't, however, surrender your independent nature in the process. Inside the bedroom and elsewhere, words are your most powerful seduction tool. You live as much in your mind as in your body, and you long to establish a deep mental connection with your bedmate along with the physical one. Your brain is your most sensitive erogenous zone. You enjoy talking about sex, and you respond as readily to tantalizing language as you do to kisses and caresses.

Tips for Your Ideal Lover

Having spicy suggestions whispered in your ear, or reading erotic literature with your lover turns you on, as does trying out all the sexy stuff you have been reading and talking about. You respond to spontaneous gestures of romance, and your lover's provocative look can be enough to trigger your impulsive sexuality.

October 4, *Libra 4*

What Makes You Tick

Partnership is a high priority. You're as romantic and idealistic as other Libras, but you can be considerably more demanding. It may take awhile to make a commitment, but when you do, you're prepared to stick around. In a close relationship, you're loving, and caring. However, you can be easily hurt if your kindness is not reciprocated or if you feel that your devotion is unappreciated.

Between the Sheets

You find it more difficult to relax and express your deepest feelings than other members of your Sun sign. Your attitude toward sex is typically passive, and you would rather attract love than pursue it. You enjoy lovemaking most when it is part of a committed, serious relationship. The promise of intimacy sparks your desire, but without an intuitive bond, the attraction can fade. While you may recoil from crude expressions of love, you're not shy once things get going and your impulse is to do everything possible to please your partner. In the bedroom, you like being surrounded by touches of simple elegance, and making love in a well-appointed room appeals to your refined tastes.

Tips for Your Ideal Lover

Your ideal lover knows when to take you out and when to remain home. Sharing an evening of sophisticated entertainment at a concert or ballet puts you in a relaxed, companionable mood. Afterward, a romantic supper for two or a moonlight swim under the stars sets the stage for blissful lovemaking.

October 5, *Libra* 5

What Makes You Tick

You crave love and companionship and probably can't be truly happy without a mate. Even so, your tendency to think in terms of we and us is somewhat diminished by an inner longing for freedom and independence. You are kind-hearted and caring, yet you project an airy detachment that your bed partner may find off-putting. Your ideal lover knows how to combine romance and sexuality with friendship and intellectual rapport.

Between the Sheets

A genuine romantic, you seem to prefer the courtly rituals of romance to the unbridled passion of earthy sexual encounters. However, when the mood strikes you, you can be as ardent and imaginative a lover as any in the zodiac. An idealist and uncompromising dreamer, you want your sexual encounters to be as close to perfect as you can make them. Gratifying your bedmate is important to you, and few other lovers are as adept at making another person feel cherished and adored. You have refined tastes, and a tendency to recoil from crude or overly aggressive expressions of sexuality. As a result, you prefer a slow, sensual approach to lovemaking.

Tips for Your Ideal Lover

Talking during sex comes naturally to you and you're turned on by provocative pillow talk. Although you thrive in the world of ideas, you also enjoy sensual pleasures. A romantic ambiance with candlelight, soft music, affectionate gestures, and loving words relaxes you and puts you in the mood for love.

October 6, *Libra 6*

What Makes You Tick

Your innate sensitivity and romantic idealism make you emotionally vulnerable in an intimate union. Should you feel let down by your lover, you may become seriously distressed. However, like other members of your Sun sign, you tend to fall out of love as easily as you fall in love. When your life partner no longer fits your idealized version of the perfect lover, the relationship begins to lose its luster.

Between the Sheets

Romance is as important to you as passion, and your refined nature prefers lovemaking that is serene and beautiful. However, thoughtfulness and even selfless devotion come easily to you. Although you prefer romance to unbridled passion, you tend to put your bedmate's wants and needs ahead of your own. In your willingness to compromise, you can lose sight of your own desires. Although you may not admit it, you want to be treated with tenderness and consideration, and if you do not receive it, you can become disillusioned. You long to be adored, courted, wooed, coaxed, pampered, and seduced with loving words and affectionate gestures in a beautiful, harmonious setting.

Tips for Your Ideal Lover

You enjoy being the object of your lover's desire, and knowing that you're loved turns you on. The charming bedmate who helps you relax and escape from the cares of the world has an edge. If he or she showers you with romance and surprises you with small gifts, so much the better.

October 7, *Libra 7*

What Makes You Tick

Although your Sun sign is about love and partnership, the number 7 is a truth-seeker, much given to solitary contemplation. As a result, some people may regard you as rather enigmatic and mysterious. Even so, in your mind there is no greater miracle than bonding with your soul mate. However, during your search for companionship, you don't neglect the other things in life you consider important, such as art, music, literature, philosophy, and helping others.

Between the Sheets

Your taste is impeccable, and you feel most relaxed and loving in beautiful, luxurious surroundings. Pleasing your significant other is important to you, and you will do almost anything to gratify your mate's desires. A gentle lover yourself, you don't expect to be swept away by wild passion. However, you do appreciate a partner who is skilled in the ways of love. Anything dull or routine turns you off; you prefer a creative bedmate who knows how to keep you guessing. Since planning ahead is not your style, your ongoing quest for new experiences gives your lovemaking a spontaneous edge. Experimenting with new positions appeals to you and adds zest to your lovemaking.

Tips for Your Ideal Lover

Versatility is your strong point and you're willing to try anything at least once. Romantic gestures add sparkle to your sexual activities and soft music, scented candles, and silky nightwear turn you on. Whether watching or participating, a sultry, sensual striptease energizes your libido and gets all your juices flowing.

October 8, *Libra 8*

What Makes You Tick

Relationships are central to your life, yet you're a dichotomy of independence versus dependence. Partnership invariably wins out, because your need to be loved is stronger than your desire for freedom. Once involved, you're a model mate with a penchant for always doing the right thing. However, it takes more than just love to hold your interest; you want to be with someone who shares your life goals.

Between the Sheets

In the bedroom, pleasing your partner is one of your main objectives. Left to your own devices, you are more romantic than ardent, but you will not hesitate to explore the wilder side of your sexuality if you think it is what your significant other truly wants. Not only do you like lovemaking to feel good, you also think it should be a beautiful, harmonious, transcendental experience for both participants. However, there is a lighthearted, playful side to your sexuality. You enjoy laughing, talking, and swapping erotic stories in bed. One part of you just wants to let go and break all the rules, and your sexual responses tend to heat up as your relationship with your lover grows and deepens.

Tips for Your Ideal Lover

With your sophisticated tastes and delicate sensibilities, you usually opt for a refined, romantic approach to lovemaking. However, your libido can be urgent and impulsive, and you appreciate an innovative, imaginative lover who is able to entice you into lustier couplings with subtle moves and provocative suggestions.

October 9, *Libra 9*

What Makes You Tick

In an intimate union, you're a thoughtful, generous partner. However, you hold some rather unrealistic ideas about love and relationships. Instead of dealing directly with disappointment, you're inclined to don rose-colored glasses and tell yourself that everything is okay, even when it clearly isn't. You need to remember that love is a partnership, and you are entitled to get as much out of it as you put into it.

Between the Sheets

Although your world revolves around loving and being loved, you are more romantic than ardent. Private time with your lover spent kissing and cuddling can be as gratifying to you as grand sexual passion. When you're with your true love, lovemaking seems to transcend the physical. Much of what you feel for your bed partner is engendered by your abstract notions of ideal love, and fantasy and dreams play a large part in your sex life. Kind and thoughtful in bed and elsewhere, you have a knack for intuiting your lover's desires and satisfying them. The bed partner who is capable of doing the same for you is the one most likely to turn you on.

Tips for Your Ideal Lover

Above all, you value tender moments of exquisite intimacy. By mixing fantasy with reality, your ideal lover can create a romantic world for you to share. A dreamy atmosphere in the bedroom with background music, soft lighting, an aromatic oil lamp, and flickering candles relaxes you and draws out your hidden sensuality.

October 10, *Libra 1*

What Makes You Tick

Affectionate and outgoing, you are considerably more passionate than most other Libras. Since you enjoy everything about the rituals of making love, you rarely lack for romantic partners. Yet while your heart craves love and companionship, your head yearns for freedom. Over the long term, however, love generally wins out because you truly need the companionship of a lasting and fulfilling romantic union.

Between the Sheets

You like the excitement of the chase and the anticipation of impending conquest almost as much as the resulting lovemaking. In the bedroom, you are full of delightful contradictions. You flash between extremes very quickly, moving from ultraromantic to superpassionate in the blink of an eye. Your ideal bed partner is able to see through your changing moods to the warm, caring lover you really are. You respond passionately to an exciting, uninhibited lover who knows how to inflame your libido with long, smoldering kisses and enticing intimate caresses. Sexy teasing and provocative suggestions on both sides add a bit of erotic spice that enhances your lovemaking.

Tips for Your Ideal Lover

Your refined Libra nature never quite overcomes the lustiness of the number 1 vibration that lurks just beneath the surface. There are times when you long to break all the rules with a wild free-for-all that gratifies your most primal urges. A savvy, imaginative bedmate will initiate an occasional bedroom romp to satisfy your deeper cravings.

October 11, *Libra 2*

What Makes You Tick

A genuine romantic, you tend to think in pairs and probably don't feel complete without love in your life, yet you rarely rush into anything. Although you enjoy flirting, you expect to remain loyal and faithful to your mate. However, if the relationship no longer fits your idealized version of what true love should be, the romance could fade.

Between the Sheets

Although you are warm-hearted and sensuous, you may feel a bit hesitant about making the first move. You would rather attract love by turning on the charm, than by pursuing it openly. You know how to create an ambiance for lovemaking that engages all the senses, and your innate gift for artful seduction allows you to express your physical desires in a dignified, refined, and alluring manner. Moreover, your sexual passions seem to surface more readily in beautiful, harmonious surroundings. The wise bedmate knows how to whet your appetite for loving. Kissing and cuddling make you feel secure, and just a hint of your lover's intentions can spark your interest and draw out hidden passions.

Tips for Your Ideal Lover

Sexual arousal may begin with subtle flirting and mildly provocative suggestions. Long, rapturous foreplay or a slow, languid massage can bring all your deep-seated sensuality to the surface. Erotic teasing acts as an enticing turn-on, because it adds to the sexual tension that heightens ecstasy during the actual sex act.

October 12, *Libra 3*

What Makes You Tick

Normally, your head rules your heart, yet in romantic relationships you rarely take time to analyze your feelings. Instead, you tend to jump right in. As long as your chosen mate offers you companionship and plenty of intellectual stimulation, you should get along fine. However, problems may arise if you get bored and decide you want some alone time to pursue your own interests.

Between the Sheets

In your bedroom encounters, good communication is as important to you as romance. As far as you're concerned, an ongoing relationship needs to grow and change. An innovative lover, you get off on trying new moves that can add spice to your sex life. Since giving is as important to you as receiving, you are not content unless you know that your bedmate is also satisfied. You're turned on by the sexual tension that builds while you and your mate are in the company of others, and sharing an evening out puts you in a relaxed mood for the intimacy to follow. Once behind closed doors, pent-up desire surfaces in a blaze of passion.

Tips for Your Ideal Lover

You enjoy being pursued in the game of love and secretly long to be swept off your feet by your bedmate. Sometimes all it takes to trigger your impulsive sexuality is a provocative look from your lover. Spicy pillow talk and whispering sweet nothings in bed engages both your mind and your body.

October 13, *Libra 4*

What Makes You Tick

You want an honest, harmonious, lasting romantic partnership. However, you hold off on making a commitment until you're sure your feelings are reciprocated. Once the commitment is made, you are a faithful, devoted mate or partner. Sensitive and aware of your spouse's needs, you do your best to gratify them. You thrive in an equitable union and expect your significant other to be attentive and loving to you, too.

Between the Sheets

A sophisticated idealist, you bring glamour, elegance, and romance into the bedroom. Your discriminating tastes and gift for artful seduction add a touch of class to your sexual encounters. However, there are aspects of your character that make you seem cooler and more controlled than you actually are. Beneath the refined façade, there is a good deal of smoldering sensuality waiting to be released. Your ideal lover has a skillful touch that draws out all your hidden passions. Work and responsibility can claim so much of your time and energy that there appears to be little left over for loving. But an occasional getaway to someplace serene and beautiful can put you back in the mood.

Tips for Your Ideal Lover

An evening of dining and dancing, followed by a sensuous sexual encounter in a harmonious setting is a certain turn-on. You tend to remember the ambiance and moods evoked during sex rather than the actual technique. A bedroom with a romantic touch makes it a sacred space for rapturous lovemaking.

October 14, *Libra 5*

What Makes You Tick

A loving relationship gives you a sense of completeness; you prefer being half of a couple to living alone. Still you're unlike other Libras because a committed union is not the end-all of your existence. Moreover, your romantic idealism makes it easy for you to fall in love with love. When this happens, you become disillusioned if the reality doesn't live up to your fantasy.

Between the Sheets

You're ardent and loving, yet in control of your emotions. At times, you actually seem to prefer the romantic rituals of love to the unbridled passion of a steamy sexual encounter. Moreover, you're quite capable of putting your own sexual needs on hold to accommodate your lover. Your seduction techniques may be laid-back, but they're determined. You simply prefer allurement to blatant pursuit. The setting has to be right, and nothing that is cheap or tacky can do it for you. Your good taste and refined sensibilities respond a lot more readily in tranquil, harmonious surroundings. Soft music, sensual perfume, and silken fabrics can all serve as seductive additions to your private love nest.

Tips for Your Ideal Lover

Talking during lovemaking comes naturally to you, and expressing your desires through erotic language can be quite thrilling. Your ideal mate creates the right atmosphere for lovemaking by appealing to your appreciation of beauty and romance. Your frenetic energy responds favorably to gentle foreplay that includes a calming aromatic massage and slow, tender kisses.

October 15, *Libra 6*

What Makes You Tick

Since you don't like spending time alone, relationships play a major part in your life. You thrive on the love and approval of your significant other, and a failed romance can upset you to the point of making you ill. Nevertheless, if an intimate union becomes unpleasant, you may not hang around to fix it. Instead, you could go off in search of more congenial company and surroundings.

Between the Sheets

A natural romantic, you're exceedingly idealistic. Your approach to lovemaking is laid-back and alluring. Ambiance and mood are as important to you as sexual technique. You appreciate the rituals of courtship and enjoy being wooed with finesse and sophistication. Affectionate gestures and loving words draw out your hidden passions and get your juices flowing. Although you enjoy being the object of your lover's attention, you're as concerned about gratifying his or her physical desires as your own. Since you are probably an accomplished lover and adept at pleasing your other half, this should present no problem. In return, you like being told that you are admired and appreciated.

Tips for Your Ideal Lover

Your ideal bedmate understands and responds with alacrity to your secret romantic fantasies. A special night of lovemaking in a beautiful, harmonious setting with moonlight and whispered words of love and affection is a genuine turn-on, and the lover who plans an exotic romantic getaway knows the best way to please you.

October 16, *Libra 7*

What Makes You Tick

You don't feel complete without a loving relationship in your life, yet you need to be truly comfortable before you'll commit. Although you want to be loved, you need a partner who understands your moodiness and occasional desire for seclusion. Since you are rather more solitary than other Libra natives, there are times when you feel misunderstood. Moreover, you would rather be on your own than with the wrong person.

Between the Sheets

Affectionate, romantic, and sensitive to the feelings of others, you make a thoroughly generous and thoughtful lover. Even though you may not be the lustiest of bed partners, you always seem to know exactly what your significant other wants, and you are more than happy to provide it. However, you expect to receive a similar amount of attention and consideration in return. Balance is truly important, and you yearn for an intimate relationship with just the right degree of give-and-take. Your artistic temperament and appreciation for beauty and harmony make you particularly susceptible to the various accouterments of old-fashioned courtship. Music, candlelight, perfume, silky sheets, and filmy nightwear turn you on.

Tips for Your Ideal Lover

An imaginative bedmate helps bring out the impulsive side of your nature, and slow, skillful touching and stroking with a feather can raise your sexual temperature to a fever pitch. Adding a light touch to your lovemaking relaxes you, and you enjoy laughing and swapping erotic pillow talk with your lover.

October 17, *Libra 8*

What Makes You Tick

Since Libra is a dual sign, those of you born under the scales of justice can have several distinct sides to your personalities. The problem is that although one part of you may long for love and affection, there is another side to your ambitious nature that is more interested in work and worldly success. Nevertheless, with the right partner, you are generous, caring, protective, and capable of absolute devotion.

Between the Sheets

A romantic idealist with high standards, you have rather lofty ideas about what an intimate union should be. However, when you find the person who suits you, you willingly dedicate yourself to his or her happiness. Smoldering just beneath your serious façade, there is a sizzling sexuality waiting to be released. Your physical desires may run hot and cold, but when they are hot, they really rock. During your wilder bedroom moments, you pull out all the stops and give full expression to your impulses. A well-orchestrated seduction goes a long way toward waking up your libido and making you forget about the work-a-day world and all the stress it engenders.

Tips for Your Ideal Lover

A sexy but elegant striptease or a sensuous massage with aromatic oils triggers the spark that turns you on. An elegantly appointed bedroom with a romantic ambiance is the perfect setting for transcendent lovemaking. Heaven is brought down to earth when your sensuality is heightened by a deep emotional connection with your beloved.

October 18, *Libra* 9

What Makes You Tick

You possess a mysterious, chameleonlike personality that captivates and confuses potential partners. As romantic as you are compassionate, you are quite capable of falling passionately in love with an ideal. Then, when reality refuses to live up to your expectations, you may be deeply disappointed and liable to retreat into yourself. However, your periods of solitude usually don't last long, because you are an exceptionally sociable person.

Between the Sheets

Your attachment to your significant other is intensely emotional, and you regard good sex as a transcendent experience. No one believes in love more than you do, and merging your body with that of your beloved is your idea of heaven on earth. As a thoughtful, caring, and considerate bedmate, you're more interested in pleasing your partner than yourself, and you're happy to go along with whatever your mate wants. In return, you expect lots of attention and affection. In your imagination, you can create a bliss-filled place that is more real than anything around you. A sensitive lover discovers the details of your favorite dream scenarios and acts them out with you.

Tips for Your Ideal Lover

Comfort and luxury in the bedroom tend to draw out your sensuous side, and nothing delights you more than a full-body massage with aromatic oils. Deeply romantic, you prefer a harmonious atmosphere with candlelight and soft music, and fantasy and role-playing games can add all sorts of erotic pleasures to your lovemaking.

October 19, *Libra 1*

What Makes You Tick

You're considerably more passionate than other Libras and probably don't lack for romantic partners. You delight in pleasing your bedmate, and you're generous with compliments and flattering remarks. However, the successful suitor will realize that you also like being flattered and having your ego stroked. In a committed union, you're loyal and caring, but if the spark dies, you may begin looking elsewhere.

Between the Sheets

Establishing a loving and intimate union is genuinely important to you. You believe that if pleasure is to be any good it must be shared, and you are prepared to provide a satisfying romantic experience for yourself and your significant other. Typically, you feel things as readily with your intellect as with your emotions. Thus, a successful relationship requires striking a delicate balance between heart and mind. Even so, you are turned on by rituals of courtship such as words of love whispered in your ear. Subtle perfumes, candles, incense, and aromatic oils arouse all your senses. Perusing erotic drawings and reading provocative literature with your lover inflames your deep-seated desires.

Tips for Your Ideal Lover

Your sensuous nature is full of delightful contradictions, and your ideal mate knows how to switch gears to match your sexual rhythm. With an innovative, imaginative bed partner, your libido ignites like a five-alarm fire. While you are mostly aroused by elegant lovemaking, the occasional no-holds-barred free-for-all satisfies your most primal cravings.

October 20, *Libra 2*

What Makes You Tick

Sexy and affectionate, you're seemingly made for grand passion. However, it is difficult for you to let down your barriers and allow anyone to get close to you. In a romantic union, you are generous and devoted, if somewhat demanding. Casual love affairs hold little interest; you crave the type of caring and devotion that can only be found in a long-term relationship.

Between the Sheets

More intense and emotional than you appear, sex is a transcendent experience. Your magnetic appeal and flair for the dramatic rarely fail to make an impression, and your amazing physical stamina can keep your lover satisfied throughout the night. Sharing intimate pleasures and confidences with your mate refreshes your body and renews your spirit. The bed partner who plies you with sensual delights knows how to turn you on. Your lusty libido responds amorously to the prospect of acting out all your favorite erotic fantasies. With an obliging lover, you glory in the ecstatic gratification of your secret wishes and desires, and then you reply in kind.

Tips for Your Ideal Lover

You respond to a slow, elegant courtship that builds toward a peak of sexual desire. Your ideal lover knows how to bring body and mind together in an artful way. Creating sensuous comfort in your love nest may include music, soft lighting, luxurious fabrics, scented candles, and luscious edible tidbits on the bedside table.

October 21, *Libra 3*

What Makes You Tick

One part of you wants freedom, and the other part wants commitment. As a result, you may go through a string of romances before deciding to settle down with one person. Friendship and mental companionship are as vital to you as love and romance, yet you are an incurable romantic. Even so, once you are seriously involved with a partner, you tend to stay that way. Overall, you make a thoughtful, considerate lover.

Between the Sheets

Your clever mind and fluency with language make you a master of verbal seduction. Your approach to lovemaking is typically lighthearted and playful, and your natural curiosity and diverse interests prompt you to keep trying exciting new things. High drama, however, has little or no place on your sexual agenda, and you avoid intense emotional scenes whenever possible. If you are faced with a choice, you would rather leave than stay around to fight with your significant other. Easily bored by empty glamour, a smart suitor garners your interest with intelligence, wit, and charm. By and large, you prefer an ongoing loving relationship to one-night stands.

Tips for Your Ideal Lover

Spoken sexual enticements turn you on, and a provocative look or a few whispered words of desire speak volumes to you. Since you enjoy being wooed, you respond amorously to spontaneous romantic gestures. The lover who offers you sweet gifts and meaningful compliments knows the way to your heart.

October 22, *Libra 4*

What Makes You Tick

It's important to you that your closest relationship helps you escape the stresses of your everyday world. When you work, you work hard. You also like to party hard and enjoy going out. However, once you're home, you want to be able to close the door and relax with your partner in a harmonious atmosphere of love and romance.

Between the Sheets

In your private world for two, passion and romance tend to exist side by side. You love flirting with your significant other, and provocative teasing helps you keep your union fresh and alive. You thoroughly enjoy the mating game, and every aspect of a well-executed session of foreplay excites you. You are an intense and passionate lover and something of a sexual explorer. Since you believe that loving is about making the other person happy, giving and sharing in the bedroom and elsewhere is very important. You expect equal consideration in return, and the mate who gives back with similar thoughtfulness will sustain your affection and devotion.

Tips for Your Ideal Lover

A well-orchestrated seduction turns you on. From an intimate striptease or flavored sensual oils to a teasing feather, you are open to any bedroom move that enhances your sensual experience. For you, the undertow of desire is already there, and skillful touching and stroking raises your sexual temperature to a fever pitch.

October 23, *Scorpio 5*

What Makes You Tick

Although you love with your whole heart, it may be difficult for you to give all of yourself to another person. Even in your most intimate moments, you hold something in reserve. You think long and hard before entering into a committed union, and when you do, you expect absolute loyalty and fidelity from your partner. While you are devoted, and passionate, you can also be jealous and controlling.

Between the Sheets

The amorous intensity of your Scorpio nature smolders just beneath the surface of a cool outer facade. On one level, your blood boils for an all-consuming passion that takes your breath away. Yet another part of you yearns for a mental connection. In private, you are intrigued by anything that bursts the barriers of sexual propriety. An enticing, seductive lover, you know all the best ways to arouse your bedmate. The very idea that your friends might be scandalized if they knew what you were doing behind closed doors actually turns you on. Erotic experimentation is your forte, and you want a lover who knows how to gratify your unconventional side.

Tips for Your Ideal Lover

When you find a bed partner you love and trust, your red-hot libido inflames your passion and keeps the fires stoked. You enjoy midnight or early-morning lovemaking, and a spontaneous quickie when you wake up can provide all the impetus you need to keep going throughout the day.

October 24, *Scorpio 6*

What Makes You Tick

Since your capacity for solitude is low, an intimate relationship is pretty much a necessity. Although you yearn for a close, permanent union, you need to feel comfortable and in control before committing yourself. With your romantic and sensual nature, you have a lot to give in a loving relationship. Although your surface personality is easier going than most other scorpions, your inner toughness swiftly surfaces when challenged.

Between the Sheets

You expect a great deal from your significant other, and he or she could find your demands somewhat overwhelming. Still you tend to be more sensitive to your mate's needs and desires than is typical of other members of your Scorpio Sun sign. Since romance and sex are integrally intertwined in your psyche, you use your body and mind together in an artful way. Moreover, your particular combination of passion and romantic idealism makes you an extremely creative lover. Intuitive and imaginative, you always seem to know exactly what your partner wants, and you are more than capable of providing it. You find the glamour of romance quite intoxicating; you prefer a sophisticated, well-orchestrated seduction to a carnal free-for-all.

Tips for Your Ideal Lover

You appreciate a bedroom companion who takes the trouble to create a romantic setting for lovemaking. On the sensual side, reading together from sexy books can lead to refreshing sexual experimentation. Anything enticing from a sensuous massage with flavored oils, to teasing feathers, to a slow, sultry striptease, turns you on.

October 25, *Scorpio 7*

What Makes You Tick

You may idealize your romantic partner and place him or her on a pedestal. Then if the relationship turns sour, you are likely hurt and disappointed. Despite being perfectly capable of loyalty and lasting affection, you can be rather moody and you require occasional periods of tranquility and solitude. At times, you may feel pulled between your inclination toward fidelity and your naturally flirtatious, independent spirit.

Between the Sheets

Initially, you may conceal your hot-blooded sexuality and emotional vulnerability behind a mask of cool detachment. An air of mystery and secrecy guards your feelings, at least until you are sure that you can trust your mate completely. Eventually, you will begin to reveal the true depth and breadth of your ardent nature. Once this happens, you're able to surrender totally to the smoldering desires welling up inside you. Your appetite for sensual pleasure grows more insistent as your comfort level increases. Sharing your lustiest sexual fantasies can provide you with an imaginative outlet for your volatile inner passions, and just following the whims of your libido will take you to the edge of intense sensual pleasure.

Tips for Your Ideal Lover

With an imaginative, free-spirited bed partner, erotic dancing becomes delicious foreplay. An aromatherapy massage can be relaxing and arousing as you respond eagerly to teasing, touching, and caressing of all your erogenous zones. You thrive when your intense emotions find easy expression and sexual release makes you feel reborn.

October 26, *Scorpio 8*

What Makes You Tick

Playing the field does not really interest you, because you are looking for a long-term partner who takes love as seriously as you do. Nevertheless, when you find your soul mate, the intensely private portion of your superemotional nature can make it difficult for you to reveal your true feelings. Moreover, insecurity or lack of trust could cause you to act in a jealous, possessive, or controlling manner.

Between the Sheets

Your libido is white-hot, yet your courtship style is careful and cautious. Although you feel things deeply, a lack of trust may cause you to hide your true feelings behind a mask of nonchalance. However, once you find the love you seek, you are anything but shy. You expect to be the one calling the shots. Power and success act as aphrodisiacs for you, and you are drawn to potential partners who are as ambitious and capable as you are. A born sensualist, your sexuality comes to life behind closed doors. Alone with your mate, you feel free to let down your guard, set aside daily cares, and surrender to your physical desires.

Tips for Your Ideal Lover

With your ideal mate, you shed your cautious exterior and reveal the deeply passionate side of your love nature. Nevertheless, you refuse to be rushed during sex, and a smart lover eases you into moments of relaxed sensuality. Erotic play and sensual massage oils add spice to your lovemaking.

October 27, *Scorpio 9*

What Makes You Tick

Instinct and intuition provide you with an eerie insight into people that borders on the psychic. You're sincerely devoted to those you love, and if necessary you're prepared to sacrifice everything for them. In an intimate union, you are more likely than other Scorpio natives to idealize your partner. If disappointment forces you to face up to a negative reality, however, you may be left heartbroken.

Between the Sheets

At times, the diverse facets of your character seem to conflict. Your idealistic side seeks perfection from both your partner and yourself. However, your devilish part is attracted to mysteries and longs to unravel all the secrets of a dark and dangerous lover. Moreover, your craving for a sense of togetherness can make you seem emotionally needy. Your colorful, chameleonlike moodiness notwithstanding, between the sheets you are a sensual, passionate, considerate lover, dedicated to making your bedmate's wildest dreams come true. Moreover, your passion and enthusiasm during intimate moments tend to be contagious. Acting out your most exotic secret fantasies, together with your bed partner, is usually all it takes to turn on both of you.

Tips for Your Ideal Lover

Your perfect mate possesses an almost-telepathic sense of how to arouse you; once sparked, your tireless libido spurs you on to ecstatic lovemaking. Slow massage, leading to delicate teasing of your erogenous zones, builds an aching sexual tension, causing the passions simmering beneath the surface to boil over in frenzied excitement.

October 28, *Scorpio 1*

What Makes You Tick

In an intimate union, you're loving and passionate but also quite demanding and not very easy to please. Although basically independent and self-contained, you prefer committed relationships to casual ones, and your romances tend to be serious and long lasting. A true Scorpio, you are a strongly sexed, somewhat controlling lover. Nevertheless, you are intensely loyal, and when you allow yourself to get deeply involved, you make a steadfast, loving, and reliable spouse.

Between the Sheets

Few can match either your amazing sexual prowess or your powerful intensity in the bedroom. For you, love and sex need to be all or nothing. Once aroused, your lusty libido shoots off fiery sparks of desire. Typically, your unflagging physical stamina leads to long nights (and days) of ecstatic lovemaking. Your ideal bed partner must be capable of matching your reckless abandon, and the lover who cannot equal your sexual vigor could end up out in the cold. Since you are considerably more sexy and passionate than romantic, it takes physical stimulation and erotic excitement to really turn you on. You yearn for an enthusiastic partner, who is willing to try just about anything in bed.

Tips for Your Ideal Lover

A playful romp between the sheets releases pent-up aggressions and puts you in the mood for even more potent lovemaking. Your idea of a good time is an evening of breathless adventure, leading to passionate foreplay, and culminating in a meteoric shower of sexual fireworks.

October 29, *Scorpio 2*

What Makes You Tick

At parties, you're charming, but in an intimate union, you have difficulty expressing your true feelings. Since you're naturally possessive, your struggle for dominance places a severe strain on romantic alliances. Moreover, you have an all-or-nothing attitude that can make your partner feel hemmed in. Nevertheless, intimacy is important to you, and you're more than willing to work with your mate to make the relationship successful.

Between the Sheets

Determined to make your beloved the center of your universe, you're a considerate lover who considers your partner's needs as important as your own. You love unconditionally, so commitment and security are truly important. Only when you feel safe, can you let yourself go and open up completely to your spouse. Sensuality is your middle name, and you long for a relationship that involves a great deal of touching and caressing. For you, sex plays a primary role in any intimate union. The bed partner who projects an air of mystery intrigues you, and you thrive during those moments you and your mate spend locked away from the world in your love nest.

Tips for Your Ideal Lover

You respond sensually to deliberately provocative situations and you may become sexually aroused when viewing a romantic or erotic movie with your bedmate. Discussing the dynamics of the onscreen character's sexual interactions is an enticing and imaginative way to get you both in the mood for some exquisitely hot hanky-panky of your own.

October 30, *Scorpio 3*

What Makes You Tick

In a loving union, you're torn between your inclination toward fidelity, and the carefree flirtatiousness of your independent spirit. In a close relationship, the paradoxes of your personality puzzle even your staunchest admirer. Although you need the fulfillment of a deep, transforming emotional involvement, you resist commitment for as long as possible. You take your time before you settle down, but once you do, you stick around.

Between the Sheets

In the bedroom and elsewhere, you bring the shrewdness of a detective to your quest to understand what makes people tick. You use this skill to best advantage when aiming to please your mate. No desire is safe from your intensive probing. You don't give up until you've uncovered every last detail of your partner's dreams and wishes. Then, of course, you do everything possible to turn those erotic dreams into a reality you can enjoy together. Your mind is as sensitive an erogenous zone as the more obvious parts of your body, and your ideal lover dazzles you mentally as well as physically. Provocative verbal suggestions excite you as much as enticing caresses.

Tips for Your Ideal Lover

You're turned on by an alluring suitor who begins with sultry pillow talk and progresses to urgent, fiery passion. More than anything, you crave variety in your lovemaking and even a hint of dull routine puts you off. Erotic play and sensuous massages with aromatic oils can add spice to your bedroom activities.

October 31, *Scorpio 4*

What Makes You Tick

In relationships, your tendency is to follow your instincts and emotions rather than reason or logic. Due to the complexity of your inner nature, you actually seem to thrive on the mystery and intrigue of a life lived on the edge. In a committed union, you are sexy, ardent, affectionate, and more than a little possessive. Although you crave love, you are deathly afraid of exposing your inherent vulnerability.

Between the Sheets

You are passionate, sensual, romantic, and demanding. When you find the person you want, you will stop at nothing to make the relationship a reality. Once smitten, you are a sexual dynamo and quite capable of making every close encounter amazing and memorable. Your ideal partner is the one you believe worthy of your trust, someone in whom you can confide and share your secrets. A laid-back mate is not for you. You long to be swept away on a tidal wave of passion, and an ardent display of sexual desire turns you on. You're especially responsive to a commanding lover who swoops right in and assumes control in the bedroom.

Tips for Your Ideal Lover

You come alive in the arms of your lover where the catharsis of lovemaking opens you to deeper intimacies. Experimenting with exotic sexual techniques turns you on and helps keep your lovemaking fresh and exciting. Exchanging erotic stories with your significant other can serve as tantalizing foreplay for a night of heightened sensuality.

November 1, *Scorpio 1*

What Makes You Tick

In a close relationship, you are loyal and loving. However, you need to feel secure in the belief that you are in charge of your own destiny. You have a lot to give, but you expect to get as much in return. You long to establish a loving relationship, and when you find it, you pledge undying devotion. Nevertheless, a potential life partner may find your spurts of jealousy a bit overwhelming.

Between the Sheets

A highly sexed, demanding lover, your strong physical vitality thrives on high-energy lovemaking. Your obsessive, all-or-nothing approach to bedroom activities is likely to captivate some and repel others, and your lusty libido requires a nimble partner. An intimate relationship that is overly peaceful bores you out of your skull, and when you are deeply in love, your ardent intensity can take your partner's breath away. In addition, the darker side of human nature fascinates you, and you require lots of deep drama in bed to keep your sexual batteries going at full tilt. Since it takes a great deal of erotic stimulation to hold your interest, acting out your fantasies provides a creative outlet for your passions.

Tips for Your Ideal Lover

The ardent lover who exudes an air of mystery and a hint of danger has the edge with you. Smoldering kisses and caresses are your trademark, and slow, sensuous teasing of your erogenous zones can stir up a frenzy of sexual excitement that leads to hours of passionate, ecstatic lovemaking.

November 2, *Scorpio 2*

What Makes You Tick

You're as stubborn on the inside as you are pleasant and charming on the outside. Most of your actions are determined by your highly charged emotional nature, and your ongoing struggle for dominance can place a severe strain on your love life. Eminently dependable, you can be relied on to look after and provide for your beloved. However, so much caring can make you seem overly concerned and jealous or possessive.

Between the Sheets

With your lusty libido, sex is rarely far from your thoughts. However, you're searching for more than just physical release. You regard lovemaking as an emotionally transcendent experience, and casual affairs hold little interest for you. What you really want is to merge with your lover in an intimate bond of total union. Once aroused, your sensual, tempestuous lovemaking makes for steamy moments of intense sexual pleasure. Moreover, your vitality and enthusiasm can keep you going throughout the night. Secrets, mysteries, and erotic taboos of all kinds fascinate you. You willingly fall under the mesmerizing spell of the bed partner who intrigues you with smoldering charm and sultry moves that hint of inconceivably sexy, sensuous delights.

Tips for Your Ideal Lover

Your fascination with the darker side of sex can lead you to explore all sorts of exotic erotic activities, and an uninhibited, open-minded bed partner suits you to a T. However, the enigmatic lover with the deep penetrating gaze promising hidden secrets is the one most likely to capture your imagination.

November 3, *Scorpio 3*

What Makes You Tick

In an intimate union, you're ardent, demanding, and protective of your beloved. However, there's a paradoxical aspect to your nature that puzzles those close to you. You may find yourself torn between contradictory messages you receive from your head and your heart. On one hand, you yearn for the emotional fulfillment of a committed relationship. On the other, you crave variety and change and enjoy playing the field.

Between the Sheets

As much of a chameleon in bed as elsewhere, you're an odd combination of passion and intellect. Despite your hearty sexual appetite, you require mental titillation along with physical release, and a dazzlingly brilliant mind can be as much of a turn-on as pure animal magnetism. At times, you come off as playful and lighthearted, yet at other times, nothing seems to matter except your intense sexuality and desire for physical gratification. Some nights, your bedmate is treated to little more than good conversation. However, on many other nights, he or she is provided with ample evidence of your amazing sexual prowess and expertise. Either way, no partner of yours has to worry about boredom in the bedroom.

Tips for Your Ideal Lover

You are as likely to be aroused physically by witty pillow talk and provocative erotic suggestions as by kisses and caresses. Your ideal bed partner entices you with spicy verbal banter and innovative ideas for erotic fun and games. Exchanging sexy stories can serve as foreplay for a night of sultry sensuality.

November 4, *Scorpio 4*

What Makes You Tick

Although you feel things very deeply, sometimes you come off as distant and mysterious. This is particularly true if lack of trust causes you to hide your vulnerability under a mask of feigned nonchalance. Even so, with your wit, intelligence, and passion, you attract suitors like a magnet. In an intimate union, you are loving and affectionate; if and when your mood changes, your attention can begin to wander.

Between the Sheets

You put up emotional barriers that few are able to cross, and despite your ardent nature, jealousy and possessiveness can make close relationships difficult for you to sustain. You tend to keep your emotions under wraps until you're sure they are reciprocated, so a potential lover may have a hard time gauging your true feelings. Once you're sure your amorous intentions are shared, you delight your mate with many fantastic nights of delicious lovemaking. In the privacy of the bedroom, pleasing your partner comes easily. A born sensualist, you're readily aroused by the feathery touches and tender caresses from your lover's skillful hands.

Tips for Your Ideal Lover

Sharing sensual pleasures behind closed doors turns you on, and the lover who approaches slowly and takes the time to draw out your hidden passions has the edge. An erotic massage with aromatherapy oils soothes your jangled nerves and also serves as stimulating foreplay for a night of lovemaking.

November 5, *Scorpio 5*

What Makes You Tick

You are passionate and rarely indifferent or indecisive; once you make up your mind, it is almost impossible to change it. Although you crave sexual fulfillment as much as other Scorpios, you really want conversation as well. At times you may feel torn between a desire for freedom and a yearning for a committed relationship. However, once you find Mr. or Ms. Right, you willingly pledge undying devotion.

Between the Sheets

Even though you think sex is meant to be a transcendent experience, your bedroom mood tends to swing between hot and cold. You're more inclined to surrender to your primal desires when you feel relaxed and comfortable with your bedmate. Once trust is established, your lusty libido keeps the erotic fire burning. You have an intuitive understanding of what your partner likes in bed, and you're happy to provide it. Taking reckless chances with your bedmate turns your wildest fantasies into spicy realities, and the thrill increases in proportion to the likelihood of being interrupted by someone when you two are in a compromising position.

Tips for Your Ideal Lover

When you are feeling lustful, your sexual intensity has a powerful undertow. You enjoy a lover who will not hesitate to initiate sex during the night or early in the morning. One sultry glance is usually enough to trigger your desire for an amorous quickie.

November 6, *Scorpio 6*

What Makes You Tick

You are more partnership oriented than other Scorpios. While you may not live for love alone, it's certainly at the top of your list. Despite your Sun sign's sexy image, you are extremely discriminating when it comes to getting seriously involved. Nevertheless, when you find the one you consider your soul mate, you willingly pledge your undying devotion.

Between the Sheets

Above all, you crave intensity in your most intimate relationship. Although you may try to conceal your true feelings, your strong sexual appetite tends to bring your extreme emotions to the surface. With the right person, you are sensuous, daring, and sexually accommodating. Your love deepens when you know that you are truly cared about, and as trust develops between you and your significant other, the sex gets better and better. Eager to explore all the mysteries of sexuality, you will try almost anything to enhance the experience, and your clever mind conjures artful ways of adding exotic ambiance to your bedroom setting. However, if your love is rejected, or you feel betrayed, you're not likely to accept defeat graciously.

Tips for Your Ideal Lover

Your ideal mate matches your sexual impulses and enjoys spicing things up with seduction and role-playing. From sex toys to flavored sensual oils and teasing feathers, you're always open to the idea of using pleasure-enhancing props, and you respond hungrily to the delights of erotic touch and oral stimulation.

November 7, *Scorpio 7*

What Makes You Tick

Although a loving relationship is important to you, you would rather be alone than subjugated to another person's will. Inherently secretive, you have your own way of doing things. Much of the time, even those close to you are unaware of what's actually going on beneath your composed façade. Even so, you're capable of long-lasting affection, and when you make a firm commitment, you stick to it.

Between the Sheets

Despite Scorpio's reputation for smoldering sexuality, you can sublimate your strong physical desires when it suits your purposes. You understand the power wielded by your magnetic sex appeal, but you also understand the power of celibacy. Since your attitude regarding intimate relationships tends to be all or nothing, you may alternate between frequent sexual activity and abstinence. Although not especially romantic, you are a passionate, agile lover and eminently capable of providing your bedmate with great deal of physical pleasure. Your fascination with sex inspires numerous exotic fantasies of sultry seductions. Acting out these scenarios with your lover provides a creative outlet for your powerful imagination, in addition to being a guaranteed turn-on.

Tips for Your Ideal Lover

Easily intimidated lovers need not apply. The spouse who instinctively understands your many moods and is not bothered by your jealous nature has the edge. Your ideal mate can enjoy your powerful sexuality without being scared off or swallowed up by its intensity.

November 8, *Scorpio 8*

What Makes You Tick

Although you are an exceedingly sensual lover, you have a rather paranoid aspect to your personality that makes it hard for you to reveal your deepest feelings. When you do commit to someone, you are generous and affectionate. Nevertheless, you are not easy to live with, and lack of trust can cause you to act in a possessive, controlling manner. Once your craving for emotional security is satisfied, you make a loyal, devoted partner.

Between the Sheets

Even though you seem rather distant and mysterious, your deeply passionate nature and obvious sex appeal attracts suitors like a magnet. Power is the name of the game. You have to be the one calling the shots, inside the bedroom and everywhere else. Eventually, however, you must realize that you can't micromanage your feelings and emotions. With a partner who is content to go with the flow, you are an ardent, considerate, and extremely skillful lover. Success oriented and hardworking, you channel most of your passionate intensity into achieving your worldly goals. At home, however, you shed your professional reserve and revel in the deeply sensual side of your nature.

Tips for Your Ideal Lover

Although you refuse to be dominated in any way, you can be enticed into lovemaking by a bedmate who understands your deep-seated need for the dramatic catharsis of total intimacy. Moreover, a lusty bedroom romp with your beloved restores your vital energies and makes you feel alive.

November 9, *Scorpio 9*

What Makes You Tick

You're strongly sexed and extremely romantic, and love and intimacy play a very important role in your life. Since you're among the most sensitive members of the zodiacal family, your feelings determine everything you do, and your emotional nature is so complex that your love life can be as turbulent as a soap opera. You may display a poignant vulnerability one moment and become possessive and demanding the next.

Between the Sheets

You are a sensual, passionate, considerate lover. Yet despite your strong libido, physical satisfaction is not the primary focus of your lovemaking. You crave a spiritual union that connects you to your partner body and soul. Since you are searching for the complete soul-mate experience with your one true love, nothing less will suffice. However, while your angelic side is seeking the ultimate in perfection, the devilish part of you longs to unravel the mysteries of a dark and dangerous love. Predisposed to place your partner on a pedestal, you could be left heartbroken if he or she disappoints you.

Tips for Your Ideal Lover

You possess an exceedingly intense erotic imagination and an exceptional flair for the dramatic that gives you a talent for role-playing games and acting out fantasies. With an uninhibited bedmate who is creative enough to devise innovative and exotic pleasures, you raise the sex act to an art form.

November 10, *Scorpio 1*

What Makes You Tick

As a lover, you're devoted, passionate, and affectionate but also aggressive, demanding, and controlling. When you find someone that suits you, you pursue the object of your affection with unremitting zeal, and you overcome obstacles to your success by barreling through them. Because you prefer committed relationships to casual ones, your romances tend to be serious and long lasting. However, you won't commit unless you are convinced the person is right for you.

Between the Sheets

A bold bedmate, you blend determination with sultry erotic seduction. Your amorous intensity smolders beneath the surface, but its irresistible force is felt by your partner as strongly as a physical tug. When you project your magnetic charm, few can match your ability to capture and hold your mate's total attention. The passionate lovemaking you engage in requires a vital bed partner with unflagging physical stamina. Your enticing athletic foreplay ultimately culminates in a climactic shower of exploding sexual fireworks. Tempestuous lovemaking channels your intense emotions as it satisfies your lusty libido, and the lover capable of matching your passion and sensuality is the one who holds the key to turning you on.

Tips for Your Ideal Lover

Your sexy romps typically include playful struggles for power and control that help you release tension and pent-up aggression. For you, the mate who provides lots of excitement and stimulation is a sure-fire turn-on. Your ideal partner knows how to stand up to your unpredictable volatility without extinguishing your sexual fervor.

November 11, *Scorpio 2*

What Makes You Tick

A generous lover, you know intuitively what your partner wants and you are more than willing to provide it. In an intimate union, you are ardent, affectionate, generous, and totally devoted to your beloved. Since you are the quintessential immovable force, you need to learn to curb the controlling aspects of your nature. Nevertheless, when you set your mind to something or someone, nothing can divert you from your chosen course.

Between the Sheets

When you find the person you want, you go after him or her with single-minded determination. Once involved, you crave lots of action and excitement in the bedroom. However, your all-consuming approach to relationships can make your romantic partner feel hemmed in and resentful. Affectionate and physically expressive, you thrive in a passionate union, and lovemaking is rarely far from your thoughts. You have an innate understanding of the sexual side of life, and an approach that is direct and uncomplicated. Although it doesn't take much to entice you, your partner's gratification is as important to you as your own. The right mate knows how to satisfy your cravings for affection and the joys of tactile sensuality.

Tips for Your Ideal Lover

Given the opportunity, you will dive right in and sample all the delights of earthy pleasure. Relaxing in an exotic atmosphere of luxuriant comfort causes you to open yourself up to sensuous exploration, and touching and stroking makes your body shiver in delicious anticipation of the satisfaction to follow.

November 12, *Scorpio 3*

What Makes You Tick

You are versatile and quick-witted; people are attracted to your keen intelligence and magnetic personality. In romantic relationships, the paradoxes in your nature may puzzle even those closest to you. Although you may long for the emotional security of a permanent union, your flirtatious, independent side craves variety and change. Consequently, you may not be as quick to settle down as other members of your Sun sign.

Between the Sheets

Even though you truly enjoy playing the field, once you decide to make a permanent commitment, you stick with it. Between the sheets, you are innovative, creative, and imaginative but also passionate and demanding. Your uniquely curious mind requires freedom and excitement, and you resist being tied down to anything approaching routine. Playfulness in bed gives your sexual technique a delightful spontaneity. Variety spices up your love life, and your busy mind works overtime thinking up new ways to arouse and please your partner. First, you entice your lover with provocative verbal suggestions and then follow up with the real thing. Bedtime gossip about other people's amorous exploits fascinates you; just talking about it turns you on.

Tips for Your Ideal Lover

Trying out new sex toys with your bedmate satisfies your curiosity and enhances your bedroom experience. Your decidedly witty and eminently naughty observations about other people's love lives can add spice to your own. Taboo practices intrigue you, and with the right partner, you enjoy exploring the darker side of sexuality.

November 13, *Scorpio 4*

What Makes You Tick

You're sensitive but passionate, and your carefully concealed intensity usually manages to confound potential suitors. You're uninterested in meaningless sexual interludes. Instead, you need a partner who returns your love in equal measure. Love is a serious business where the words casual and sex don't appear in the same sentence. However, a close union with you may not be easy, because you can be controlling and possessive.

Between the Sheets

As a lover, you're sensual, demanding, and caring, sometimes to the point of obsession. Once you find a partner whose desire for intimacy matches your own, you'll do everything you possibly can to make love last a lifetime. Your libido may be red-hot, but your courtship style is careful and cautious. You like to think things over carefully before settling into a serious romantic alliance. However, once you find the love you seek, you're anything but shy. You expect to be the one calling the shots, in and out of the bedroom. Power and success act as aphrodisiacs, and you are drawn to those who are as ambitious and capable as you.

Tips for Your Ideal Lover

A born sensualist, your ardent nature comes to life behind closed doors. Alone with your mate, you let down your guard and surrender to your erotic desires. Your ideal lover is the one you deem worthy of your love and trust; someone in whom you can confide and share your sexual fantasies and hidden secrets.

November 14, *Scorpio 5*

What Makes You Tick

Even though you appear cool and detached on the outside, your intense emotions are smoldering just beneath the surface and they won't lie dormant for long. In romantic situations, you're passionate but also controlling and possessive. There is a secretive, mysterious aspect to your character that makes intimacy more difficult than it needs to be, and fear of being misunderstood can cause you to shy away from commitment altogether.

Between the Sheets

You are an inventive and enthusiastic lover. Even so, there are times when you feel conflicted between your intellectual awareness of sex as a purely physical act, and your emotional ideal of lovemaking as a transcendent union. As a result, you may be wildly passionate one day and seemingly disinterested the next, and your frequent mood swings are likely to confuse and confound the mere mortal who shares your bed. Although you yearn for the emotional fulfillment of a deep, transforming long-term affair, you also crave variety and change. Moreover, while demanding independence for yourself, you can be jealous and controlling where your significant other is concerned.

Tips for Your Ideal Lover

Your ideal bedmate enjoys bursting through barriers of sexual propriety to explore the limits of eroticism. Taboo areas of sexuality intrigue you, and emotional power games turn you on. Behind closed doors, you happily surrender to your primal desires, and acting out shared sexual fantasies provides a creative outlet for your lusty libido.

November 15, *Scorpio 6*

What Makes You Tick

Your unique blend of passion and detachment presents an intriguing challenge to potential partners who are trying to figure you out. Sometimes you're not sure what you want; at other times, you're jealous and possessive. However, the glamorous aura of sex and romance you project is utterly captivating and draws suitors to you. Yet love is serious business, and you never take relationships lightly.

Between the Sheets

You're an irresistible combination of passion and romance. The glamour of courtship intoxicates you, and you're forever conjuring up new ways to add romantic touches to your ardent lovemaking. Despite your sexy image, you're actually quite discriminating when it comes to getting seriously involved. Nevertheless, when you find the one you consider your soul mate, you willingly pledge undying devotion. Since your love is limitless, your commitment may turn into obsession. If your love and devotion are rejected, you feel betrayed, and you're not likely to sit back and accept defeat graciously The burning love you once felt will turn to ice in the blink of an eye.

Tips for Your Ideal Lover

Red-hot passion and old-fashioned romance make an irresistible combination. Your amorous nature thrives on the rituals of traditional courtship, and sensuous accouterments such as sultry nightwear, silky sheets, and soft lighting excite you. With the stage set, you readily indulge in the many erotic pleasures love has to offer.

November 16, *Scorpio 7*

What Makes You Tick

You're generous and exceedingly loyal in love, but you refuse to be subjugated to another person's whims. As a result, a romantic alliance with you isn't easy. Nevertheless, few people are capable of generating the passion and excitement that come so naturally to you. You may laugh off your own possessiveness, yet you demand absolute fidelity from your mate, and if you don't get it, you could leave.

Between the Sheets

An agile, accomplished lover, you possess an almost-psychic intuition that allows you to tap into your bedmate's deepest needs and desires and satisfy them. However, you are interested in more than just the physical side of love-making. You regard the sex act as a transcendent experience, one that allows you to merge with your partner on all levels: physical, mental, emotional, and spiritual. Despite Scorpio's reputation for smoldering sexuality, you're quite capable of sublimating your strong physical desires if and when it suits your purposes. In the bedroom and elsewhere, you have your own way of doing things. While you realize the potency of your magnetic sex appeal, you also understand the power of celibacy.

Tips for Your Ideal Lover

You enjoy mystery and secrecy and may be drawn to a slightly dangerous lover. You thrive when your intense emotions find expression, and the resulting physical release can make you feel reborn. Sexual arousal may begin with an erotic body massage and delicate teasing of your erogenous zones that makes you tingle with anticipation.

November 17, *Scorpio 8*

What Makes You Tick

Your hallmarks are loyalty and dependability. You don't wear your heart on your sleeve, and it takes a very special person to penetrate your cool exterior. However, once Mr. or Ms. Right has won your heart, you make a loving, steadfast, and reliable partner. Although you love deeply, it is often difficult for you to express your feelings in words, and you usually prefer letting your actions speak for themselves.

Between the Sheets

You are something of a sexual dynamo, with an exceedingly lusty libido. Since you view sex as a means of merging two souls, you aim to possess your lover body and soul. In the bedroom and elsewhere, you enjoy being in control, and the bedmate who understands and accepts this has an edge. While chemistry is important, you need to feel connected to your significant other emotionally and intellectually as well as physically. You expect a lot from your spouse, but you're willing to give a lot in return. Above all, you require stability in an intimate union, and once trust has been established, you expect your romance to endure forever.

Tips for Your Ideal Lover

An inventive lover, you're always eager to try different techniques to excite and please your mate. A partner who is as enthusiastic and willing to make love anytime suits you best. Alone with your lover, you become aroused very quickly, and ardent kisses and passionate embraces drive you wild with desire.

November 18, *Scorpio 9*

What Makes You Tick

You're highly sexed and exceedingly romantic, and love and intimacy play a major role in your life. Your emotional nature is so complex that your love life is often as turbulent as it is passionate and intense. In the bedroom and elsewhere, everything you do is guided by feelings and intuition. Consequently, you may display poignant vulnerability one moment and become quite possessive, demanding, or jealous the next.

Between the Sheets

Your dreamy demeanor and soothing approach to lovemaking do little to hide your steamy sexuality. However, the passions simmering beneath the surface are driven as much by emotional needs as physical ones. You crave the complete package with your soul mate, and nothing less will suffice. When you find it, you willingly surrender to the ardor that consumes and transforms both you and your partner. Since you like unraveling mysteries, you may be drawn to a secretive and slightly dangerous lover. You are turned on by the idea of exploring some of the darker aspects of your own sexuality. With just one sultry glance from alluring bedroom eyes, you can barely wait to dive into precarious waters.

Tips for Your Ideal Lover

Romantic fantasy tends to play a large part in your sex life, and the ebb and flow of your emotions finds a satisfying outlet in erotic role-playing games. Your ideal mate uses his or her innate creativity to devise all sorts of exotic pleasures as an escape from boring routine lovemaking.

November 19, *Scorpio 1*

What Makes You Tick

In an intimate union, you are loving and ardent but also demanding and not easily pleased. Because you prefer committed relationships, your romances tend to be serious and long lasting. As a member of one of the most passionate Sun signs, you are a strongly sexed, somewhat controlling lover. Nevertheless, you are intensely loyal, and once you get deeply involved, you make a steadfast, reliable mate.

Between the Sheets

Your charm and magnetic personality make you a much sought-after bed partner. Few can match either your amazing sexual prowess or your powerful intensity in the bedroom. For you, love and sex need to be all or nothing. Once aroused, your lusty libido is on fire, and your unflagging physical stamina can lead to long days and nights of thrilling lovemaking. Your ideal lover is innovative and totally capable of matching your reckless abandon. Your bedmate must equal your extraordinary sexual vigor or end up out in the cold. Since you are considerably more sexy and passionate than romantic, it takes physical stimulation and erotic excitement to really turn you on.

Tips for Your Ideal Lover

Your hair-trigger libido and amazing sexual stamina make you yearn for an equally enthusiastic, aggressive bed partner who is willing to try just about anything that pleases you both. A playful bedroom romp can release your pent-up desires and put you in the mood for even more potent lovemaking.

November 20, *Scorpio 2*

What Makes You Tick

You're inherently dependable and can be always relied on to look after your beloved. However, the price you extract for caring reveals excessive concern and possessiveness that can make your partner feel overwhelmed. This tendency to hold on too tightly makes living with you rather difficult. You think you want loyalty and devotion from your mate, but you're actually seeking concrete proof of his or her love for you.

Between the Sheets

With your lusty libido, sex is rarely far from your thoughts. Even so, you regard lovemaking as a transcendent experience, and casual affairs hold little interest. What you really want is to merge with your lover on all levels. Once aroused, your sensual, tempestuous lovemaking makes for steamy moments of intense sexual pleasure. Moreover, your vitality and enthusiasm can keep you going throughout the night. You are, however, as stubborn and single-minded on the inside as you are pleasant and charming on the outside. Most of your actions are determined by your highly charged emotional nature, and your ongoing struggle for dominance and control can place a severe strain on a loving union.

Tips for Your Ideal Lover

Secrets, mysteries, and taboos of all kinds fascinate you. The enigmatic lover with the penetrating gaze will most likely capture your imagination. You willingly fall under the mesmerizing spell of the partner who intrigues you with smoldering charm and sultry moves that hint of inconceivably sexy, sensuous delights.

November 21, *Scorpio 3*

What Makes You Tick

You are less intense and more able to rationalize your emotions than other scorpions, and your unique mix of insight and humor helps you get along with all kinds of people. In close relationships, you may find yourself torn between your love of personal freedom and the inclination to be possessive of your beloved. One part of you longs for emotional security, while another part craves freedom, excitement, and change.

Between the Sheets

You approach your love life with all the zeal of a detective investigating an important case. An accomplished listener as well as a great talker, you channel as much of your bedroom energy into intellectual communication as you do into physical contact. Using your intuitive powers, you probe your lover's psyche for information that can clue you in to his or her sexual predilections. In addition, every inch of your mate's body becomes the subject of your sensual inquiries. Your lovemaking may begin with slow, sensitive touching and stroking, but once your passions are let loose, you display a robust libido that grows more urgent and demanding as you move toward culmination.

Tips for Your Ideal Lover

You respond enthusiastically to a partner who provokes you with enticing suggestions, and sharing erotic discoveries and trying out new positions with your lover turns you on. Since your mind is your primary erogenous zone, you like discussing what you enjoy doing in bed, and teasing games with sex toys provide steamy foreplay for your lovemaking.

November 22, *Sagittarius 4*

What Makes You Tick

In social situations, your humor and apparently easygoing nature make you a charming companion. Whereas casual friends may see only your sunny side, those who know you well are aware of your hidden depths. You're pulled between a desire for independence and the security of committed intimate union. Since you look before you leap more readily than most other archers, you prefer to weigh all your options before getting involved in a romantic alliance.

Between the Sheets

While you don't always show it, you have a serious side, especially where relationships are concerned. Torn between inherent caution and a taste for erotic thrills, you are hesitant yet eager to expand your sensual horizons by exploring all sorts of sexual practices. Although actually willing to go along with most anything in the bedroom, you may be too shy to come right out and say so. Your ideal bedmate inflames your passions by luring you into previously untested sexual territory. Variety is an essential part of your lovemaking, and you make sure that it never becomes routine. You're more likely to allow your uninhibited sensuality to surface when you have a lover's trust and confidence.

Tips for Your Ideal Lover

Exotic role-playing games intrigue you, and a romantic evening of not-so-subtle seduction turns you on. A sultry striptease inflames your physical desire as it builds sexual excitement. Using your creative minds, you and your ideal mate can devise new sensual pleasures inspired by your mutual flights of fantasy.

November 23, *Sagittarius 5*

What Makes You Tick

You rarely admit to being fickle, yet your fear of intimacy may keep you from settling down. When you do choose a mate, he or she is likely to be a friend as well as a lover. In a romantic union, you're generous and passionate but wary of anything that impinges on your personal freedom. While no one will ever own you, an understanding partner can win your loyalty and devotion.

Between the Sheets

Despite being an ardent and essentially uninhibited lover, sex is rarely your number-one consideration. In the bedroom, you are inventive and imaginative. However, romance often begins for you as a marriage of two minds and only later progresses to a merging of bodies. With your low tolerance for boredom, you are always hungry for fresh experiences and you're eager to try new things. Having fun comes easily to you, and telling jokes and exchanging funny stories in bed relaxes you and heightens your physical pleasure. Like most archers, your brain is your ultimate erogenous zone. While exotic potions, naughty toys, and flavored massage oils may intrigue you, talking about sex really turns you on.

Tips for Your Ideal Lover

You enjoy wild love play that is spontaneous and whimsical, and your ideal lover is a fun-loving flirt with a clever mind and a wild imagination. You are at your best with a bed partner who is adept at creating a steamy atmosphere for lovemaking with provocative looks and spicy sexual banter.

November 24, *Sagittarius 6*

What Makes You Tick

You don't like being alone, and without an intimate relationship in your life, you feel incomplete. You crave companionship, and the romantic in you dreams of finding the perfect mate. As a result, you're prone to falling in love with an ideal. Then if the real person fails to live up to your dreams, you feel devastated and it can take awhile for you to put your life back together.

Between the Sheets

You're more affectionate and fun loving than passionate. Intensity of any kind is simply not your style. Your easygoing, relaxed nature prefers an atmosphere of serenity to the emotional ups and downs of a soap opera romance, and you thrive in an open-ended, carefree love union. You long to be wooed and courted not captured and caged. The harmonious ambiance of a tasteful décor, with candlelight, soft music, and fresh flowers helps put you in the mood for love-making. A gentle lover who wants to please and who is able to draw out all your hidden passions turns you on, and you respond amorously to affectionate gestures and whispered words of love and desire.

Tips for Your Ideal Lover

You're extremely sociable and not inclined to spend every night snuggled up in front of the TV with your lover. As far as you are concerned, there is time enough for lovemaking after a night out. Although you crave profound moments of physical pleasure, you also expect sex to be fun.

November 25, *Sagittarius 7*

What Makes You Tick

In a loving union, you are easygoing and generous. Relationships are important to you, but you also require some alone time. Consequently, you may have difficulty finding a partner who's tuned to your wavelength and able to adjust to your shifting moods. Archers are natural hunters, and although you mean to be true, coping with day-to-day realities isn't your strong point. If your lover makes too many demands, you may leave.

Between the Sheets

You can be faithful in a successful romantic relationship, but only if you feel free and unfettered. Your sex drive is strong but erratic. While physical attraction sparks your interest initially, it takes intellectual stimulation to hold it indefinitely. Boredom is an anathema to you, both inside and outside the bedroom. As an adventurer, you want to explore all sorts of sexual practices. Even so, spontaneity and fun matter more to you than grand passion, and you would rather take part in a spirited conversation than a dull sexual experience. Your ideal lover knows the best way to please you is to alternate periods of hot sex with a variety of interesting, exciting nonsexual activities.

Tips for Your Ideal Lover

Your ideal mate thinks nothing of joining you on a trip to exotic faraway places. Even a short getaway with your beloved relaxes you and soothes your restless spirit. Spending time outdoors with your lover, camping, hiking, and making love under the stars, revitalizes you and restores your good humor.

November 26, *Sagittarius 8*

What Makes You Tick

In you, the typical archer's restless nature and enthusiasm for roaming is tempered by the levelheaded caution of the number 8 vibration. Since you have less of a roving eye than others of your Sun sign, you're more willing to commit to a permanent romantic union. Although you may crave excitement and independence in your life, you also need the emotional security of a long-term loving alliance.

Between the Sheets

Your tendency is to remain steadfast and devoted to a lover who provides you with understanding and true intellectual rapport. Even so, you need to retain a certain amount of freedom and independence in all your relationships. Otherwise, you could begin feeling stifled or trapped by love. You like the idea of indulging in wild, rapturous sex, but you may be a little hesitant when it comes to making it happen. There is a shy side to your nature that makes you less direct about expressing your physical desires than the typical Sagittarius native. Your ideal lover is bold and spontaneous and unafraid when it comes to initiating lovemaking or experimenting with innovative ideas for increasing sensual pleasure.

Tips for Your Ideal Lover

Your approach to loving begins slowly but soon grows into a raging fire. Sultry glances and sexy suggestions from your lover remind you that all work and no play is no fun. Getting past your reserve can take time, but the patient suitor will be well rewarded for stimulating your lusty sexual appetite.

November 27, *Sagittarius 9*

What Makes You Tick

You are intuitive and sentimental, and so devoted to your loved ones that you would willingly sacrifice everything you have to make them happy. More than anything, you want a meaningful, loving romantic union in your life, yet you also need time on your own to restore your equilibrium. Prone to falling hopelessly in love with an ideal, you can be quite devastated if the real person doesn't live up to your mythological image.

Between the Sheets

Once sparked, your tireless libido spurs you on to moments of exquisite intimacy, and you use your unique creativity to invent exotic ways to please and be pleased in bed. Your dreamy approach to lovemaking demands a romantic atmosphere for sexy bedroom trysts. In carefully setting the stage for loving, you provide the perfect backdrop for your emotionally charged nature. A chameleonlike flair for the dramatic gives you a talent for role-playing and acting out your favorite fantasies. The tactile pleasures of erotic massage with aromatic oils calms your harried mind as it eases your body into a state of deep relaxation. Playful teasing with a feather adds a touch of whimsy to your sensuous foreplay.

Tips for Your Ideal Lover

Besides letting your lover know what you like doing or having done to you, expressing your lusty desires verbally really turns you on. Your ideal mate understands and responds to your highly creative style of lovemaking, and erotic play and fantasy engage you mentally as well as physically.

November 28, *Sagittarius 1*

What Makes You Tick

You view life as a continuous adventure, and you like having the freedom to sample exciting new experiences. In an intimate union, you're ardent and generous. Even so, you're driven by your impetuous nature and can leap in and out of romantic relationships without much thought for the future. Still you're able to remain loyal to Mr. or Ms. Right as long as he or she doesn't try to chain you to hearth and home.

Between the Sheets

You enjoy being surrounded by fun and excitement, in bed and elsewhere. Inherently passionate and excitable, you make love as exuberantly as you do everything else. Once aroused, your libido is like a fire that keeps burning throughout the night. Although happy to seize the initiative between the sheets, you appreciate a lover whose bedroom style is as bold and direct as your own. Easily bored by repetition and dull routine, your appetite for sexual novelty demands imagination and experimentation. However, you are unlikely to confine your lovemaking to the bedroom. You enjoy participating in vigorous activities with your partner as a prelude to sex, and your favorite playground is actually the great outdoors.

Tips for Your Ideal Lover

An evening together on the dance floor gets your blood pumping and can be a very effective erotic turn-on. Later on, in private, you might extend the night's dancing into something a bit more seductive, such as a slow, sultry belly dance or an exotic striptease.

November 29, *Sagittarius 2*

What Makes You Tick

Although you need emotional security, you also crave freedom and independence, and despite a desire for roots, you become bored if you stick close to home for too long. Your ideal partner understands your restless nature and love of adventure. You truly want a loving companion to share your life, so you can be quicker to commit to a long-term partnership than others of your Sun sign.

Between the Sheets

Even if you're a traveling archer who spends lots of time on the road, home is where your heart remains. You're idealistic enough to believe in true love and romantic enough to make your mate feel adored. Giving and sharing affection means a great deal to you, and you revel in the intimacy that lovemaking engenders. You flourish with a partner who is as eager as you to explore the many possibilities offered by innovative sexual experiences. Your penchant for fantasy and romantic imaginings can help keep your bedroom relationship fresh and lively. The partner who turns you on is willing to explore the world of your imagination.

Tips for Your Ideal Lover

Even the slightest suggestion of erotic touching and stroking is usually enough to spark your fire. An evening of sexual banter and teasing turns you on by adding to the anticipation. While you and your lover delve into each other's bodies, you like pretending that you're in some exotic place you've both dreamed about.

November 30, *Sagittarius 3*

What Makes You Tick

Naturally outgoing and flirtatious, you love to party and pursue an active social life. Like most Sagittarians, you make a charming, sexy lover with an affectionate manner. Given your amiable nature and interest in other people, you probably have lots of friends and potential lovers. However, you prize your independence more than anything or anyone. With your freedom on the line, you may think twice before committing yourself to a long-term relationship.

Between the Sheets

Even at your most romantic, you thrive on the idea of adventure, challenge, and excitement. You pride yourself on your spontaneity, and creative, innovative, imaginative sex is your forte. However, your apparent nonchalance in the bedroom may sometimes be misinterpreted as shallowness or a lack of deeper feeling. Nevertheless, nothing could be further from the truth. Physically, your passion burns very brightly. But on an emotional level, you are unusually careful; you keep the key to your heart well hidden until you're ready to give it away. Inherently open-minded, you enjoy experimenting with new ways to increase sensual pleasure. A free-spirited, exciting bed partner with few inhibitions knows what it takes to turn you on.

Tips for Your Ideal Lover

You are likely to become enamored of a lover with a quick wit and the ability to turn you on with hot, spicy sexual banter. Playful fantasy and role-playing games are a means of keeping your imagination engaged during lovemaking, and reading erotica in bed tantalizes and intrigues you.

December 1, *Sagittarius 1*

What Makes You Tick

A witty conversationalist, your fine mind is perpetually open to new ideas. You set such a fast pace mentally and physically that the people around you feel that they have to struggle to keep up. In an intimate relationship, you're a passionate, inventive lover. However, you'll stick around only as long as your partner holds your interest. If you become disillusioned, you may suddenly drop everything and move on to someone new.

Between the Sheets

Whirlwind romance is your specialty, and you thrive on fun and excitement. You have few qualms when it comes to pushing the envelope of your sexuality. Even in a long-term union, you need variety and change. Curiosity and an adventurous spirit prompt you to experiment with erotic fantasy and innovative sexual techniques. Romance often begins for you as a marriage of minds as well as bodies. You possess great physical endurance; once you get started, you can keep going into the wee hours. Your active, adventurous nature craves a dynamic, spontaneous lover. Acting on your fantasies ignites your vivid imagination and makes your lovemaking more colorful, and experimenting with new positions liberates your hidden sensuality.

Tips for Your Ideal Lover

An aura of excitement surrounds you, and your active nature calls out for feats of romantic daring. Your ideal mate doesn't hesitate to wake you during the night with all-over kisses and sensual caresses. Spicy talk and sex toys appeal to your desire for fresh experience in the bedroom and elsewhere.

December 2, *Sagittarius 2*

What Makes You Tick

You like people and they like you. Moreover, you have a wonderful sense of humor, so long as the joke's not on you. Although exciting and full of fun, you're also reliable and dependable. You go back and forth between wanting freedom to roam the world and needing the safety of a secure, committed union. However, once you reconcile your conflicting impulses, you make a loyal and loving partner.

Between the Sheets

Your ideal mate understands the duality of your nature and shares or supports your love of travel and adventure. As a sexy, generous Sagittarian, you have an instinct to please and be pleased. Just being with you is apt to make your partner feel sexy and alive. Since variety is an essential ingredient in your bedroom approach, you are always willing to try something new and unusual between the sheets. An expert at sensuous foreplay, your specialty is enticing your bed partner with a seductive smorgasbord of exotic delights. For you, playful erotic fun with your lover is the ultimate turn-on. Together with your mate, you happily explore novel ways to enhance each other's bedroom experience.

Tips for Your Ideal Lover

You are an affectionate and generous lover. Fooling around with sex toys and naughty novelties stirs your imagination and energizes your libido. Spicy pillow talk liberates your quick wit and adds to your anticipation of the delights to follow. Teasing and touching awakens your desire and heightens the ensuing ecstasy.

December 3, *Sagittarius 3*

What Makes You Tick

In a romantic union, you're a passionate, generous, eager, and loving partner. However, you are also something of a rolling stone, with a relaxed attitude toward all relationships. It generally takes both intellectual and physical stimulation to keep you interested over the long term. Too much intimacy or emotion can scare you off, and if the closeness becomes cloying, you may leave in search of greener, less restrictive pastures.

Between the Sheets

Lighthearted, restless, uninhibited, and adventurous, you are as endlessly curious about sex as you are about everything else. Totally convinced that variety is the spice in your life, you're constantly on the lookout for new challenges and adventures. You make love with the same fiery passion you have when approaching   s all your interests. Having sex is one of your favorite things, right up there with rousing debates and exotic foreign travel. You enjoy the thrill of the chase as much as the hot sex that follows. Your ideal lover is affectionate, cheerful, and open-minded. Sharing a few laughs under the covers sparks your lusty libido, whereas a gloomy bedmate turns you off.

Tips for Your Ideal Lover

The lover who isn't easy to catch turns you on. Your preferred sex fantasy involves traveling with your beloved and making love in romantic, exotic places. Your ideal life companion always has a bag packed and is prepared to go off with you at a moment's notice.

December 4, *Sagittarius 4*

What Makes You Tick

You long to find your soul mate, but few potential partners are able to live up to your high expectations. Once involved in an intimate union, you tend to be more dependable than the typical archer. Although you vacillate between wanting freedom and independence and needing the safety of a secure and committed relationship, once you reconcile your conflicting desires, you make a generous, caring spouse.

Between the Sheets

The paradoxes in your temperament extend to the bedroom, and you can be carefree and romantic one moment and quite serious the next. Your fiery sensuality simmers below the surface, but with a little encouragement, you begin to reveal the true extent of your passion. Although something of a daredevil with regard to sexual exploration, you tend to be considerably more hesitant when it comes to establishing deeper ties. Your love of nature provides you with a splendid backdrop for expressing and exploring your hidden desires, and your ideal lover satisfies both your lusty libido and your sexual restlessness by creating a setting for lovemaking that is out in the open air, yet sheltered from prying eyes.

Tips for Your Ideal Lover

The lover who showers you with attention in bed knows how to spark the flames of your desire and keep them burning. You enjoy trying new ways of expanding your erotic horizons, and it just takes a little encouragement to get you to drop your reserved façade.

December 5, *Sagittarius 5*

What Makes You Tick

You are physically ardent but emotionally cooler than the average Sagittarian. Companionship is as important to you as romance, and your sociable nature can make a fling seem more appealing than a long-term alliance. You regard love as a glorious experience, but your need for personal freedom may make fidelity difficult to sustain. Although no one will ever own you, a tolerant mate can win your love and loyalty.

Between the Sheets

In the bedroom and elsewhere, you are open-minded and willing to try just about anything at least once. A loving partnership begins with a true meeting of minds. You view sex as a pleasure to enjoy and not something to be taken too seriously. You believe that the real bond between lovers comes from sharing all the wonderful things life has to offer. Your ideal mate is as capable of engaging you in a lively conversation on diverse subjects as he or she is of making love to you in various and sundry positions. Starting off with mellow foreplay arouses you slowly while enhancing your anticipation of the many erotic delights still to come.

Tips for Your Ideal Lover

Sultry foreplay relaxes you and calms your frenetic energy, and intimate moments of subtle teasing and caressing inflame your desires as nothing else can. Sharing physical activities such as dancing or even exercising with your mate starts your blood pumping and helps heighten your pleasure in the lovemaking that follows.

December 6, *Sagittarius 6*

What Makes You Tick

Naturally outgoing, amiable, and friendly, you adore parties and other fun-filled social gatherings. In an intimate union, you are romantic, affectionate, and warm-hearted. However, you often feel as if you are being pulled in two opposite directions at once. Part of you yearns for a loving companion to share your journey through life, yet your more independent part resents being tied down and may be prompted to shy away from permanent commitment.

Between the Sheets

Grand gestures are not your style. Although physically passionate, loving, and romantic, you tend to avoid any relationship that is emotionally heavy or angst ridden. You believe life is meant to be fun and is much too short to waste on excessive drama and unhappiness. While you want a close union with your beloved, you refuse to put up with a mate who attempts to control you. Your freewheeling nature responds most readily to a lighthearted approach to love and sexuality, and your ideal lover is as ardent and free spirited as you are. For you, a setting of casual elegance strikes just the right note for an evening of sensual pleasure.

Tips for Your Ideal Lover

Your quest for new and exciting sexual experiences gives your lovemaking a spontaneous style, and experimenting with innovative positions gets all your juices flowing. You might start the activities by sharing an invigorating shower with your lover, follow up with an erotic massage, and then end with a sexy romp beneath the covers.

December 7, *Sagittarius 7*

What Makes You Tick

You waver between craving a secure home life and longing for independence. Moreover, you have a thirst for adventure and your threshold for boredom is low. While you may think you want to stay in one place, it's hard for you to resist the allure of the open road. Once you reconcile your conflicting impulses, you make a loyal and caring romantic partner.

Between the Sheets

Sexually, you're beguiling, exciting, and responsive. You are as attracted by your bed partner's friendship and ability to exchange thoughts and ideas as by his or her sexual prowess. Consequently, you may come off as a libertine, especially if the friendship with benefits you offer is misconstrued and mistaken for everlasting love. An adventurous lover, you are always eager to expand your sexual horizons. You thrive with a dynamic bedmate who is your equal in enthusiasm and physical vitality. Once assured of his or her affection, your prowess and uninhibited sensuality in bed keeps your lover enthralled. Although you prefer romantic alliances that don't tie you down, you are capable of fidelity and long-term commitment.

Tips for Your Ideal Lover

Your exuberance and candor in the bedroom allow you to express your desires quite openly. Despite your seemingly casual attitude toward sexuality, you long to be swept away on wave of ecstatic lovemaking. The free-spirited lover, whose lack of inhibitions matches your own, knows how to gratify your secret desires.

December 8, *Sagittarius 8*

What Makes You Tick

Typically, you are not as flighty or flirtatious as other solar archers. In an intimate alliance, you are warm-hearted but highly critical of anyone who cannot measure up to your high standards. Fun loving without being frivolous, you like the excitement of an independent existence, yet you long to settle down to a permanent union with a partner who shares your life goals and ambitions.

Between the Sheets

You are a bit of a paradox when it comes to making love. You can be playful and teasing one moment, and passionately serious, even somewhat demanding the next. Getting past your emotional armor may take some time, but once you feel comfortable with your lover you willingly throw caution to the wind. You have a healthy appetite for sensual delights, and you appreciate a lusty bed partner who shares your interest in trying out various sexual techniques. When you work, you work hard. When you play, you're serious about having fun. In fact, you can be more fun in bed than just about anyone, and you get off on experimenting with novel ways to enhance sexual pleasure.

Tips for Your Ideal Lover

From decadent edibles and naughty toys to seductive attire, you are open to just about any steamy idea that adds to the erotic enjoyment of lovemaking for both partners. High-energy sexual activity brings you to peaks of ecstasy enhanced with a strengthened bond of emotional intimacy between you and your bedmate.

December 9, *Sagittarius 9*

What Makes You Tick

Physically, you are warm-hearted and passionate, but emotionally, you are so impressionable that close relationships can be rather difficult for you to sustain. Naturally concerned and compassionate, you are deeply sensitive to your partner's needs. Moreover, you lead an intense inner life of sentimental dreams and crusading ideals. Although you long for the intimacy of a committed union, your inner archer requires occasional periods of freedom for contemplative withdrawal.

Between the Sheets

Inherently kind and caring, you make a generous, devoted lover. However, you have so much affection to give that your partner may not be able to share your depths of emotion. Since you are more romantic and fanciful than most other Sagittarians, imagination plays a huge part in your sex life. You enjoy using your innate creativity to devise exotic scenarios to act out with your bedmate. You long to be swept away on a wave of ecstasy. A dreamy atmosphere in which to share moments of exquisite intimacy arouses you and adds to your sensual pleasure. Tantalizing feathery caresses and slow, enticing kisses that build slowly to a rapturous crescendo are a real turn-on.

Tips for Your Ideal Lover

You view sex as an art form, and playful fantasy engages your mind and imagination along with your body. An herbal soak with your lover, in a hot tub or spa surrounded by flickering candles or lamps filled with scented oils, could become a favorite way to relax before making love.

December 10, *Sagittarius 1*

What Makes You Tick

Although work is an important part of your life, you rarely let it get in the way of a good time. In a committed union, you're passionate and affectionate, and you make a devoted partner for as long as you stick around. However, you prefer relationships that don't tie you down. If you start to feel hemmed in, your inclination is to leave and not look back.

Between the Sheets

For you, sex is mainly fun and games. Uninhibited exuberance marks your style of lovemaking, and your bedroom approach is bold and spontaneous. You express your sexual desires freely and passionately, as a natural part of your joie de vivre. Since your fiery sensuality simmers just beneath the surface, you are always ready for a quickie. Versatility is your strong point, and you're enough of a daredevil to try just about anything, in bed or out. Your impetuous, active love nature craves adventure and excitement. Your ideal lover is a sparring partner who continually challenges you physically and intellectually. Change thrills you, and traveling to exotic places with your partner spices up your love life.

Tips for Your Ideal Lover

Something of a romantic, you're perpetually on the lookout for the ideal lover to rescue you from the banality of everyday life. Outdoor amour appeals to your liking for making love in open spaces. Since you enjoy a little spontaneous tomfoolery, a sultry glance can trigger some exciting erotic moments.

December 11, *Sagittarius 2*

What Makes You Tick

Sometimes you feel confused about what you want in life. Although your heart yearns for freedom and independence, your more practical head prefers a settled existence with roots and a firm foundation. Even so, you tend to become bored and restless if you stick close to home for long periods. Your ideal mate understands the duality of your nature and shares your love of travel and adventure.

Between the Sheets

In a romantic union, you are cheerful, exciting, and fun loving, yet reliable and dependable. An ardent and generous lover, you possess an innate understanding of intimate relations and a willingness to invest a great deal of energy in satisfying your own and your partner's sexual desires. You're extremely sensual with a deep appreciation for the good things in life; you respond amorously to the beauty and comfort of sumptuous surroundings and the tactile pleasures of lush, luxurious fabrics. Any gesture of physical contact with your lover is likely to spark your desire. Erotic touching re-energizes you and inflames your lusty libido. A slow, languid aromatherapy massage relaxes you into a state of heightened receptivity.

Tips for Your Ideal Lover

Lovemaking is joyful, lighthearted fun, and laughing and joking with your bedmate is a prelude to deeper intimacy. Together you happily explore novel ways to enhance your mutual pleasure. Subtle teasing adds to your anticipation of what is to follow, and delving into your collection of sexy toys incites your passion.

December 12, *Sagittarius 3*

What Makes You Tick

Where love is concerned, you are ardent, caring, open-hearted in your affections, and loyal in your attachments. Although you may be slow to make promises, when you do make them, you tend to keep them. It's important to live life to the fullest, experiencing everything you possibly can. In a romantic relationship, you are eager for love, however, it takes both intellectual and physical stimulation to keep you interested.

Between the Sheets

In love as in life, you are not afraid to act on your hunches. Moreover, you're surprisingly lucky when you do. You believe in taking chances on love, and if things don't work out, you pick yourself up, dust yourself off, and move on to someone new and even more exciting. In bed, you are a tender, considerate lover. Your sexual approach begins as a tiny spark and slowly builds to a raging fire. Fulfilling your sexual cravings in a stable relationship allows you to indulge your erotic fantasies with a partner you trust. You enjoy experimenting with diverse ideas, and trying out novel ways to add to your own and your lover's sensual pleasure.

Tips for Your Ideal Lover

You view sex as fun and games, and you are eager to expand your sexual horizons by exploring all sorts of amorous practices. Your ideal bedmate is spontaneous and innovative in his or her approach, and together your creative, uninhibited lovemaking can take you both to new levels of physical gratification.

December 13, *Sagittarius 4*

What Makes You Tick

In social situations, your humor and easygoing nature make you an utterly charming companion. However, the serious side of your character emerges once you are away from the spotlight. At heart, you are hardworking and determined to succeed in life. Inherently more cautious and prone to look before you leap than other archers, you like to weigh all your options before getting involved in any romantic alliance.

Between the Sheets

A homebody with a touch of the adventurous thrill-seeker, you are eager to expand your sensual horizons by exploring all sorts of sexual practices. Your ideal bedmate inflames your passion by luring you into previously untested erotic territory. You are more likely to allow your uninhibited sensuality to surface when you have prior assurance of your lover's willingness to go along. A romantic evening of not-so-subtle seduction turns you on. An erotic strip-tease inflames your physical desire as it builds sexual excitement. Your talent for the dramatic makes it possible for you to engage in exotic role-playing games. Using your creative minds, you and your lover can devise new sensual pleasures inspired by mutual flights of fantasy.

Tips for Your Ideal Lover

High-energy lovemaking takes you to peaks of ecstasy. Working up a sweat relaxes you as it satisfies your innate desire for physical activity. Dancing or exercising together can provide a playful prelude to exciting lovemaking. Your perfect lover is loyal and dependable in public and sensual and uninhibited in the bedroom.

December 14, *Sagittarius 5*

What Makes You Tick

An open-minded free spirit, you're always on the lookout for new adventures. The seeker in you enjoys experimenting, and you generally have an anything-goes attitude toward sexuality. Consequently, you may have had your share of unconventional liaisons, and you probably wouldn't want it any other way. Since you require a lot of independence in an intimate union, settling down with one person may be difficult.

Between the Sheets

You're an innovative, inventive, and enthusiastic lover. Even so, physical love-making is not as important to you as mental rapport. Although you regard the sex act as extremely liberating, pleasurable, and fun, you expect a long-term intimate relationship to be based as much on common interests and ideals as on love and romance. You are wary of any commitment that curbs your ability to move around freely and without restraint. No matter how close you get to your mate, there is always a part of you that you reserve only for yourself. Inherently future oriented, you rarely waste time lamenting relationships that didn't work out. When a romance is over, you move on without regrets.

Tips for Your Ideal Lover

A bed partner who appeals to your intellect definitely has the edge. Relaxing and soaking together in a scented hot tub, before or after sex, gives you a chance to share thoughts and ideas without outside interruption. Spicy verbal foreplay turns you on, as it heightens your anticipation for the lovemaking to follow.

December 15, *Sagittarius 6*

What Makes You Tick

Fun loving and sociable, your amiable nature swiftly breaks down barriers between people. When personally involved, you thrive in an equitable union where each partner respects the other's personal space. Heavy emotional scenes aren't your style, so the lover who hopes to hold you needs to keep things light. Even so, you want a loving companion to share your life, and eventually you'll commit to Mr. or Ms. Right.

Between the Sheets

You play well with others, and you are not inclined to stay home nights snuggled up in front of the TV. You want to be out on the town, where you can meet interesting new people. In the bedroom, pleasing your mate is important to you, and you will do most anything to gratify his or her desires. Dull or routine sex turns you off. You prefer a creative lover who knows how to keep you guessing. You may not expect to be swept away by wild passion, but you do appreciate a skilled bed partner. Your open sensuality responds amorously to relaxed, playful touching and stroking. Spontaneous romantic gestures add sparkle to your activities between the sheets.

Tips for Your Ideal Lover

You express passion ardently, happily tumbling into bed with your mate after a day of exertion. Whether you are watching or actually participating, a sultry, sensual striptease energizes your libido and gets your juices flowing. Sexy banter liberates you, and experimenting with new positions appeals to your desire for variety and change.

December 16, *Sagittarius 7*

What Makes You Tick

Experience is considerably more important to you than stability or security. Emotionally, you are a bit of a paradox. Although you regard love as a glorious adventure, your need for freedom and independence makes your loyalty difficult to sustain. As with other things, you're better at starting a romantic relationship than maintaining one. While your intentions are sincere, you may lose interest once the initial excitement has worn off.

Between the Sheets

In an intimate relationship, intellectual companionship counts as much with you as physical compatibility. Your lovemaking style is wildly experimental, and you're always interested in discovering new ways of expanding your sexual horizons. Making love in different locations is a turn-on, and you dislike being restricted to the bed when there are many equally appealing places in which to have sex. You need to find a partner who is willing to put up with your restless nature, because you're more likely to stay committed to a mate who grants you some breathing space both in the bedroom and elsewhere. Moreover, if you feel trapped in a romantic union, you could decide to leave.

Tips for Your Ideal Lover

Sexually and otherwise, versatility is your strong point and you're always ready to try something different. You pride yourself on your innovative approach to lovemaking, and appreciate a lover with a similar bedroom philosophy. Spicy pillow talk turns you on, and you may enjoy discussing other people's sex lives while engaging in your own.

December 17, *Sagittarius 8*

What Makes You Tick

You crave the emotional security of a permanent union, yet you're rather guarded when it comes to intimate relationships. Getting past your emotional armor may take some time, but once you feel comfortable with your partner, you throw caution to the wind. Although you enjoy a good time as much as anyone, when you work, you work hard. Still, when you take time to party, you can be more fun than anyone.

Between the Sheets

In an intimate alliance, you're affectionate, warm-hearted, and idealistic. You're also something of a paradox, both inside and outside the bedroom. You can be playful, flirty, and teasing one moment, and passionately serious, even somewhat demanding, the next. You get off on experimenting with exciting new ways to enhance sexual pleasure for yourself and your lover. You have a healthy appetite for sensual delights and appreciate a lusty bedmate who shares your interest in trying out innovative erotic techniques. From decadent edibles and naughty sex toys and devices to provocative attire, you are open to just about any hot, spicy idea that enhances sexual gratification and adds to the enjoyment of lovemaking.

Tips for Your Ideal Lover

Lighthearted fun in the bedroom brings out your uninhibited sensuality. Intelligence and a nimble mind are invaluable assets in a lover, and you respond as readily to sexy verbal banter as to physical stimulation. Sex is something of a game, and you play it with imagination and gusto.

December 18, *Sagittarius 9*

What Makes You Tick

You are romantic, intuitive, imaginative, and sentimental. More than anything, you want a meaningful intimate relationship in your life. Intellectually, you're clever; emotionally, you are impressionable. However, you can become so devoted to your beloved that you would sacrifice everything you have. Too much emotional involvement tends to sap your vitality, and then you require time on your own to reconnect with yourself and restore your equilibrium.

Between the Sheets

You use a unique combination of intuition and creativity to invent exotic ways to please and be pleased in bed. In carefully setting the stage for your trysts, you provide the perfect backdrop for your emotionally charged sensuality. You have a flair for the dramatic and your talent for acting during role-playing games adds spice to your favorite erotic fantasies. Once sparked, your tireless libido spurs you on to moments of exquisite intimacy. The tactile pleasure of a sensual massage with aromatic oils calms your harried mind as it eases your body into a state of deep relaxation. Telling your lover what you like to do, or have done to you, really turns you on.

Tips for Your Ideal Lover

You like to take your time in bed and out. You dislike rushing to dessert before you have had a chance to enjoy a satisfying meal of tender, romantic foreplay. Exotic vacation trips and weekend getaways lift you out of your mundane environment and make for memorable moments of intimacy.

December 19, *Sagittarius 1*

What Makes You Tick

You are one of those fools who rush in where angels fear to tread. Although charming and sociable, you set such a fast pace that your companions often struggle just to keep up. Despite being highly opinionated, your mind is open to new ways of doing things. In an intimate relationship, you're passionate and loving, but you're only likely to stick around as long as your partner holds your interest.

Between the Sheets

You thrive on fun and excitement and have few qualms when it comes to pushing the envelope of your sexuality. Even in a long-term union, you crave variety and fresh experience. Curiosity prompts you to experiment with erotic fantasy and innovative sexual techniques, and your adventurous nature craves an equally dynamic bed partner. You possess great physical endurance; once you get started, you are able to keep going all night. Acting on your fantasies ignites your vivid imagination and makes your lovemaking more colorful. Experimenting with new positions liberates your innate sensuality. Sexy talk and toys appeal to your desire to experience everything life has to offer, both inside the bedroom and elsewhere.

Tips for Your Ideal Lover

Sexually, you are something of a walking incendiary device, but slowing things down can help maintain your red-hot libido at a steady boil. Your sexual prowess gives you the strength for late-night amour, and you enjoy a lover who wakes you up with sizzling all-over kisses and erotic touching and stroking.

December 20, *Sagittarius 2*

What Makes You Tick

To hold you, a loving relationship must be challenging and interesting. Your ideal mate is your best friend as well as your lover. Sexually, you are something of a free spirit. You detest routine and like being able to make love when the mood seizes you. Yet, despite your breezy, laid-back public persona, you can be quite demanding and more than a little possessive in an intimate union.

Between the Sheets

In a close relationship, you make a warm, ardent, generous lover. Although rather flirtatious and welcoming of change and excitement, once you find the person who's right for you, you're inclined to stick around over the long haul. More passionate than romantic, you tend to be pretty direct about your sexual needs and preferences. Your ideal bed partner shares your adventurous nature as well as your desire to explore all facets of sexuality. However, you aren't only interested in the physical side of sex; the emotional side matters as well. Lovemaking is a transcendent experience. Your aim is to establish a deep understanding with your lover, an understanding capable of reaching your very souls.

Tips for Your Ideal Lover

Slow, languid massage relaxes you and helps you tune in to the deeper rhythm of your inherently sensual nature. Lovemaking is an erotic feast for the senses. You get off on the delicious tension that builds during teasing, tantalizing foreplay, and you might also enjoy sharing edible aphrodisiacs that enhance arousal.

December 21, *Sagittarius 3*

What Makes You Tick

As a lover, you're kind, generous, and ardent but something of a romantic gypsy. Consequently, you could be here today and gone tomorrow. What you really care about is companionship and the experience of love. More than anything, you yearn to test uncharted waters, meet interesting new people, and try exciting new things. You may choose freedom and independence over either love or security.

Between the Sheets

Your attitude toward love and sexuality is easygoing and relaxed. An excess of intimacy scares the wits out of you. Although you are strongly sexed, the physical act alone rarely fulfills you. A romantic partnership works best for you when it's firmly rooted in friendship and intellectual rapport. You are adventurous in all areas of your life, and this naturally carries over to the bedroom. As a result, you refuse to take your erotic activities too seriously. Sex is a wonderful game, but an excess of intense emotion is more of a turn-off than a turn-on. You enjoy expanding your sexual horizons while having a good deal of fun in bed.

Tips for Your Ideal Lover

You're eager to expand your horizons and explore all sorts of sexual practices. Versatility is your strong point, and you're willing to try just about anything. Since nothing turns you off more completely than dull routine, your ideal bed-mate depends on variety, innovation, and spontaneity to keep you interested.

December 22, *Capricorn 4*

What Makes You Tick

Afraid of rejection, you hold back to keep from appearing vulnerable, and it is not at all unusual for you to close yourself off emotionally rather than risk being hurt. Moreover, you have a secretive side that makes it difficult to share your deepest feelings. Nevertheless, when you are feeling safe and secure in a committed relationship, you make an ardent lover and a generous, dependable mate.

Between the Sheets

Your sex drive is strong and uncomplicated. Beneath your hands-off, somewhat uptight public persona, you are warm and sensual and capable of intense sexual passion. While you may be a bit inhibited emotionally, you can be relentless and abandoned in your pursuit of physical fulfillment. The horny goat's seduction technique tends to be straightforward and direct. In the privacy of your bedroom, you expect your lover to be responsive and receptive to your desire for down-to-earth sex with a touch of ribald playfulness. With your reserve melted, your initial detachment swiftly turns into lusty passion. Sexually, you possess all the patience, vitality, and staying power typical of your Sun sign, but also Capricorn's controlling, possessive, demanding nature.

Tips for Your Ideal Lover

There's nothing more stimulating than a sensuous back rub from the attentive hands of a loving partner. You find the feel of silky fabrics against your skin extremely pleasurable, and both the front and back of your knees are particularly responsive to erotic touching and stroking.

December 23, *Capricorn 5*

What Makes You Tick

You're interested in a wide range of people, yet choosy about the ones with whom you spend serious time. Since you are gregarious on the one hand and self-sufficient on the other, you're something of a mystery to everyone who knows you. Despite your outgoing personality, there is a reserved inner goat standing guard over your privacy and independence, and you rarely allow anyone to get too close.

Between the Sheets

Intelligence, shared interests, and a quick wit are more likely to catch and hold you than a beautiful face or a to-die-for body. You want a partner who sees through your reserve to the passionate, affectionate person beneath. Sometimes you get so caught up in other things that you forget about love and sex altogether. However, it usually only takes a small reminder to spark your latent desires. With just a few sexy suggestions to get you started, you become an impassioned, inventive lover. Your brain is your most sexually responsive organ, providing you with the unusual talent of being able to "feel" with your mind. Where it goes, your body automatically follows.

Tips for Your Ideal Lover

With a lover you trust, you exhibit the earthy side of your lusty libido. Your ideal mate initiates spontaneous bedroom encounters with sexy words and steamily passionate touches. Tender caresses may mellow you into a relaxed sensuality, but a little playful roughhousing between the sheets stimulates you and gets all your sexual juices flowing.

December 24, *Capricorn 6*

What Makes You Tick

Even though you enjoy occasional bouts of solitude, partnership and team-work come naturally to you. You like being half of a couple, and you thrive on the attention and affection of your significant other. While very protective of your beloved, you can also be demanding and controlling. Since you're a bit of a perfectionist where love is concerned, it can be difficult for a prospective partner to live up to your expectations.

Between the Sheets

You are laid-back but determined in your approach to lovemaking. In bed, you take charge in a quiet, seductive way that leaves little room for doubt about your intentions. You like knowing that you are admired and appreciated, but you are not particularly free with flattery or compliments in return. It is a lot easier for you to deal with your physical passions and sexual desires than with your emotions. Your ideal lover has the ability to tune in to your true feelings. Your tastes and sensibilities are more sophisticated and refined than those of the typical goat. A graceful, harmonious atmosphere turns you on, and coarse vulgarity turns you off.

Tips for Your Ideal Lover

Like fine wine, your sensuality grows richer over time. The intensity of your desires goes through high and low cycles, depending on what is happening in other areas of your life. Since you truly enjoy being courted and coaxed, your libido is particularly responsive to an artful and elegantly staged seduction scene.

December 25, *Capricorn 7*

What Makes You Tick

In an intimate union, you are affectionate and devoted, with a humorous side that makes you lots of fun to be around. Your deepest desire is to love and be loved, yet there's an aspect of caution in your makeup that makes its difficult for you to follow through on your feelings. Because you require more time for yourself than the average Capricorn, you select your companions with considerable care.

Between the Sheets

You are not one to jump in and out of casual affairs, but neither are you predisposed to fall in love with the first person you meet. You are as discriminating and selective in love as you are in other life areas. You are also less conservative and more open to alternate ideas and sexual experimentation than most other goats. Even so, your bedroom activity may fluctuate wildly between extremes, as you try to balance your passionate nature with the traditional vibrations of your Capricorn Sun sign. You dislike the feeling of being trapped, either emotionally or physically, and respond more readily to a relaxed approach to lovemaking than to one that is demanding or possessive.

Tips for Your Ideal Lover

In the comfort of hearth and home, your passions slowly erupt with playful abandon. However, you don't like to be rushed into an ecstatic embrace. A spa soak with your lover relaxes you into a loving mood, and the tender caresses of an erotic massage help you reconnect with your lusty physicality.

December 26, *Capricorn 8*

What Makes You Tick

Despite a need to love and be loved, you are cautious with regard to your intimate relationships. Used to being in control, you dislike the feeling of vulnerability, and you don't let down your guard until you feel secure enough to trust your lover completely. Moreover, any potential partner must meet your high expectations. However, when you find the person who is right for you, you make a passionate, caring mate.

Between the Sheets

You work at love with the same diligence you apply to other areas of your life. Emotionally, you're somewhat rigid, but you are ardent and responsive physically. You consider coquettish game-playing and sappy romantic overtures a waste of time. Highly sexed and quickly aroused, your usual approach to lovemaking, although respectful and refined, is no-nonsense direct. Whatever you lack in the romance department, you make up for in skill and sexual prowess. Even given your businesslike attitude toward your sexuality, you can be vamped or seduced. Once with your Mr. or Ms. Right, you throw all caution to the wind and give full reign to your earthy sexuality.

Tips for Your Ideal Lover

You like to take your time during sex. Being hurried between the sheets makes you feel flustered and can even get you out of the mood altogether. Since you enjoy the rituals of formal courtship, you appreciate a lover who moves slowly with skill and precision.

December 27, *Capricorn 9*

What Makes You Tick

More romantic and idealistic than others of your Sun sign, you fall passionately in love with the very idea of love. If reality doesn't live up to your expectations, you can be deeply disappointed. What you're actually seeking from a loving union is a genuine soul mate. When you find him or her, you'll sacrifice your own interests to keep your beloved happy.

Between the Sheets

An unselfish lover, you're considerate of your mate's preferences. You're proud of your sexual prowess and ability to satisfy your partner, but your feelings are rather sensitive, and you welcome a bit of ego-boosting encouragement in return. Although basically conventional in your lovemaking, you enjoy a bit of sexual experimentation now and again. When you feel secure in an intimate relationship, you may allow the kinkier side of your nature to emerge. You like making love in a romantic atmosphere, and nothing turns you on faster than a well-staged seduction scene with all the traditional trimmings: sexy attire, dim lighting, soft music, scented candles, and a properly chilled bottle of champagne.

Tips for Your Ideal Lover

While your passionate side remains hidden in public, your ideal bedmate knows how to light your fire behind closed doors. Slow, erotic massage relaxes you and draws out your earthy sensuality. Your libido may need a little coaxing after a hard day at work, but once ignited you have stamina to burn.

December 28, *Capricorn 1*

What Makes You Tick

You're accustomed to winning, and your competitive spirit spills over into your love life. Yet you're a romantic at heart, and you want everyone to like you. When you meet Mr. or Ms. Right, you refuse to take no for an answer, and one way or the other, you wear down any resistance to your charms. Once committed, you make a generous and caring but also controlling and possessive life partner.

Between the Sheets

Your libido is strong and your sexual energy is high. You possess a type of animal magnetism that swiftly surfaces behind closed doors. In an intimate union, you're a fiery lover. Your seduction technique is straightforward and direct. As a sensualist, you seek the heights of love through sheer physical passion. Although your romantic side enjoys many of the elegant courtly rituals of love, you want no part of emotional games. Your sensuous nature is earthy and erotic. You don't require a lot of foreplay to become physically aroused. In fact, you are perfectly willing to skip the appetizers altogether and go directly to the main course.

Tips for Your Ideal Lover

Although your sensitive nature may swing from fiery passion to controlled reserve, you are actually rejuvenated by regular sexual release. A provocative look or a playful ribald suggestion can ignite your combustible libido, and a clever mate knows how to release tension and lure out your sexy side through touching and stroking.

December 29, *Capricorn 2*

What Makes You Tick

Your sensitive, romantic nature accentuates your desire to be involved in an intimate relationship. Yet you tend to be somewhat hesitant in interpersonal situations. Ultimately, your need for structure and emotional stability helps you conquer your doubts and seek a committed relationship. Since love and affection are so important, you are best suited to a partner who is encouraging and able to help you overcome your shyness.

Between the Sheets

Your emotions run deep and you keep them well hidden. Moreover, your sensitivity and emotional fragility may prevent you from opening your heart totally to another person. You function best and feel happiest when partnered with someone who understands your moods and shares your interests and ideals. Beneath your hesitancy and restraint, there's a smoldering sensuality waiting to be released. Even so, you like being in control of your feelings and actions. You also like being in charge, even in the most intimate situations. Consequently, you won't put up with a mate who is overly aggressive. When you find the compliant, understanding lover you're seeking, you make a generous, affectionate bedmate.

Tips for Your Ideal Lover

The intensity of your libido goes through cycles according to your mood swings. During a low cycle, your partner may reawaken your inherent sensuality by gently trailing a large feather or a sumptuous bit of fur or silky fabric over your skin, especially in the ultrasensitive areas behind the knees.

December 30, *Capricorn 3*

What Makes You Tick

You are a genuine romantic with a genial manner and a disarming sense of humor. You look carefully before you leap, but once committed, you expect love to last forever. Although you consider intellectual accord as important as sexual harmony, your ardent nature demands a bed partner who is passionate as well as bright and funny. Your perfect match is highly sexed yet capable of holding your interest through sharing thoughts and ideas.

Between the Sheets

With the right mate, you are able to throw off your inhibitions and allow the red-blooded, lusty side of your nature to come to the forefront. You enjoy sex games and want an exciting, innovative lover who is able to keep up with you. In your most intimate moments, you are predisposed to try just about anything that might be fun. Since you also have an active fantasy life, your responses can be heightened by a combination of verbal foreplay and the imaginings of a fertile mind. Outside the bedroom, however, the reserved side of your nature swiftly asserts itself, and you expect modesty and decorum from your significant other.

Tips for Your Ideal Lover

You respond passionately to erotic touching and stroking and to lighthearted bedroom romps and imaginative role-playing games that bring out your earthy sensuality. Soaking together with your lover in an aromatic bath relaxes you and prepares your body and mind for the deeper nuances of sexual pleasure to follow.

December 31, *Capricorn 4*

What Makes You Tick

A need for structure prompts you to seek a committed, long-lasting love union. Yet even in your most intimate relationships, you warm to people slowly and may be perceived as emotionally aloof. Moreover, you have a secretive side that makes it difficult for you to share your deepest feelings. In addition, the controlling aspects of your personality may make your beloved feel constrained.

Between the Sheets

When you're feeling secure in a steadfast relationship, you make an ardent lover and a dependable mate. Underneath your reserved public persona, you are sensual and capable of intense sexual passion. While you may be somewhat inhibited emotionally, you can be relentless and abandoned in your pursuit of physical fulfillment. In the privacy of your bedroom, you expect your partner to be responsive and receptive to your need for lusty, uncomplicated sex with a touch of ribald playfulness. You don't require a great deal of foreplay, but after a day's work, you do enjoy relaxing in a luxurious bath or shower for two. Just add a brisk toweling, and you are ready for a perfect night of lovemaking.

Tips for Your Ideal Lover

A romantic evening of seduction and role-playing is guaranteed to stir your earthy passions. A witty, creative lover ignites both your libido and offbeat sense of humor with bawdy stories. Since your sexual stamina is probably one of your strongest assets, you need a bed partner capable of staying the course.

About the Author

Phyllis Vega (Miami, FL) is a practicing astrologer and tarot reader, and has been a New Age counselor for more than three decades. She is the author of numerous books, including *Erotic Astrology*; *Lovestrology*; *Celtic Astrology*; and *Romancing the Tarot*.

BEYOND HERE

Sure, this world is fascinating, but
what's beyond is even more intriguing...

Want a place to share stories and experiences about all things strange and unusual? From UFOs and apparitions to dream interpretation, the Tarot, astrology, and more, the **BEYOND HERE** blog is the newest hot spot for paranormal activity!